THE ART OF SPECULATION

THE ART OF SPECULATION

BY
PHILIP L. CARRET
Author of "Buying a Bond"

BARRON'S
The National Financial Weekly

BOSTON NEW YORK PHILADELPHIA

1927

Marketplace Books
Columbia, Maryland

Preface

The man who looks upon speculation as a possible means of avoiding work will get little benefit from this book. It is written rather for the man who is fascinated by the complexity of the forces which produce the ceaseless ebb and flow of security prices, who wishes to get a better understanding of them.

Successful speculation requires capital, courage and judgment. The speculator himself must supply all three. Natural good judgment is not enough. The speculator's judgment must be trained to understand the multitudinous facts of finance. It is the hope of the author that this book will be of assistance in this connection.

P. L. C.

Contents

From the Publisher

(2007 Edition)

Less than a year before this book was released in 1930, America was rocked by a financial crisis that made paupers out of millionaires and sent more than a few people reaching for that top drawer bottle of gin. After the shock, and even before the mind numbing malaise of the Great Depression had fully set in, there entered Phillip L. Carret with—what else, a book on stock speculation. But wait, wasn't it the speculators who bet it all and ended up on a shovel crew for the WPA? Not exactly. Carret's classic work on the true essence of speculation shows just how subtle this art is, and how a little knowledge about human tendencies can make you rich.

Our desire to reprint this book was based on many levels of thinking. First and foremost, the fallacy of the perceiving the professional trader as a "gambler" is one that should be addressed. Philip Carret dedicated his life to proving that intelligence, logic, and a careful accumulation of data can, in fact, make stock speculation no more uncertain than opening a corner drug store. To back this up, Carret went on to create a business empire out of the process of trading.

Throughout his 101 years (according to his profile at Carret Asset profile, LLC), he lived and prospered through 31 bull markets, 30 bear markets, 20 recessions, and a depression; all while creating and managing the first mutual fund the world had ever seen—a fund that he managed and grew for more than 50 years. Carret did this by understanding the true underlying psychology of the market and by becoming one with the cycles and indicators that mark the swings. He understood the mind of the trader like no other, documenting their passion, their optimism, their naiveté—and eventually—exactly when they would panic and sell, or with what intensity the masses would cling to a stock like needles to a magnet.

But just like any great leader, a developed intuition is not the only making of success on the trading floor Successful leaders in any discipline—boardroom or battlefield—must have a complete knowledge of the intricacies of their business. They must know the history of their profession and most importantly, they must know the terms and tools of their trade. Carret makes this point often and he reviews the fundamentals of the core stockpile of the trader's arsenal: bonds, securities, derivatives, and stocks. This book doesn't miss a detail.

Warren Buffet, a man who many consider a virtual Patton of the financial battlefield, once said that Carret had the best record of any long term investing going. This is no slight praise, especially because he rode the financial catastrophe of 1929 in a manner unshaken by the banter of Wall Street critics and the downtrodden trader masses. Philip L. Carret loved to trade. It's as simple as that. You'll see his passion in every word of this book. He understood the prime factor in winning: keep your eyes on the prize. Sports players call it "the zone," and for him, it was his "money mind." Whatever the final phrase may be, this book will teach, elevate, and inspire.

Chapter I

What Is Speculation?

A treatise on investment needs no defence. Everyone who is not a socialist or communist realizes more or less vividly the vital part which capital plays in the modern world. It is readily admitted that the investor is entitled to a fair return for the use of the wealth accumulated by his self-denial. The average intelligent person recognizes fully the justice of permitting the hundreds of thousands of investors who make possible the unceasing growth of our telephone system a return, on the average, of 8% on their money. Such a person also recognizes the necessity of supporting the elaborate machinery which transmutes the hard-saved thousand dollars of a New York school-teacher into the equipment of a California hydro-electric plant. It is only the economically illiterate who regard bond salesmen, brokers and the other specialists of the financial world as "parasites" or "non-producers."

The case is different with speculation. It is by no means clear to the average man that the successful speculator contributes anything to the world's welfare by way of compensation for his financial gains. So far as he is personally familiar with speculative operations the average man sees more of losses than of gains. As there seems, on superficial consideration, to be no benefit to society from speculative operations, it is commonly believed that in speculation as in gambling the gains of the successful merely offset the losses of the unsuccessful. It is small wonder that Jay Gould, Daniel Drew and other noted speculators have never been popular figures.

A Flyer in Lumber

It is unfortunate that the word "speculation" immediately suggests the word "stocks" to most people. When his neighbors read in the local paper the income tax returns which show that Henry Robinson, the well known lumber dealer, paid a large sum to the public treasury last year, their natural comment is that Henry is a shrewd business man. It occurs to no one to say that Henry is a successful speculator, though the profits indicated by his income tax return may be due quite as much to a rise of $2 a thousand feet in the value of Henry's inventory as to his business acumen. In such a case a large part of the lumber dealer's profits are essentially speculative, though the speculation is incidental to his main business.

The "Dance of the Millions"

No profound research is necessary to indicate that this sort of speculation enters in very large degree into the operations of every business. On the rising sugar market that culminated with $22^1/_2$-cent sugar in 1920 it was literally impossible for any producer or refiner of sugar in the world to escape a fleeting prosperity. There resulted in Cuba the orgy of extravagance known as the "Dance of the Millions." In the debacle of 1921, with sugar at two cents a pound, it was quite as impossible for any sugar producer to make money. Such extremes as these are fortunately unusual, but fluctuations in the prices of every commodity are constantly occurring. In varying degrees every business man, whether he be a manufacturer of steel or the proprietor of a notion shop, is affected by price fluctuations of the things in which he deals.

Speculators by Necessity

It is a commonplace that the success of a cotton mill depends almost as much on the shrewdness with which its manager purchases his raw material as on the efficiency with which he operates his plant. The successful manufacturer of cotton textiles must then be to a considerable degree a successful speculator in raw cotton. If he buys cotton at the wrong time or fails to buy it at the right time, his profits will be small, or non-existent.

This is so much a matter of course that it is taken for granted, even by those who voice their disapproval of the speculator in stocks.

It will at once be suggested that there is a vital difference between the stock speculator and the business man. The latter, it will be said, is not a speculator by choice. Certain speculative risks are inherent in his business, and those he must minimize by the exercise of good judgment. They are incidental, however, to his main business. The textile manufacturer does not run a cotton mill as an excuse for speculating in cotton. He runs it to supply the world with cotton goods. The speculation is a necessary evil. The speculator in stocks, one may be told, has no such respectable excuse for his operations. He is merely a buyer and seller of intangibles which are not transformed in any way while in his possession. If the stocks he sells fall in price, he has merely enriched himself at the expense of the unlucky purchaser. If those he buys advance, no credit is due him for the fact. In fact, he is an idler who should be busy, a capitalist whose funds might more usefully be employed.

Familiar observation of the sources whence a stock broker's customers are drawn lends force to the indictment against the speculator. The lawyer whose partner neglects his practice to spend profitless hours poring over the quotations in the morning paper and haunting his broker's boardroom is one strong critic of stock speculation. The business man who has seen a promising subordinate lose interest in his job as he caught the fever of the ticker is another. Then there are the well known figures, whose origin no one seems to know, but whose authenticity no one questions, that 95% of traders in stocks lose money in the long run. These are readily available to the critics of stock speculation.

The Investor Must Speculate

Is there, however, no one to whom speculation in securities is as inevitable an accompaniment of his normal business as speculation in cotton to the textile manufacturer? There is! The investor is just as much a speculator by necessity as any business man. If he says proudly, "I never speculate," he is an ignorant speculator, and probably an unsuccessful one. Just as changes in commodity prices are constantly occurring with far-reaching effects on the fortunes of business men, so changes in security prices are likewise constantly occurring. The widow who bought 4% bonds at 95 in 1914 had an inkling of the truth when she asked her banker some time later to explain to her the phrase "yield to maturity." She was told that in addition to the $40 interest each year there was included in the return on her investment part of the $50 difference between the price she had paid and par, that her bonds were theoretically worth a little more each year as they approached maturity. "That sounds very well'" she commented, "but really they've gone down." Even in the highest-grade securities there is a certain inescapable speculative risk. It is not decreased by burying one's head in the sand like an ostrich and saying, "I never speculate !"

What the Dictionary Says

What, after all, is speculation? The redoubtable Webster gives a number of definitions. Among them we find (1) "mental view of anything in its various aspects; intellectual examination"; (2) "the act or practice of buying land or goods, etc., in expectation of a rise of price and of selling them at an advance." To the second he added the complacent observation that "a few men have been enriched but many have been ruined by speculation." According to Webster, the motive is the test by which we must distinguish between an investment and a speculative transaction. The man who bought United States Steel at 60 in 1915 in anticipation of selling at a profit is a speculator according to Webster, though he may have changed his mind about selling and added the stock to his list of permanent investments. On the other hand, the gentleman who bought American Telephone at 95 in 1921 to enjoy the dividend return of better than 8% is an investor, though he may have succumbed to the temptation of a 10-point profit a few weeks later. Although the outcome of the transaction may contradict the original intention of the party chiefly interested, it is obviously impossible to omit the factor of motive in defining speculation. For the purposes of these articles speculation may be defined as "the purchase or sale of securities or commodities in expectation of profiting by fluctuations in their prices." The purchase of a crate of eggs for the purpose of distributing them to the ultimate consumer a dozen at a time at a price a few cents higher is not speculation, though the merchant may derive a speculative profit if the egg market rises before the crate is sold. Neither is the purchase of a carload of eggs in June to be sold from storage in a carload lot in December speculation, though here again the fluctuations of the egg market vitally affect the profit involved. Pure speculation involves buying and selling in the same market without rendering any service in the way of distribution, storage or transportation.

ORGANIZED MARKETS

Though one may speculate in cheese, paper, coconut oil or almost any other imaginable commodity, the great bulk of speculation occurs in stocks and in commodities for which there are organized markets. The Chicago Board of Trade affords a market for the speculator in wheat, corn, oats, pork and other provisions, the Cotton Exchanges of New Orleans and New York a market for the cotton speculator, the New York Coffee and Sugar Exchange a market for trading in those commodities. To obviate the necessity of delivering huge quantities of goods or even warehouse receipts to the speculator, trading on these Exchanges takes the form of trading in contracts for future delivery. Since these contracts must be standard it is possible to organize Exchanges for trading only in commodities which may readily be graded. Such an important commodity as wool, for example, is not susceptible to such grading. There is, therefore, in the wool trade no counterpart of the Cotton Exchange.

Most important of the organized markets are the Stock Exchanges, headed by the New York Stock Exchange. More than a thousand stocks and an even greater number of bonds are listed on this greatest of organized securities markets. Other hundreds of securities are the subjects of trading on the New York Curb and the various provincial Exchanges. The strict rules of these Exchanges make certain requirements in the matter of publicity of the companies whose securities are listed, limit the commissions which their members may charge the trading public and in every way seek to foster the maintenance of a free and open market.

A Democratic Institution

The machinery of the Stock Exchange is available alike to the investor and the speculator. The broker neither knows nor cares into which category his customer falls. He knows, of course, whether his customer buys for cash or avails himself of the privilege of trading on margin, but even this distinction does not define the position of the customer. The purchaser for cash may buy primarily with an eye to enhancement in value, the buyer on margin may later pay the broker the debit balance, take up his stock and hold it permanently for income. One may safely assume that the man who buys nothing but high-grade bonds is primarily an investor, though even he must assume certain speculative risks. On the other hand, the margin trader who is constantly shifting his position in the market is certainly a speculator, if not a gambler. Between these two extremes are an infinite number of gradations, of buyers and sellers of securities whose motives are more or less mixed. It is quite impossible to draw a sharp line and say of those on the one side, "These are investors!" and of those on the other, "Those are speculators!"

HOPE OR JUDGMENT?

The two dictionary definitions of speculation already noted are more closely allied than might appear at first glance. An "intellectual examination" of the circumstances surrounding the security or commodity in which he is to deal is the first step of the speculator. Let it be noted that Webster does not speak of the "hope" of a rise in price, but of its "expectation." The man who places $100 on "Spark Plug" at 1 to 10 odds may hope that the thoroughbred will be first at the finish. In dealing with anything so uncertain as horse flesh he can have no logical ground for expecting so happy an event. He is, therefore, a gambler and not a speculator. If this same individual buys 100 shares of Mack Trucks or any other stock on hope rather than on judgment, he is likewise a gambler. The fact that his purchase may have been stimulated by the perusal of a tipster's sheet or even the unintelligent reading of a reputable broker's market letter does not alter his status.

In fact, gambling is a common form of stock market activity. Those who decry stock market speculation usually have stock market gambling in mind. The speculators are those who use brains as well as ink in writing the order slips for their brokers. They perform a service of substantial value to society.

ADVANCE AGENT OF THE INVESTOR

Just as water always seeks its level, answering the pull of gravity, so in the securities markets prices are always seeking a level of values. Speculation is the agency by which the adjustment is made. Has a new industry arisen, filling a new demand, adding new wealth to society, requiring new capital in generous volume? The alert speculator discovers it, buys its securities, advertises its prosperity to the investing public, and provides it with a new credit base. Is a once prosperous company falling upon evil days, its profits dwindling, its management declining in competence? The speculator is looking for such hidden weak spots in the market. He pounces upon it, advertises the difficulty on the stock ticker, and gives timely warning to the investor. In this fashion the speculator is the advance agent of the investor, seeking always to bring market prices into line with investment values, opening new reservoirs of capital to the growing enterprise, shutting off the supply from enterprises which have not profitably used that which they already possessed.

INCREASING MARKETABILITY

One great benefit stock speculation and stock gambling alike confer upon the investor is increased marketability of his holdings. Other things being equal, the greater the number of people interested in a given security the better will be its market. Perhaps marketability may be defined as the ability of a security to maintain its price level in the face of an unusual volume of offerings. It is probable that the market for United States Steel common would yield less under the impact of a sudden offering of 10,000 shares than a gilt-edged well known railroad bond like Atchison general 4s under pressure of offering of a $1,000,000 block. This high degree of marketability for the stock is principally the result of speculative activity.

In his work of bringing prices into line with values, the speculator is psychologically akin to the investor who seeks to obtain a better than average return on his money. The intelligent investor who succeeds in this quest is sure to grow a crop of speculative profits. Being an investor by intent he may not be so quick to reap his harvest as the avowed speculator, but it is apparent that the successful investor differs from the intelligent speculator in degree rather than in kind.

Speculation and the Cost of Living

"It is easier to make money than to keep it" is the frequent plaint of the man who has made his "pile" and is somewhat bewildered as to the best means of preserving it. His problem is not made less difficult by the recent researches of such students of investment as Kenneth S. Van Strum, whose "Investing in Purchasing Power" first appeared in *Barron's*. This and other studies of the subject stress the necessity not only of maintaining intact the dollar value of an investment fund but of maintaining its purchasing power in the face of constant fluctuations in the cost of living. The traditional policy of making bonds and mortgages the exclusive vehicles of conservative investment has suffered a rude blow at the hands of these modern authorities. They insist that sound investment policy requires the inclusion of common stocks in any fund. A sustained advance in the cost of living will then be offset by a compensating rise in the value of and dividend income from these stocks. In other words, the conservative investor must give himself an opportunity to reap speculative profits if he would maintain the real as well as the nominal value of his fortune. By this doctrine the difficulty from a practical standpoint of differentiating between the investor and the speculator has once more been emphasized.

When the investor has fully grasped the point that he must buy with an eye to at least occasional speculative profit he is likely to go one step further. Both to protect himself against the rare casualties which occur even among "gilt-edged" securities and to protect the real value of his funds against possible increased living costs, the investor must purchase at least a portion of his securities with the expectation of profit. It will not be possible for him to reap profits which will exactly offset the occasional losses and the increased living cost. In the face of this impossibility he will naturally wish to err on the safe side, to produce some net gain in his fund over a period of years. He has now crossed the border line. In some degree he has surely become a speculator. The degree to which he will seek capital gains will depend in part upon temperament, in part upon the amount of time and effort he will be able to give to the study of security values.

The Road to Success

The road to success in speculation is the study of values. The successful speculator must purchase or hold securities which are selling for less than their real value, and avoid or sell securities which are selling for more than their real value. The successful investor must pursue exactly the same policy. The one seeks primarily the increased return over a period of years which may be expected from an undervalued as compared with a fully valued security; the other seeks primarily the capital gain which will accrue to him when the price of the undervalued security adjusts itself to the line of values.

The time requisite for the accomplishment of the adjustment of prices to values is a factor of great weight with the speculator. Here he parts company with the investor, to whom it is of little concern, while adding to the complexity of his problem. There are styles in securities as there are in clothes. A security may be undervalued, but if it is also out of style it is of little interest to the speculator. He is, therefore, compelled to study the psychology of the stock market as well as the elements of real value.

How Stocks Resemble Real Estate

Innumerable factors affect the value of securities. The amateur trader who expects to become a successful speculator will not find the study of values an elementary one. He will find it fascinating and profitable, however, as well as intricate. Essentially the determination of values in securities is a matter of comparison, just as it is in any other field. The competent real estate appraiser compares a given piece of property with others in the same neighborhood whose value he knows by recent sales. It is not exactly like any one of them, but by making proper allowance for the points of unlikeness the expert can make a reasonable estimate of its true value. In the securities market the competent trader similarly compares one security with others as nearly like it as he can find and allows for the unlikenesses and estimates a figure at which it should be selling. He is also vitally concerned with the trend of the general level of security prices. Here again he must determine the trend by a comparison of current conditions in the securities market with periods in the past when like conditions prevailed.

In a single chapter it would be impossible to discuss even the most important factors affecting the value of securities and the trend of the price movement. Perhaps enough has been said, however, to answer the question, "What is Speculation?" In fact, speculation is inseparable from investment. The investor must assume some degree of speculative risk, the intelligent investor will seek a certain measure of speculative profit. If he has the time, the temperament, the ability, the investor may go a step further and seek speculative profit in preference to dividend and interest income from his capital. In so doing he is performing a valuable service to the investor, acting as his advance agent in seeking the most profitable channels of investment, increasing the marketability of investment holdings, and helping to support the financial machinery which is designed primarily for the service of the investor.

CHAPTER II

THE MACHINERY OF MARKETS

G o into the financial district of any of the dozen largest cities of the country and look at the signs on the doors and windows which are visible to the passerby. Under the firm and corporate titles there will be seen a great variety of legends. "Members of the New York Stock Exchange" will be seen frequently. Among other descriptions will be found "Brokers," "Investment Securities," "Investment Bonds," "Bankers," "Dealers" and "Specialists" in securities of various types. Two firms which use exactly the same word or phrase to describe their business may actually be as far apart as the poles in the type of securities they handle, the quality of service they render their customers. The multitude of firms who thus offer their services to the investor or speculator are a part of the great machinery of investment and speculation which distributes $6,000,000,000 annual savings of the American people into more or less profitable channels and maintains a market for the still greater billions of securities already outstanding. So complex is this machinery, so numerous its possible points of contact with the individual, that it is not surprising that blind chance rather than intelligent choice most frequently determines into which door the individual with ready money shall turn his steps.

THE GLORIFIED ERRAND-BOY

Generally speaking those who deal in securities may be divided into two classes: merchants, or so-called investment bankers, and brokers. Firms of the former type buy securities on their own account in large blocks and resell them to the investing public in smaller amounts. Fundamentally this is exactly the same type of business as that of the corner grocer who buys sugar by the barrel and retails it in five-pound lots. The broker renders an entirely distinct type of service. He is a sort of glorified errand-boy. On receiving a buying or selling order from a customer he seeks to find a buyer or a seller at the most advantageous price to his customer. For this service he receives a small commission. In relation to the amount of money involved in the transaction the broker's commission is usually only a small fraction of the profit legitimately taken by the investment banker. Despite the fact that the functions of broker and investment banker are distinct, many firms are engaged in both types of business. The leading firm of brokers in the country is also active in merchandising securities, both bonds and stocks. One of the leading bond houses of the country has an active stock department which will execute orders on a commission basis in any of the leading markets.

Merchant Bankers

The merchants of securities are for the most part bond houses. The long-term loans which our cities, towns, counties and states, our railroads, public utility and industrial corporations raise are almost invariably obtained by the process of selling bond issues to the great merchant bankers of the country. Stock issues are seldom created in this way, rarely distributed to the investing public in the same manner as bonds. A large number of investment banking houses consequently deal exclusively in bonds and there are hundreds specializing in one or another type of bond, as in municipals, in real estate mortgage bonds, or in public utilities. The bond houses send out thousands of salesmen to seek out investors in their homes, shops and offices, to sell securities which they have bought and must resell at a profit. Such salesmen, and the firms they represent, are primarily interested only in the securities which they have purchased. They are not likely to have detailed knowledge of or, informed opinion about other securities.

THE AMATEUR IN BONDS

Bond houses are concerned little or not at all with the speculator. The securities they offer carry for the most part a fixed return and afford little opportunity for capital appreciation. It may sometimes happen in an advancing bond market that an issue of bonds will be received with such enthusiasm that the market price will immediately advance two or three points. The investor who habitually takes his small profit in such cases is not regarded as a desirable customer by the bond houses. They prefer customers who buy bonds for income and usually hold them more or less permanently. The man who buys bonds for a quick profit is dubbed a "rider." He seldom makes any substantial profits by such trading and usually places himself in a position where he cannot expect favors from any of the houses with whom he deals. Speculative operations of this character are typical of the amateur bond buyer who has acquired just sufficient smattering of bond lore to fancy himself a professional.

STOCK FINANCING

The average bond house handles an occasional issue of preferred stock as well as the senior type of security. Preferred stock issues are created and sold in the same manner as bonds by companies which wish to raise new capital. In order to maintain a strong capital structure the growing corporation which must look to the public for new capital is compelled to sell a certain amount of stock, common or preferred, to support its growing funded debt structure. In recent years the public utility companies have found it possible in many cases to sell their own stock directly to their customers, maintaining permanent departments for handling such flotations. A company which needed new capital only at occasional long intervals could obviously not afford to use anything other than the conventional method for disposing of its stock.

Common stock equities, particularly in the case of industrial companies, are ordinarily built up by the continual reinvestment in the business of surplus earnings. The company which finances its capital requirements by the sale of common stock is the exception rather than the rule. The unusually successful company, such as American Telephone & Telegraph, is able to do so, but this sort of financing is far from common. When it does occur the offering of stock is usually made direct by the company to its existing stockholders rather than to the general public. An offering of this sort may be underwritten by investment bankers, who agree for a small commission to take any stock not subscribed by stockholders.

How Common Stock Issues Originate

The sale of a large block of common stock by a firm of investment bankers usually results from the disposal by the dominant interests in a company of all or a part of their stock. An individual who has built up a successful business may wish to retire and put his estate in more liquid form through reinvestment in diversified securities. A large corporation may sell the stock of a prosperous subsidiary whose control is no longer essential to the parent company. The recent sale to the public of a large block of stock of the National Cash Register Co. is a concrete example of the first type mentioned. A year or two ago a large block of stock of the Eastman Kodak Co. was sold by the educational institutions which had acquired it as a gift from Mr. Eastman and offered to the public by banking houses. Usually firms which are engaged in business both as brokers and as bankers make such offerings.

16

ORGANIZED MARKETS

Besides the firms which acquire securities—bonds or stocks—in wholesale lots and retail them to their customers, there are a great many firms which serve exclusively as brokers. The bulk of these firms are members of one or more of the organized Stock Exchanges of the country, chief of which is the New York Stock Exchange. Besides the premier Stock Exchange of the country, the New York Curb provides an organized market for an ever-growing list of securities, and in all the other important cities from Boston to San Francisco there are Exchanges of greater or less importance. By far the greatest volume of speculation in securities occurs in the form of trades made on the floors of these Stock Exchanges.

UNDER THE BUTTONWOOD TREE

The New York Stock Exchange proudly traces its history back almost to the American Revolution. Like every other war, that struggle was followed by the funding of the national debt. In this case $80,000,000 in 6% stock was issued and absorbed by the investing public. The close of the war was also speedily followed by the organization of banks, both in Philadelphia and in New York. Inevitably a market for government securities and for bank stocks was created and a number of individuals were soon making their living by acting as brokers for the buyers and sellers of these securities. By some accident of chance they formed the habit of meeting under an old buttonwood tree which stood at what is now 68 Wall Street. Doubtless some among them were tempted to seek business by cutting the commissions charged their patrons to an unremuneratively low level. Whatever the cause they were impelled to form some crude sort of organization. Accordingly on May 17, 1792, twenty-four of them signed the following agreement:

> We, the Subscribers, Brokers for the purchase and
> sale of Public Stock, do hereby solemnly promise and
> pledge ourselves to each other that we will not buy
> or sell, from this day, for any person whatsoever, any
> kind of public stock at a less rate than one quarter per
> cent, commission on the special value, and that we
> will give preference to each other in our negotiations.

From this small beginning, progress was for many years slow. Not for twenty-five years did the member brokers find it necessary to provide a roof over their heads. Of the early years of the Stock Exchange but meager records remain. The infant institution seems to have occupied many quarters, including at one time following a fire temporary refuge in a hayloft. The great institution whose marble palace towers aloft at Broad and Wall streets, upon whose floor billions in securities change hands each month is thus after all of humble origin. Its growth has been an inevitable consequence of the growth of the United States. Such a free market as it provides for instruments of credit and of ownership is an absolute necessity to modern civilization.

A Strict Code of Ethics

On reading the original agreement of organization of the Stock Exchange, it appears that two motives actuated its founders, protecting their scale of commissions and guarding against competition from outside their membership. The elaborate constitution of today likewise fixes a scale of commissions and in effect secures to members a monopoly of dealing in securities admitted to trading on its floor. In line with modern business practice it is also largely concerned with protecting the interests of the customers of member brokers. Probably no business today is conducted on a higher plane of ethics than that of the members of the New York Stock Exchange.

Perhaps the Stock Exchange may logically be regarded either as a trade union or as a private club. The latter is the usual simile.

The Exchange is an association of 1100 members. It furnishes the mechanical facilities for the transaction of their business and prescribes high standards for their business conduct toward one another. An additional professed object is "to promote and inculcate just and equitable principles of trade and business." A governing committee with despotic powers and various subsidiary committees control the government of the Exchange. A member found by a majority of the governing committee guilty of a wilful violation of the constitution or of any resolution of the governing committee or of any conduct "inconsistent with just and equitable principles of trade" may be suspended or expelled. Not only is a misdemeanor on the part of any member visited with swift and severe punishment but the Stock Exchange authorities are equally swift to take any action necessary to maintain the Exchange as a free and open market. If some misguided individual attempts to corner a listed stock, he may suddenly find himself with no market for his holdings as a result of action of the governors in suspending trading in the issue. There have been one or two occasions of extreme crisis when the Stock Exchange itself was suspended, notably for several months following the outbreak of the war in 1914.

Broker Starts in Business

A broker who wishes to become a member of the Stock Exchange must first purchase a "seat" from some retiring member at a figure ranging up to $150,000, depending on market conditions. He must then convince two-thirds of the committee on admissions that he is a citizen of high character and otherwise eligible. Having passed these tests he may now put the legend "Members of the New York Stock Exchange" under the firm name on his office door or window. He has now the right to go upon the floor of the Exchange to execute the orders of his customers. In case he finds it to his advantage to seek orders rather than to execute them he may instead handle all his customers' orders through a "two-dollar broker." The latter is a broker who executes orders for other members, charging them a fraction of the commission paid by the non-member customer with whom the transaction originated.

The Broker's First Order

Let us suppose that J. Madison & Co. have just become members of the Stock Exchange through the election of James Madison. He is now upon the floor of the Exchange when the firm's first customer enters the office and gives an order for the purchase of 100 shares of Atchison. The order is immediately transmitted by private wire to the firm's telephone booth on the edge of the floor. The telephone clerk has Mr. Madison's number flashed on the two annunciator boards on the wall and the broker hastens to the booth and gets the order. Next he goes to the Atchison post. He may find there another broker with a selling order or he may purchase from the specialist in Atchison. If the order is limited by his customer at a price some distance away from the market at the moment, Mr. Madison may leave the order with the specialist, who enters it in his book and ultimately executes it in the role of a two-dollar broker. The specialist is a dealer in Atchison and perhaps in several other stocks dealt in at that post. He may either buy or sell for small profits on his own account or act as a two-dollar broker. Orders given him for execution in the latter capacity take precedence under Stock Exchange rules over his own trades and he is also forbidden to make both a dealer's profit and a commission on the same transaction. The existence of the specialist assures the maintenance of a continuous market in each listed security.

Handling an Odd Lot

The next order received by J. Madison & Co. may be for the sale of 25 shares of General Electric. This order is promptly relayed by the telephone clerk at the edge of the floor to the representative at the General Electric post of the odd-lot house with which J. Madison & Co. deals. There are a number of such odd-lot houses, which stand ready at all times to buy or sell any odd lot—less than 100 shares—of any stock. If the next sale of General Electric is at 82, the odd-lot house will take the 25 shares at $81^7/_8$. The eighth—increased to a quarter or more in the case of higher-priced or less active stocks—compensates the odd-lot house for the risk that by the time it has purchased in this way 100 shares the market may have declined below this purchase price. Thanks to the odd-lot houses, the small investor or trader is able to buy or sell listed stocks at a minimum disadvantage as compared with the customer whose orders are for a 100-share lot. Odd-lot trading is an important factor in broadening and stabilizing the market for listed stocks, contributing a large part of the total volume of business. Mechanical limitations forbid the reporting of odd-lot transactions by the stock ticker, which is barely able in an active market to handle the transactions in round lots.

In the case of the 100-share purchase of Atchison the seller may be neither the specialist nor another commission broker but a floor trader. Such a trader is a member of the Stock Exchange who trades for his own account, seeking only small, quick profits. He roams the floor ever on the alert for opportunities for a "turn." Stock transfer taxes are a serious handicap to the floor trader. On each sale of 100 shares of $100 par value the state and federal governments levy a tax of $4. A gross profit of ⅛ on 100 shares thus becomes a net profit of $8.50, while a loss of ⅛ is equal to a loss of $16.50. Barely to break even the floor trader must thus be right in his judgment on two out of three trades. Before the imposition of these taxes there were upward of 200 floor traders, but today the number is greatly reduced.

STRICT DELIVERY RULES

When James Madison has purchased a block of stock for a customer from another commission-house broker, from the specialist in the stock, from a floor trader, from an odd-lot house or through a two-dollar broker there is still much to be done before the transaction is completed. The next step is delivery. Under the rules of the Stock Exchange the seller must deliver the stock to the purchaser by 2 p. m. on the following day. This is "regular" delivery. The buyer and seller may contract otherwise. An investor in California with his securities in a San Francisco safe-deposit box obviously cannot make delivery on the day following the sale. Possibly the New York office of his broker may have sufficient of the stock in its possession on behalf of other customers to make delivery, borrowing enough stock temporarily from other accounts pending arrival of the western customer's certificates. If this arrangement is not feasible, the sale may be made "seller 7 days," giving the seller the extra time in which to get his stock to New York. The price will obviously differ somewhat from the price for regular delivery. In the case of a sale for regular delivery the purchaser has the right to buy in the stock "under the rule" if the stock is not forthcoming on time. Traders who sold Northern Pacific against expected later delivery from European holders in the famous corner of 1901 received an expensive lesson in the rigidity of the Stock Exchange's delivery rule.

CLEARING STOCK TRANSACTIONS

To minimize the actual labor in delivering certificates of stock following transactions on the floor of the Stock Exchange in 1892 organized a system of clearances. All the most active listed stocks are cleared for members by the Stock Clearing Corporation. Suppose J. Madison & Co. sold 300 shares of U. S. Steel to John Q. Adams & Co. while the latter firm had sold 300 shares to B. Franklin & Co. Each firm would send the clearing corporation at the end of the day a deliver ticket for each block of stock it had sold and a receive ticket for each lot it had purchased. The deliver ticket would order the clearing corporation to deliver stock to the purchaser for account of the seller, the receive ticket would order the clearing corporation to obtain stock from the seller for account of the purchaser. On comparison of the tickets received from all clearing members it would be found that many could be canceled. In the instance given the clearing corporation would direct J. Madison & Co. to deliver the 300 shares of Steel to B. Franklin & Co. direct, thus saving one delivery which would be necessary without a clearing system.

THE BOARD AND THE TICKER

Having described very sketchily what takes place on the floor of the Stock Exchange and how deliveries between brokers are effected, let us return to the broker's office. The average customer seldom understands the complicated mechanics behind the scenes. In the typical broker's office will be found a board-room with a large black-board on which transactions in leading stocks are posted. A clerk stands at a ticker, which prints on a strip of paper transactions in stocks as they occur on the floor of the Stock Exchange. He reads off transactions in leading stocks and boys post the latest prices on the board. The customers standing in front of the board have at any time a history of the market for leading issues for the day, opening, high, low and latest quotations of the stocks quoted. The board shows the daily history of the market, the ticker itself a picture of the market at the moment. So speedy are executions on the floor of the Stock Exchange, so perfect the reporting system, that a trader in a distant city may under normal conditions put in an order, receive a confirmation of its execution and watch the report printed on the ticker, all within two minutes. Unfortunately the rapid increase in the number of stocks listed and the growth in the volume of trading has outstripped the ability of the ticker to report in active markets. On such a day as March 2, 1926, when an avalanche of stocks were sold in a frenzy of liquidation, the ticker may sometimes be fifteen or twenty minutes behind the actual market. Under such conditions the trader may by no means be sure that his order will be executed within a fraction of the price quoted on the ticker at the moment of giving it.

TRADING ON MARGIN

The customer who gives an order for the purchase of 100 shares of Steel may be a cash customer, but it is more likely that he is buying on credit. In certain unenlightened sections of public opinion it is regarded as a reproach to a man that he trades in securities on margin. It is unfortunate that the word is used only in connection with securities. One never says that a man has bought a house, a car, a radio set on margin. The use of credit in the case of such forms of wealth differs not at all fundamentally from the use of credit in connection with the purchase of securities. In each case an initial cash deposit is required. With such rapidly depreciating forms of wealth as cars and radio sets repayment in full of the loan made to the buyer by the seller must be made by installments. A house is a more permanent form of wealth and a mortgage for a moderate proportion of its value may run indefinitely. When securities are bought on credit the broker merely requires that the margin between their value and his loan shall be kept good.

Fraudulent vendors of worthless securities frequently preach eloquent sermons against margin trading. With the unsophisticated, who confuse speculation with gambling, such sermons make a favorable impression. From the promoter's standpoint their importance lies in the fact that the stocks he is attempting to sell would not be accepted as collateral by any responsible bank or broker.

The trader who buys 100 shares of Steel at 125 as his first purchase must first have deposited a minimum sum of probably $1500 with his broker as margin. Disregarding commissions he then owes a balance of $11,000, which is supplied by his broker. The latter in turn has probably borrowed $10,000 of his bank. He will charge his customer a slightly higher rate than he pays on his bank borrowings, thus earning something on the interest account as well as by commissions. Since the broker's requirements of bank accommodation are widely fluctuating he obtains the greater part of it by demand or call loans, renewed daily. The call-loan renewal rate is published daily on the stock ticker and is one of the interesting indices of the market's technical condition watched closely by traders. Collateral loans on Stock Exchange securities are practically risk-proof and hence are utilized by banks throughout the country as a medium for the investment of their surplus funds. Though call loans provide the bulk of the sinews of speculation a considerable volume of funds is borrowed on time. The term of such loans may be sixty days or six months.

OVER-THE-COUNTER TRADING

The catalogue of dealers in securities is by no means completed with a brief discussion of investment bankers and Stock Exchange firms. The thousands of stocks and bonds listed on the leading Stock Exchanges of the country are outnumbered many times over by unlisted securities which are more or less widely held by investors. Just as there are brokers who deal only or principally in listed securities so there are brokers and dealers in unlisted securities. In any financial publication the reader will notice the advertisements of such brokers in the form of long lists of stocks wanted and stocks offered. If a certain broker lists among his offerings the stock of the Continental Gadget Co., it may indicate that he is seeking a market for a customer or that he is offering stock on his own account. The investor or trader in unlisted securities should remember that the dealers and brokers are not governed in their transactions by any such rigid rules as those of the New York Stock Exchange. They seek to buy cheap and sell dear. Neither their profits nor commissions are limited by anything except their consciences and competition. In the unlisted market there is no Continental Gadget post beneath which all transactions in that stock are made under the scrutiny of a hundred eyes. *Caveat emptor* is the rule in the unlisted market.

The dealer in unlisted securities seeks to make an honest commission or profit where he can. The telephone is his principal tool. He is constantly checking the market for securities in which he is dealing by seeking quotations from other dealers. If he finds that one broker will supply him with Continental Gadget at 81 while another will take it at 82, the situation is meat and drink to him. It may sometimes happen that a broker in New York will be buying stock from a Philadelphia broker and selling it to another Philadelphia broker in the very same building at a profit. The average investor is at something of a disadvantage in dealing with so shrewd and nimble-witted a specialist, particularly if he is not a regular customer. At the same time the investor or speculator should learn to trade in the unlisted market, if only for the reason that its very obscurity often conceals genuine bargains.

THE STOCK AUCTIONS

In New York, Boston and Philadelphia the auctions provide a public market for the unlisted securities which is of some importance. These auctions are usually held weekly. Odd lots of local unlisted stocks usually provide the bulk of the trading. The auctions are also a convenient dumping ground for obscure and frequently almost worthless issues when an estate is being settled. Sometimes a long list of such securities will be offered "in one lot." The auctions attract bargain-hunters who frequently find wheat among the chaff. Occasionally such a trader will buy for five or ten dollars securities which turn out to be worth thousands thereafter. In the case of well known unlisted stocks the auction prices provide a good check on the quotations of dealers.

HOW TO FIND A RELIABLE BROKER

The great majority of the reputable investment bankers of the country are members of the Investment Bankers Association of America. Membership in this body is no such guaranty of re-liability as membership in the New York Stock Exchange, but it does carry assurance that a firm has reasonably adequate capital, has been in business at least two years, bears a good reputation with its competitors. The investor is justified in making searching inquiry as to why a particular firm of investment bankers is not a member of this body. In the case of the speculator in listed securi-ties, membership in the New York Stock Exchange may well be demanded of his broker. Under the rules of that organization members may not split their commissions with non-members. There is thus no legitimate way in which a non-member firm can profit by specializing in listed stocks. A member of an out-of-town Stock Exchange may make a reciprocal arrangement with a New York Stock Exchange firm by which he will give them all his customers' business on that board in exchange for all their customers' business on the local board. Any reputable firm will get an order in a listed stock executed as an accommodation for a customer. The firm which goes after business in listed stocks but is not a member of any Stock Exchange is a firm without visible means of support. Like a man without visible means of support, such a firm is the legitimate object of suspicion. If the amateur speculator learns nothing else of the machinery of speculation, let him at least learn enough about classifying brokers and investment bankers so that he will not be caught in the failure of a bucket-shop.

Chapter III

The Vehicles of Speculation

Limitless horizons stretch before the would-be speculator. All the commodities of commerce are possible subjects for his trafficking. If, however, he confines his dealings to bonds and stocks, he is by no means curtailing the scope of his activities to any narrow field. The values and the prices of securities are affected by a multitude of factors. Is he interested in jute? He may find securities whose value is affected by the state of the weather in India as well as the commodity itself. Does he fancy himself an expert on cotton? The rise or fall of fertilizer stocks, textile stocks, certain railroad stocks are all affected by the forecast of the cotton crop just as much as the quotations of cotton futures themselves.

Among securities he will find issues ranging in quality and in possibility of price appreciation from penny mining stocks to government bonds. His broker stands ready to buy these or anything between the two extremes at his bidding. He is by no means confined to bonds and stocks. Rights, puts, calls, option warrants also afford him a field for speculative activity. Among bonds he will find many sub-classifications inviting him—mortgage bonds, debenture bonds, income bonds, convertible bonds, bonds with warrants. An almost equally great profusion exists among types of stocks, preferred, common, class "A," participating preferred and many others. Before attempting to risk money on actual purchases and sales of securities, the trader should at least know what all these names mean, have some notion as to the risks and possibilities of profit involved in each general class.

When the Sky Is the Limit

The first broad classification in the securities field is between bonds and stocks, between evidences of obligation and evidences of ownership. The bond is a promise to pay a fixed sum at maturity, a fixed rate of interest. Generally speaking the debtor will do no more than fulfill these major promises while the sky is the limit for the profits of ownership in a well managed business. This is the basis for the ancient belief that bonds are essentially investments and stocks essentially speculative. A debtor must fulfill his promise or invite legal action looking toward its enforcement while the profits of ownership may be non-existent.

Broadly speaking then the possible profit in the purchase of a bond is the difference between the price at which it sells and the figure at which it will be paid at maturity or at which it may be redeemed. The possible loss is as easy to calculate, the difference between the selling price and zero. If the bond is a sound investment whose coupon or stated rate approximates the market rate for money on such security, it will sell at or close to par and the chance of profit in its purchase will be negligible. If it is equally a sound investment but carries a coupon rate considerably under the market rate for money, it will sell at a discount. The difference between the market price and par will not represent a prospective speculative profit, however, but merely an offset to the low coupon rate. A conscientious bond house feels perfectly justified in considering the discount as deferred income and calculates the theoretical yield accordingly in offering the issue to its customers.

Profits in a Defaulted Bond

When the discount at which a bond sells is more than sufficient to offset the low coupon rate borne by the bond the difference is obviously compensation for risk of default. Such a situation may afford the alert speculator an opportunity for profit. If an investigation of the situation convinces him that the risk of default is much less than the price indicates, then the security is a purchase. Suppose that the default may really be expected or has actually occurred. Still the price of the bond may be unreasonably low. An instance will suffice. In March, 1924, the Virginia-Carolina Chemical Co. went into receivership. That event had been preceded by a sharp drop in the market for its bonds. The drop continued for some weeks after receivership and carried the first mortgage 7s to a low of 53⅛ in the last week of May. At this price a first mortgage of $22,500,000 on the entire property of the company was selling in the open market for less than $12,000,000. The investing public had valued the properties of the company at the low prices of 1919—a year of prosperity in the industry, to be sure—at more than $50,000,000. The company had lost its 1919 earning power entirely, it had lost part of its 1919 working capital, but its fixed properties were intact, its product was still an essential article of commerce. It would have been a fair guess that in the case of a basic industry a company with large fixed investments and a huge established volume of business would find a way to replace its working capital, would ultimately recover its earning power. So it turned out and Virginia-Carolina Chemical first 7s recovered to more than double their 1924 low.

WHEN PATIENCE IS NEEDED

It took less than two years for the speculator in Virginia-Carolina Chemical first 7s to reap his reward. If he had bought instead another first mortgage industrial bond, American Writing Paper first 6s, 1939, he would have had to exercise a much greater degree of patience. That company went into receivership several months before the big fertilizer company. When the latter had triumphantly emerged with a revamped capital structure American

Writing Paper's reorganization was still an event of the nebulous future. The mere fact that a mortgage on a large piece of fixed property is selling for much less than the cost or even than the fair value of the property does not necessarily indicate a possibility of a quick profit. There must also be a good prospect of recovery of earning power and reorganization on favorable terms.

In the reorganization of a bankrupt company it often happens that bonds are issued which prove to be attractive speculative vehicles. At first the fact of the recent bankruptcy over-shadows in the mind of the investing public the equally important facts of the surgical operation which has been performed and the convalescence which is in process. If the bankers who arrange the details of a reorganization are competent financial surgeons, they will be pretty sure to fix the new capital set-up on such a basis that the company can easily earn interest on all its bonds. In the case of the Brooklyn Rapid Transit Co., for example, the reorganization resulted in creation of a new junior mortgage under which $92,000,000 45-year 6s were issued. Despite the fact that on the new set-up the company had earned its interest charges by a wide margin in preceding years, the bonds sold in 1923 in an extreme range between 65¼ and 74⅜. At the average of these prices they yielded barely under 9%. Within two years they were selling above 90.

Origin of Income Bonds

A favorite device of reorganizers who are not sure of the margin of earnings above interest charges under the proposed new set-up is to make part or all of the new bonds income bonds. Interest on such bonds is payable only when earned and declared by the directors, though there are sometimes stipulations that the directors shall not fail to declare a certain minimum proportion of the available earnings. Bonds of this type are really a cross between real bonds, which they resemble in having a definite maturity and sometimes a mortgage lien, and preferred stocks. Such bonds attain the position of high-grade investments over a period of years. Atchison adjustment 4s, 1995, rank as gilt-edged bonds today though they are still merely income bonds whose coupons are paid, in theory, only at the discretion of the directors. Income bonds of this type frequently afford excellent speculative opportunities. In 1922 the Missouri-Kansas-Texas Railroad was reorganized, $55,820,000 adjustment 5s, 1967, being issued in the process. Under receivership the road's 1921 earnings were equal to 7.88% on the new adjustments, yet those bonds sold under 50 in 1922. Three years later they sold above 90.

In the case of the Missouri-Kansas-Texas adjustments one factor in the advance was the privilege carried by the bonds of converting into the company's 7% preferred stock par for par. Bonds carrying a convertible privilege are increasingly popular with the investing public. Such a privilege permits the speculative investor to remain a creditor or become a partner in the business at his option. If the business is increasingly prosperous, he may profit to a theoretically unlimited degree by exercising a right to convert into common stock; if the expected prosperity fails to materialize, he keeps his status as a creditor, entitled to prompt payment of interest and principal in priority to the stockholder. The right to convert into preferred stock is obviously more limited in its possibilities than the right to convert into common stock, since a preferred stock issue normally carries a fixed dividend rate. Occasionally, however, as in the case of the Missouri-Kansas-Texas adjustments, such a privilege may have value.

From the standpoint of the issuing corporation convertible bonds offer an attractive means of financing for several reasons. It frequently happens that a bond issue with a junior mortgage position or no mortgage security at all can be sold with a convertible provision as a "sweetener" which otherwise could not be sold at all. Thereby the way is left open to senior financing in the event of an emergency. Moreover, there is a good chance that the bonds will ultimately be converted, eliminating a substantial part of the company's fixed charges and improving its capital structure and credit.

Sure-Thing Speculations

From the standpoint of the speculative investor the convertible bond may be described as a "sure-thing speculation." In purchasing it he buys a fixed income with security which may range all the way from fair to good. His risk of loss is no greater than it would be in purchasing any number of other bonds devoid of a conversion privilege. At the same time he is obtaining all the profit possibilities that are contained in the common stock, less the difference between the conversion price and the current market for the stock. With minimum risk he is thus obtaining unlimited opportunity for profit.

In the past some very handsome profits have been made in convertible bonds, ranging as high as several hundred percent, on the price at which the bonds were originally sold. Of course not every convertible issue has proved profitable to investors. The speculator must never forget that he is buying primarily a bond and only secondarily an option on a stock. Having first satisfied himself that the bond is reasonably secure in itself he may next consider whether the conversion privilege offers reasonable opportunities for profit, whether the price of the bond is close enough to the price at which the bond might reasonably be expected to sell without a conversion privilege so that he is not paying an exorbitant price for the option. While the convertible bond as a type may properly be termed a "sure-thing speculation" in the sense that a good convertible bond offers theoretically unlimited chance for profit with minimum risk, it is clear that no investor is justified in buying a bond merely because it is called "convertible" any more than an investor with a different temperament is justified in buying a bond merely because it is entitled "first mortgage."

THE RECORD OF TWENTY CONVERTIBLES

The speculator who bought one each of the 20 convertible bond issues offered to the public in 1922, for example, would have suffered a good many nervous moments in the following three years. Of the 20 issues four defaulted within that period and two other companies whose securities were on the list went through voluntary reorganizations. This is a far higher mortality rate than that suffered by bond issues in general. Despite this showing the 20 bonds were worth in the aggregate a trifle more on December 31, 1925, than their cost at the original offering prices. In making the calculation it was assumed that bonds called prior to the end of 1925 had been collected at their call prices or converted into stock, whichever was the more profitable procedure. Where bonds had been converted the equivalent value of the stock was taken as the price of the bond. Making these assumptions it appears that 20 bonds costing $19,667.50 were worth $19,740.00. The original offering prices ranged from 88 to 101¾, the prices on December 31, 1925, from 33 to 181⅛.

CASES OF WINDOW-DRESSING

Actually any experienced investor considering the purchase of convertible bonds in 1922 would have recognized that a number of the issues offered in that year afforded no real speculative opportunity. In seven cases out of the twenty the bonds were convertible only or principally into preferred stock. In these cases it was fairly obvious that the conversion privilege was mere window-dressing, designed to help sell the bonds without giving the bondholder any genuine chance for profit. Eliminating these seven it appears that one bond each of the other thirteen would have cost $12,877.50, while the thirteen bonds would have been worth $13,647.50 on December 31,1925. The profit herein revealed is by no means sensational, but it should be remembered that the selection was wholly at random. Moreover, the yield obtainable on the twenty bonds at their offering prices was 7.06%, a return substantially above that afforded the conservative investor in bonds in 1922. The speculator who bought every bond offered in 1922 which was convertible into common stock, without further investigation of its quality, thus fared reasonably well in the period studied.

The practical difficulty with any such theoretical study as the above is its failure to take into account the psychological factors involved. The list of 1922 offerings, for example, includes Virginia-Carolina Chemical convertible debenture 7½s, 1937. On December 31, 1925, these bonds were selling at 99¾ . In assuming that the original purchaser of one of these bonds held it until the end of 1925, however, one must assume a large amount of courage and patience on his part. Following the receivership the bonds sold as low as 27 and a holder might reasonably have supposed that a recovery of much less than 72 points from that level afforded him a decidedly good opportunity to retreat from a dubious speculative position.

DIRECT ACTION

In purchasing a convertible bond the trader is indulging in a rather cautious speculation. It will be a successful speculation only if the stock into which the bond is convertible advances substantially above the conversion price. That figure in turn is ordinarily well above the market for the stock at the time the bonds are originally offered. If the stock is expected to advance, why not purchase it directly and get the extra profit contained in the spread between the market and the conversion price? This is exactly what the average trader does, buying stocks rather than options on stocks, becoming a partner directly rather than indirectly.

There are, of course, many types of stocks available to the speculator. In general, however, the purchaser of stock in an enterprise is becoming a partner, with limited liability for the debts of the concern, perhaps with a limited voice in its management, often with a limited right to participate in its profits, but fundamentally a partner. His position thus differs in many respects from that of the bondholder.

Many Kinds of Stocks

In any classification of stocks it was formerly customary to divide them into preferred and common stocks. In recent years, however, corporation finance has grown in complexity. Today we find that there are participating stocks, prior common stocks, class "A" stocks, founders' shares, management stocks as well as preferred and common stocks appearing in any broad list of outstanding shares. Two different issues of preferred stock may differ widely in their preferences and limitations. It is, therefore, not possible to make any sweeping generalization as to the attractiveness or non-attractiveness of any one class of stocks from the speculator's standpoint. Each issue must be judged on its merits.

The typical preferred stock is entitled to dividends in priority to the common stock of the same company. Directors must declare preferred dividends at a stated rate before anything can be paid on the common. The right of preferred stockholders to dividends is frequently cumulative. If the corporation finds itself unable to pay full preferred dividends in any year, the deficiency must be made good in some subsequent year before anything can be distributed to common shareholders. A preferred stock frequently has a preferred claims to assets in liquidation. Since voluntary liquidation of a corporation is an even rarer event than a total eclipse of the sun such a provision is of no practical importance. A preferred stock is often callable at a stipulated premium above par. It does happen occasionally that a prosperous corporation desires to retire its preferred stock, so that this provision may have some importance.

Generally speaking the preferred stock is of less interest to the speculator than the bond. If the preferred stock is a sound investment issue backed by a long record of dividends and earnings, its fluctuations will be small. Since the dividend is ordinarily limited to a stated rate, increasing prosperity of the issuing corporation is of little consequence to the preferred stockholder beyond the point where safety of his dividends is assured. In 1925, for example, the speculative public discovered that the Havana Electric Railway, Light & Power Co. was a much more prosperous concern than had generally been realized. The common stock went from a low of 112 early in the year to a high of 246 in the Fall. The preferred fluctuated between 112 and 117 in the same period. On the other hand, the possible loss in a preferred stock in case the business of the issuing corporations falls on evil days is quite as large as in a common stock. Barring bank stocks, which carry double liability under American laws, the purchaser can in neither case lose more than 100% of his commitment.

CONVERTIBLE AND PARTICIPATING STOCKS

A preferred stock like a bond may carry a convertible provision. In this case the purchaser is merely obtaining an option on the common stock with somewhat less risk than by buying it directly. Somewhat different is the case with a preferred stock which enjoys a participating privilege. The holder of a participating preferred stock is entitled not only to the stated rate of dividends but to additional disbursements under stipulated conditions, as, for example, when the directors wish to declare more than a certain rate on the common stock. The market for such a stock will reflect increasing prosperity for the issuing corporation just as the common stock will, but the holder always retains his preferred position. In case the preferred is callable by the issuing corporation there may of course be a limit to its upward possibilities.

A "prior common" or "participating" or "class A" stock may in effect be a preferred stock, possibly a second or third preferred stock. The speculator must study its exact terms to understand its real position in the company's capital structure. American Brown Boveri "participating stock" is in reality a sort of second preferred issue. Armour "A" is actually a second preferred issue carrying a participating feature. The issue is entitled to $2 a share in dividends before anything is paid on the "B" issue and participates equally with the "B" after $2 is paid on that issue. On the other hand, Pan-American Petroleum "A" differs from the "B" only in the matter of voting power.

POPULAR PREFERREDS

Not only are participating and convertible preferred stocks of interest to the speculator but ordinary preferred stocks become of interest to him when they are off the dividend list because of difficulties which appear temporary. In the case of Cuba Cane Sugar Corporation, for example, it is the preferred rather than the common stock which is the popular speculative vehicle. The same is true of Central Leather Co. and many others. Particularly when a non-dividend-paying preferred stock is cumulative is it likely to become an active speculative stock. If such a stock is selling under 50 with dividend arrears in themselves equal to a large part of the market price, the speculator will find signs of recovery in the corporation's affairs well worth watching for. As a matter of fact, such arrears of dividends are seldom actually paid in cash, stockholders usually being willing to accept new securities in lieu of cash. The prospect of some arrangement equivalent to cash payment is always a good talking point for enthusiasts on such a stock during the progress of a bull market.

Uncommon Profits in Common Stock

Common stock, the customary vehicle of speculation, represents the equity in a business, the remaining assets after all debts and claims of preferred and other senior shareholders have been met, the right to net earnings of the enterprise after interest charges, taxes, rentals of leased property and preferred dividends have been paid. Since the common stockholders rank last in their claim on the assets and earnings of a business they are the first to suffer in a period of adversity. By way of compensation they and they alone profit by increasing prosperity when the claims of creditors and preferred stockholders have been satisfied. The history of business the world over is full of examples of businesses which have grown from modest beginnings to stupendous earning power. The owners of the business of manufacturing a certain safety razor have seen the value of their investment grow from $16,000,000 to more than $200,000,000 in less than ten years. Such spectacular successes are rare, but there are many businesses which double and treble in value over a period of years with the growth of the wealth and population of the civilized world. Common stockholders, not creditors nor preferred stockholders, profit by this growth.

MANAGEMENTS NEVER RESIGN

Not only do common stockholders enjoy the right to all the assets and earnings after the fixed claims of creditors and preferred stockholders have been satisfied but they also usually control in theory the management of the enterprise. Preferred stock may or may not have voting power, common stock may be divided into classes differing as to voting rights, but in general corporation managements are elected by the votes of common stockholders. This voting right is of more theoretical than practical importance in the case of companies whose stocks are widely distributed. The small stockholders vote to retain the existing management almost as a matter of course. The management thus constitutes in practice a factor in corporation affairs differing in interest from that of the common stockholders. The latter might like to receive large dividends in a period of prosperity, the management may prefer to retain the bulk of earnings in the business to further ambitions for power and prestige. The common stockholders of a business with a poor record of earnings for several years might reasonably desire to liquidate the business, get as much of their money back as possible for reinvestment in some more lucrative field. To do so would destroy the management, requiring an entire staff from president to office boy to seek other employment. This is perhaps one reason why voluntary liquidations almost never occur.

GUESSING AT POLICIES

The probable policy of the management is one factor which the speculator must consider in trying to anticipate price movements. He cannot safely assume, for example, that any given proportion of earnings will actually be distributed in dividends. He must assume that the corporation will never voluntarily liquidate. There, is, therefore, no logical basis for an assumption regarding the relation between book and market values. To determine

41

probable market values for a common stock is no such simple matter as a mere subtraction of debts and other senior claims from the book assets of the corporation.

It is in common stock that the principal interest of the speculator lies. He should know something of bonds and preferred stocks, be on the alert for favorable opportunities in these fields. The bulk of his trading, however, will be done in the thousands of common stocks listed on the Stock Exchanges of the world's principal cities and dealt in over the counter by a host of brokers.

CHAPTER IV

MARKET MOVEMENTS—RIPPLES AND WAVES

The obvious fact about security prices to any student of the market is that they fluctuate. During a period of persistently declining prices a novice asked Russell Sage whether he thought stocks would rally. "They always have," was the laconic response.

Suppose the novice makes a casual investigation of the market record of some seasoned stock like American Telephone. In the case of that particular issue he would find that over a long period of years the stock has fluctuated between an extreme low of around 90 and an extreme high of around 150. The stock has sold under 100 only in panic markets and in normal years has usually ranged between 115-120 and 135-140. "How simple!" says the novice. "I'll buy American Telephone when I can get it at 120 and sell it when it reaches 135. In that way I'll make 12½ on my money in a few months besides getting dividends at a satisfactory rate."

SEVEN YEARS FOR FIFTEEN POINTS

On paper such a plan as this seems to be airtight. In practice it would soon break down. The speculator who had proceeded on this plan in 1917 would have purchased his American Telephone at 120 without difficulty. He would then have waited seven years to collect his 15-point profit. In the meantime, to be sure, he would have been receiving a return of 6⅔% on his money, but he would have had to carry his stock through the uncertainties of a great war, a tremendous business inflation and a severe depression. Long before the seven years were up he would probably have abandoned speculation altogether or at least have modified his theories of speculation greatly.

The novice soon learns that no such simple plan of operations as this will work. His experience, however, does not shake his confidence in the axiom that stock prices are constantly fluctuating. Indeed, the next stage in the progress of the novice—a stage beyond which many traders never get at all—comes with the observation that the prices of securities fluctuate considerably from day to day and week to week. Taking a more volatile stock than American Telephone he soon notes that it may fluctuate as much as five or ten points in a few days. Here is apparently a real opportunity for profit. There are, however, several hundred fairly active stocks listed on the New York Stock Exchange to say nothing of those having an active market on the Curb or on other Stock Exchanges. Which shall the trader select as the vehicle of his operations? Shall he buy or sell?

THE COLLEGE PROFESSOR'S SOLUTION

A college professor might attack this problem by first trying to analyze the causes which influence the fluctuations of stocks. Having then determined to his own satisfaction what these causes are, his second step in a logical investigation would be an analysis of the position of each of a great many stocks to discover which was in the most favorable position for a purchase or sale. Obviously such an investigation as this would involve a great deal more time, thought, energy and knowledge than the average trader could possibly devote to it. Being, as is usually the case, a "practical" business man he would scorn such a laborious approach to the problem of speculation anyway. Didn't his neighbor, Joe Smith, make $10,000 in the stock market last year, according to the gossip of his country club locker room? If Joe, of whose business ability he has a low opinion, can make money in the stock market, it must be a simple proposition. At this point in his reasoning certain well known students of the market come to his assistance. It is a simple proposition, they assure him. All that he needs to know about the market is printed on the tape which unrolls from several thousand tickers every day. Suppose that he stands in front of the ticker and a number of transactions in Allis-Chalmers appear. He may read *"AH 5.83 2.83⅛."* Translated for the benefit of the novice this signifies that 500 shares of Allis-Chalmers common have been sold at $83 a share immediately followed by a sale of 200 shares at 83⅛. A whole book has been written based on the thesis that such a record of transactions is of deep significance. It means, says the writer, that the supply of Allis-Chalmers offered for sale at 83 has been exhausted and that would-be purchasers may obtain more stock only by bidding up for it.

READING THE TAPE

In every brokerage office may be found traders who endeavor to make money by "reading the tape." They hang over the ticker hour after hour endeavoring to base a prediction on the future course of a given stock from the record of present transactions in it. Like the hangers-on at Monte Carlo and in gambling casinos throughout the world, each has a "system" which he believes infallible and like them none is ever known to make—and keep—any substantial fortune. A moment's consideration should show how absurd is the theory that any confident prediction of the course of any given stock can be based merely on its market action. In the case of an active stock like Allis-Chalmers there are thousands of investors and speculators throughout the country who are interested in the stock and watch the course of prices more or less closely. Any one of a thousand motives may influence them to place buying or selling orders. The 700-share transaction outlined above may represent partial execution of a 1000-share order by a large investor. Five minutes after the order is filled some trader in a distant city may walk into his broker's office and give a selling order which will knock the stock down to 79¾. The man who is watching the tape does not know who is the buyer of the 700 shares, what his motives are in purchasing, how large a block of stock he is seeking to buy. Neither does he know the motives, identity, resources of the seller. As to the prospective buyers and sellers who have placed their orders a little away from 83⅛ he is still more completely in the dark.

A SPECTACULAR MARKET MOVEMENT

Granting this, the tape-reader may still contend that a record of heavy transactions in a given stock within a narrow price range over a fairly extended period of time possesses genuine significance. If a given stock sells between 110 and 118 for several weeks, it is said to be "making a line." If then it crosses either of these boundaries, this action is thought by tape-readers to be significant of a much more extended movement in that direction. For example, if the stock in question should sell at 118½, the tape-reader would immediately conclude that it was a good purchase for a substantial further rise. On the other hand, a drop to 109½ would convince him that a further decline was probable. Apply this reasoning to a concrete case. In the late winter of 1925-26 Hudson Motors fluctuated for a considerable period between 111 and 121. In the six days, February 13-19 the stock sold between 111 and 119¼ with total transactions of 329,600 shares. During the following week the range was 115⅝-121⅜ with a volume of 254,300 shares. On March 1 the stock broke out of its trading area, reaching 122½ in the face of an almost unparalleled decline in the general market. This isolated strength in the face of general weakness made a most impressive exhibition. It was accompanied by the wide circulation of rumors, denied in responsible quarters, that Edsel Ford was seeking to purchase control of the company.

So impressive was the persistent strength in the stock that one experienced trader who was short of the stock covered at 120. On March 2, however, the stock succumbed to the general crumbling of prices and broke to 103. Within a month it was selling in the 80s. A tape-reader who had construed the action of the stock in breaking out of its trading area on the upside as bullish would have suffered a severe loss.

Perhaps the defender of tape-reading is still unconvinced. The trading area taken was too narrow, he may say. The speculator should have waited a little longer for confirmation of the bullish signal given. On the other hand, he may point out triumphantly the drop to 103 on March 2 was a decisive signal on the bear side. The trader who acted on this bearish indication certainly profited by his tape-reading.

What Makes a "Line"

As a matter of fact, the novice who tries to learn how to read the tape at once runs into an obstacle. There is no one to tell him how wide may be the range of quotations within which a stock should move in order to "make a line." Worse still, he may ask dozens of traders how long such a line should run in order to be significant and he will get no intelligible response. In point of fact the whole theory of reading the tape is based on a fallacy. The tape-reader believes that he can deduce the attitude of the "insiders" or the "prominent banking interests" traditionally active in the market by the action of the stock he is watching. The line of quotations is supposed to represent accumulation of the stock in anticipation of a rise, by people in a position to know much more about the affairs of the company than the average trader. On the contrary, it may represent liquidation of the stock in a high market area.

The Devoe & Raynolds Pool

As a matter of fact, such a line may actually represent either of these things, it may be a purely accidental sequence of quotations, it may represent accumulation by a "pool" which is not close to the management and knows no more about the company's affairs than the average trader. The collapse of the Devoe & Raynolds pool in February, 1926, is illuminating. In the month of January Devoe & Raynolds "A" stock sold in a range of about eleven points between 90 and 101. In the first week of February it pushed up to 103. Here again we have a stock breaking out of a trading area on the upside. This movement occurred in the face of publication of the company's annual report showing earnings of $3.69 a share on the combined "A" and "B" stocks. Such earning power was of course woefully insufficient to justify a price of better than 100. The tape-reader who ignored fundamental values was involved in catastrophe. From the peak of 104⅛ reached February 10 the stock dropped to 40 before the month was out.

The line which Devoe & Raynolds made in January, 1926, carried no message of accumulation by insiders. It represented the insane maneuverings of a speculative clique not connected in any way with the company's management. This group of speculators had made a lot of money in the early part of the 1924-26 bull market. Attracted by the small floating supply of an obscure issue they sought to add to their winnings by a speculative coup. Not only did they suffer heavy losses in the collapse but even the brokerage houses which carried their accounts were rumored to have lost sums running into six figures.

A GREAT BUSINESS LEADER'S DISASTROUS EXPERIENCE

Even if a line actually carries a message of accumulation by insiders, it does not necessarily represent sound judgment as to the future course of the market. Successful corporate executives seldom trade in their own stocks on any important scale. The official who keeps one eye on his business and one on the stock market is not likely long to be numbered among the leaders. His judgment regarding the stock market is by no means infallible. It sometimes happens, of course, that a corporation executive does go into the stock market on a large scale. In 1919 United Drug common reached a high of 175⅛. In common with other stocks it began to decline while business in general was still very active and profitable. President Louis K. Liggett had built the company up in a period of twenty years from small beginnings to a business giant. He had seen the business go through the panic of 1907, the depression of 1914, the collapse of the war boom with its rate of growth in sales and profits almost unaffected. He felt that the decline in the stock was unwarranted and when it had gone some distance he began to add to his holdings on borrowed money. The drop in the stock to 46¼ in 1921 would have ruined a lesser man. The solid foundation he had built for his company, the good-will acquired by nearly two decades of fair dealing, pulled the Liggett personal fortune through a tight place. Thousands of retail druggists all over the country came to the rescue when ordinary bank-credit channels were closed. Their faith in a business genius was fully rewarded. Within a few years United Drug was larger, stronger, more prosperous than ever. The incident is instructive, nevertheless, as showing that the judgment of even a foremost business leader about the market movements of his own stock is by no means convincing.

POOL OPERATIONS

Reference has already been made to pool operations. It should be understood that there are two kinds of pools. The commonest kind of pool is the steadying pool, operated to maintain at all times a ready market for a given stock rather than for the purpose of making profits. A market which is subject to sudden and violent fluctuations without apparent cause frightens investors. Bankers, large stockholders and executives interested in a particular company often employ an astute broker to operate a pool which will prevent such fluctuations. In a time of unusual demand for the stock, the pool may go short to keep prices within bounds. Similarly sale of a large block of stock would cause a severe decline unless the pool stood ready to buy. Through such buying and selling operations an orderly market may be maintained and the investor assured that he will always be able to buy or sell the stock at a price close to the last quotation. Such a pool is usually self-supporting, but not a money-maker.

HISTORIC POOL IN ROCK ISLAND

The second type of pool is organized with the avowed intention of making profits through operation in a particular stock. If a particular stock appears to be selling at an unreasonably low price and general market conditions are favorable, such a pool may seek to accumulate a large block of stock. When enough stock has been obtained the floating supply will be materially diminished and further purchases will tend to force prices upward. This price movement in itself will attract the attention of the trading public and if the stock is genuinely undervalued the result will take care of itself. Such upward movements are occasionally assisted, especially when the pool is selling its holdings, by the adroit circulation of favorable reports regarding the company in whose stock operations are being conducted. Fundamentally pool operations of this type differ not at all from the attempt of the small trader to make a profit by buying a stock for less than what he considers its real value. It is obviously more difficult to accumulate thousands of shares without running the market up or to distribute the pool holdings without breaking the market than it is to buy and sell in hundred-share lots, but this is a difference of degree and not of kind. A pool may be very profitable or suffer severe loss. The collapse of the Devoe & Raynolds pool has already been mentioned. A few years ago a pool was formed in Rock Island under the management of a well known speculator. Invitations to participate were distributed, almost broadcast, and many small traders became members. The pool finally liquidated at a heavy loss. Even if a tape-reader can deduce from the action of a stock that it is being accumulated on a large scale, he has no assurance that he will be in good company on buying it himself.

How the Amateur Trades

While considerable space has been devoted to the subject of tape-reading, it is perhaps more than the subject deserves in view of the attitude of the average trader. Even so unsound a basis for buying and selling as tape-reading is beyond his knowledge.

Impatience is his dominating characteristic. The money that he has decided to risk in the stock market is burning a hole in his pocket. Having opened a brokerage account he seeks eagerly for a suggestion as to a purchase. Perhaps a business friend who is quite as much of an amateur supplies a tip; perhaps he hears a tip circulating in the board-room of his brokerage office; he may find a suggestion that appeals to him in his broker's market letter, or he may consult a customer's man in the brokerage office. Whatever the source he is sure to receive a tip very shortly unless he is both deaf and blind. Let us suppose that a bull market is in progress and that he is attracted by the suggestion that Atlantic, Gulf & West Indies is an attractive purchase. He gives his broker an order to buy 100 shares at market and gets his stock at 43⅛. If this is his first experience in trading, he will probably remain in the board-room a few minutes watching the ticker. Perhaps the market is in an excited state and before he leaves he may see a quotation of 44⅛. Easy money, indeed, he may think to himself. A profit of $100 made in a single day on a capital of perhaps $1000! Remembering the proverb "You'll never get poor taking profits," he may now enter a selling order.

Two to One Odds

On the following day the novice will receive two statements from his broker covering these transactions. If he compares their total, he will find that he has not made a profit of $100. From that gross profit he must deduct commissions of 15 cents a share on both buying and selling and transfer taxes of four cents a share on selling. The sum of these charges is $34 on a 100-share transaction. The net profit is thus *$66* and not $100. If the stock had declined one point instead of advancing, the loss would likewise not have been $100. The broker's commissions and the transfer taxes would have been charged against the customer just the same. His net loss would then have been $134. Carrying these calculations a step further it is easy to see that the trader contenting himself with one-point profits and seeking to limit his losses to a point would have to be right on two trades out of three just to break even—and this does not allow for the interest charged by the broker on a margin customer's debit balance. Since the fluctuations of the stock market within a range of a point or two may be influenced by a thousand factors which it is impossible to estimate, trading on such fluctuations is mere gambling. No gambler can possibly make money with the odds so heavily against him as two to one.

Ten-Point Swings Take Time

The larger the profit which the speculator seeks to obtain the less heavily do the odds imposed by commissions, transfer taxes and interest count against him. On ten-point swings the trader needs only be right 52 times out of 100 in order to break even. What are his prospects of forecasting ten-point swings correctly? One-point movements may be likened to the ripples of the stock market, whose occurrence may be influenced by so great a multitude of factors that it is impossible to forecast them. Ten-point movements may perhaps be compared to waves. They occur in response to a smaller number of more powerful forces and are correspondingly easier to forecast. This is by no means to say that it is easy to forecast movements of this extent. On the day before this paragraph was written the market might fairly be described as firm. Of the 528 stocks whose symbols appeared on the tape 386 advanced, 82 were unchanged and 78 lost ground. Analyzing the transactions a little more closely it appears that 56 stocks advanced from two to as many as ten points. Selecting at random a trader would have had just better than one chance in ten of selecting a stock which scored an advance of substantial proportions. Even then he would probably have seen the greater part of the gain wiped out on the following day, as most stocks then declined. It rarely happens that five such days as the one analyzed follow one another consecutively. Rather the market is likely to go in one direction for three or four days, then move in the opposite direction for a day or two. The conspicuously strong stocks of one day will be replaced in all probability by a different group in the next day or two. A ten-point profit is not likely to be won in a week unless the trader enjoys unusual luck.

THE LONG SWINGS

The novice soon learns that stocks are likely to maintain an upward or a downward trend for long periods of time with minor interruptions of the major trend. These movements are shown by averages of the price of leading stocks compiled daily. Dow, Jones & Co., publishers of *The Wall Street Journal*, have for many years compiled daily an average figure of the price of twenty leading rails and of twenty—formerly twelve—leading industrials. Substitutions in the lists of stocks composing the averages are made from time to time to keep the lists representative. While the general market may move in one direction for months at a time any given individual stock may enjoy an entirely different movement or it may compress its movement into a few weeks and lie dormant the rest of the time. In 1922, for example, the general trend of the stock market was consistently upward, reaching a peak in March of the following year. Examine in contrast the action of Gulf States Steel. In a general way, to be sure, that stock paralleled the course of the general market, rising from a 1921 low of 25 to a 1923 high of 104⅝. More than half this 80-point rise, however, was compressed into the two-week period ended January 21, 1922. During this period the stock advanced 45 points from 45½ to 90½.

TIMIDITY AND STUBBORNNESS

This is a rather unusual instance of the way individual stocks act in comparison with the general market. If a trader could select the stock which is to be the star performer for the next week or two, take his profit on that and move on to the next, he would actually find the stock market the road to fortune that many people think it is. How shall the trader select of the thousand stocks traded in the one issue which will have the largest movement in the next week or two? Nothing short of omniscience will enable him to do it. Yet this is exactly what thousands of traders are constantly trying to do. Impatiently they jump around from one stock to another taking a small profit here or a loss there and doing no better in the long run than make commissions for their brokers. A psychological factor here enters. Having no sounder reason for his purchase than a tip the average trader has little courage and is easily frightened into taking small profits. On the other hand, he is stubborn enough to feel that any stock he has purchased must at least be worth what he paid for it. He is likely, therefore, to hold on grimly in a declining market and at the end of the year find that it took a good many five or ten-point profits to offset a few twenty and twenty-five-point losses, commissions, transfer taxes and interest charges.

HOW THE SMALL FRY FARE

Wall Street is supposed to be the seat of stock market wisdom. In the light of this supposition the novice might well ponder the following quotation from the *New York Times* of April 7, 1926, discussing the possible implication of a letter addressed by Stock Exchange authorities to their members, calling their attention to the rule which forbids Stock Exchange firms from accepting accounts from employees of other members, from bank employees and employees of other similar institutions.

The *Times* said: "According to reports circulated in the financial district, the action arose from rumors of the financial straits in which employees of certain firms found themselves after the recent period of drastic liquidation. The reports had it that many clerks and minor employees of Wall Street firms were completely wiped out as a result of the recent decline."

FEAR OF THE UNKNOWN

Everyone familiar with Wall Street and the other financial centers of the country knows that "clerks and minor employees" are not the only ones who lose money in the stock market. Among the ranks of bank officials, partners in bond houses and high corporation executives may be found plenty of individuals who consistently dabble in the stock market, trading in and out for small profits and large losses and over a period of years losing a substantial proportion of the income obtained from hard work or invested funds. Reference has already been made to the timidity of the average trader in the face of a profit, his stubbornness when faced with a loss. The explanation is probably to be found in the tardiness with which the mind adjusts itself to changing ideas of values. Suppose a trader buys at 70 a stock which has already advanced from a previous low of 49. Every point further advance is, so far as his previous experience goes, a step into uncharted ground. Any sign of hesitation in the market, particularly if he is operating in large part on borrowed money, leads him to act on the proverbial advice that a bird in the hand is worth two in the bush. On the other hand, the fact that he has actually paid 70 for the particular stock automatically establishes that figure in the mind of the average trader as representing something like its true value. It is one known spot in uncharted ground. Though the stock may stray away from it in the wrong direction, the average trader will be slow to believe that prospects of its return are dubious.

STOCK MARKET GAMBLING

Perhaps enough has been said to indicate the principal difficulties which beset the speculator who attempts to profit by the short swings of the stock. For practical purposes the occurrence of ripples and waves in the price movement is unpredictable. To attempt to trade on such movements is mere gambling with the odds against the trader by a considerable margin. It is astounding that thousands of otherwise intelligent persons persist in trying to make money in this way. Commonly accepted figures of somewhat dubious origin are frequently cited to show that 90% to 95% of all margin traders lose money in the stock market. The deep-seated gambling instinct, the well founded belief that in widely fluctuating markets there must be opportunities for profit nevertheless bring fresh recruits to the brokerage offices in constant streams. A few of them ultimately learn the methods by which money may actually be made in the stock market.

CHAPTER V

The Tides of Speculation

Take any twenty active stocks, add their closing prices each day and divide by twenty. Do this each day for a dozen years and plot the figures on a chart, the vertical scale showing the fluctuations of this average and the horizontal scale for the lapse of time. Better still take the Dow-Jones averages* of twenty rails and twenty industrials—formerly twelve industrials—kept without interruption since 1897: Such a chart will show a fairly regular series of great upward and downward movements, which may be called the tides of speculation. The upward movements, known in Wall Street parlance as bull markets, have usually lasted eighteen to twenty-four months, the downward, or bear movements, from seven to eighteen months. There have occasionally been intervals of as long as four years during which the market has fluctuated somewhat aimlessly in a more or less narrow range. On the whole, however, the regularity with which a long-sustained movement in one direction has been followed by a long-sustained movement in the reverse direction is striking.

BUSINESS CYCLES IN THE BIBLE

Every Sunday-school child knows the picturesque story of Joseph, who was sold into slavery in Egypt by his brothers. Having risen to a commanding position in the Egyptian government he saved the people of Egypt from disaster by his foresight in building warehouses and storing the surplus production of seven years of good crops. This surplus carried the people of Egypt

---

*Given in "The Stock Market Barometer" by W. P. Hamilton.

through seven years of crop failures and according to the dramatic story told by the biblical author saved Joseph's own brothers from starvation. Here we have in the early records of mankind recognition of what is now known as the business cycle.

A PARALLEL IN PUGILISM

Many explanations for the business cycle have been advanced. One leading economist has even sought to connect the fluctuations in business from prosperity to depression and back with the occurrence of sun spots. As simple and perhaps as good an explanation as any is the inability of the majority of mankind to maintain a regimen of hard work in the face of easy living conditions. Just as in the realm of pugilism a few years of soft living will make a Dempsey easy prey for a Tunney so a period of prosperity contains the seeds of its own destruction. Effort slackens, wages obtained with relative ease are spent for luxuries, business men forget the painstaking care by which they have built up their enterprises and commit themselves to reckless plans of expansion; others curtail their office hours, increase their golf hours. The silk-shirt era of 1919 and 1920 was followed by the painful depression of 1921. So it has been throughout the history of the world.

The history of the United States may be written as a record of wars and battles, a chronicle of presidents and lesser statesmen or it may be written as a story of the conquest of a continent by ox-cart and railroad, the growth of industry, the development of banking, the interplay of politics and economics. In the latter sort of history there are certain important dates which every schoolboy should know, 1814, 1837, 1857, 1873, 1884, 1893, 1907, 1921. These are the years of our great panics and depressions.

Between these major interruptions to the march of progress there occur minor recessions in business so that lesser cycles of prosperity and depression occur at much more frequent intervals than the fourteen to twenty years which usually elapses between the crises and depressions of historic magnitude.

How Bryan Was Defeated

The factors that affect the state of what we call "general business" are innumerable. The man in the street who was already complaining of the "high cost of living" before the war never heard the names of the two chemists who discovered the cyanide process of leaching low-grade gold ores. Their discovery, however, was responsible for the culmination of a twenty-year downward movement in commodity prices in 1896, firmly established the gold standard in the face of Bryanism and started commodity prices on their long rise. The fabric of civilization today is woven of millions of threads. No spot in it is so strong that it will not feel some effect from a weakening at any point. Are the people of India suffering depression? Then Lancashire cotton mills must curtail operations, American cotton farmers sell their crop at low prices, fertilizer manufacturers suffer in consequence. A bumper wheat crop in The Argentine may have similar repercussions all around the world. In an obscure corner of the Balkans, as the world discovered in 1914, the act of an assassin may wipe out currencies, destroy some industries and create others thousands of miles away, open new trade routes and close many old ones, upset the whole balance of international payments, create new standards of land values in the wheat fields of Kansas.

Exceptions to the Rule

When general business is prosperous or depressed it does not, of course, mean that every individual enterprise or even every industry is in the same state. A change in the styles may cause depression among manufacturers of ginghams even when the great majority of manufacturers are prosperous. A short sugar crop may result in rising prices and abnormally large profits for refiners despite the prevalence of hard times in most lines of business. Anomalies are always to be found in the business situation. Perhaps a retail clothing merchant could explain why in February, 1926, as compared with February, 1925, net sales of men's clothing in the New York federal reserve district were 5.7% greater, while net sales of women's clothing were 24% less. To the writer the contrast appears inexplicable, but at least it is a striking example of the fact that prosperity and depression may exist side by side. The majority of industries, however, experience much the same degree of prosperity or depression together.

A FAMOUS BUSINESS CYCLE

Going back a few years it may be interesting to recount the history of a famous business cycle, that which included as its nadir the panic of 1907. In general the opening years of the century constituted a period of prosperity. A stock market panic resulted from the Northern Pacific corner in May, 1901, and a bear market known as the "rich men's panic" developed in 1903, but business continued active well into 1907. During this period the farmers of the country raised large crops and sold them at good prices. Great activity occurred in the progress of the movement toward industrial consolidations, featured by the formation of the United States Steel Corporation. Railroad construction continued active under the leadership of Harriman and Hill and the railroad mileage of the country steadily grew. As late as November, 1906, Hill could declare in all seriousness that another 115,000 miles of railroad were "urgently needed" by the United States. Agricultural, industrial and railroad prosperity were naturally accompanied by a growth in the resources of the banks. During the early years of the century the rates paid by commercial borrowers were, judged by present-day standards, abnormally low.

The Day of the Muck-Raker

Politically the opening years of the 20th century were tranquil. The defeat of Bryan in 1896 was followed by a return to prosperity which effectually disposed of radicalism for a number of years. In 1900 McKinley was re-elected by an overwhelming vote. On his assassination Theodore Roosevelt, who is often ranked with Washington and Lincoln in estimates of our presidents, took the helm. He was returned to office with little opposition in the election of 1904. During his second term a wave of political unrest swept the country. Business methods in vogue at that time became the subject of widespread condemnation. Muck-raking was the order of the day. Ida Tarbell's "History of Standard Oil" and Upton Sinclair's "The Jungle" exposed methods of business management which aroused public hostility to the "interests." Disclosure of the prevalent practice of the railroads of giving secret rebates to large shippers particularly stimulated the wrath of the public. In New York the Armstrong investigation, revealing corruption in the management of leading life insurance companies, added fuel to the flames.

A Banker's True Prophecy

The year 1906 opened with trade and industry exceptionally active, but with political conditions distinctly unsettled and with public sentiment on the whole hostile to the country's business leaders. Evidences of strain had also begun to appear in the money market. The abnormally low rates of four or five years earlier had disappeared and the drain upon the liquid resources of the country resulting from active construction of new railroad mileage and other fixed forms of wealth had resulted in higher rates. In January call money—loans to brokers secured by Stock Exchange collateral and payable on demand—was quoted as high as 60%. Referring to the gyrations of call money and the proposal to reform the currency then agitated, the noted banker, Jacob H. Schiff, said in a public speech that "unless the currency system were reformed a panic would sooner or later result compared with which all previous panics would seem like child's play." No attention was paid to this or other warnings. Prosperity continued its mad pace. On top of the 13,500 miles of new railroad constructed in the previous three years another 5400 miles were added to the country's system. Pig-iron production made a new high record during the year, business failures in percentage of firms in business were at the lowest point since 1881. Volume of foreign trade in 1906 was the highest on record and internal trade, as measured by bank clearings, reached the second highest point on record. Bumper crops were harvested and sold at good prices.

Despite the prosperous condition of business in 1906, hostility to the business interests manifested itself in many ways. The Hepburn railroad-rate bill, giving the Interstate Commerce Commission power to regulate railroad rates, was passed by Congress. That same body enacted meat inspection and pure-food laws which are sufficiently commonplace today, but were regarded as radical at the time. In New York a reduction in gas rates was ordered by the public service commission. In Chicago court decisions adverse to the validity of franchises held by the traction lines impaired confidence. Progress was made by the government in its suits brought against the American Tobacco Co., the Standard Oil Co. and the packers under the long-dormant Sherman antitrust act.

The San Francisco Calamity

In one great American city the year 1906 will never be forgotten. San Francisco was practically destroyed by earthquake and fire on April 18 with a property loss of some $350,000,000. This tremendous destruction of wealth was bound to have far-reaching effects, but they were not immediate. The strain on the money market was temporarily alleviated by heavy importations of gold from abroad, artificially stimulated by the treasury. The government also floated a $30,000,000 Panama Canal loan. In these days of large figures it seems a little strange to read in the newspapers of that time that the secretary of the treasury "used every device to help the sale." In October several European central banks, including the Bank of England, raised their discount rates to check the outflow of gold. The condition of the money market is illustrated by the fact that in October commercial paper—short-term notes of merchants and manufacturers sold to banks through note brokers—ruled at 6% to 6½%, as compared with a 4½% to 5% level a year previous.

Throughout 1906 commodity prices were advancing. They continued to advance until July, 1907. General trade as shown by bank clearings continued very active well into the panic year, the peak reached in March being followed at first by gradual recession. Railroad gross earnings each month were consistently ahead of the corresponding month of 1906 until December, the maximum increase occurring in April. Money conditions continued extremely unsatisfactory. They were not improved by the rush of the railroads to finance their requirements. In January and February the New York Central and Pennsylvania alone sold $110,000,000 of three-year notes and most of the other railroads attempted financing operations on a large scale. It later appeared that the offering syndicates of bankers were "stuck" with large proportions of these issues, which the investing public refused to take in the face of tight money and anti-railroad sentiment. In 1907 most of the southern and western states were busy passing laws fixing railroad rates and other hostile legislation. President Finley of the Southern Railway was arrested for a technical violation of such a statute. The state of Arkansas attempted to confiscate the property of the Rock Island. Minnesota brought suits against the Great Northern and St. Paul. Missouri sought to dissolve the alleged illegal merger of the Missouri Pacific, Wabash and Iron Mountain. The Interstate Commerce Commission meanwhile was busy investigating the Harriman roads and President Roosevelt characterized Harriman as an "undesirable citizen."

Increasing stringency in the money market, declining public confidence in the value of railroad and other investments foreshadowed the impending storm. In June a number of bond syndicates dissolved with the bulk of their offerings unsold. In that same month the City of New York attempted to sell $29,000,000 of bonds and failed. Two months later Boston offered $3,900,000 bonds and received bids for $200,000. Meanwhile the political situation did not improve. Attacks on the railroads were general, the President continued to advocate radical measures and a fine of $29,000,000 was imposed on the Standard Oil Co. To cap the climax, crop prospects were by no means rosy and the gold flow turned outward. In the late summer commodity prices began to drop sharply, notably the copper market.

THE HISTORIC CRASH

Catastrophe came in October. Featuring the storm was the failure of the Knickerbocker Trust Co., one of New York's leading banks whose shares had been quoted at more than $1000 each not long before. Many other banks were the victims of runs and a number of smaller New York banks failed. For a time it was practically impossible to borrow money and call money was quoted as high as 125%. A few commercial borrowers of exceptional credit were able to place their paper at 16%. New York and other cities had to resort to the issuance of clearing-house certificates to supply the shortage of real money. Failures of banks and Stock Exchange firms in New York and the interior were followed by a host of commercial failures. Of these the most important was that of the Westinghouse Electric & Manufacturing Co. There was an immediate paralysis of trade. Bank clearings in all cities outside New York—omission of New York eliminates the effect of stock market activity and gives a better picture of trade and industry—were still running ahead of 1905 in October. The effect of the panic was immediate. November clearings showed a 17.6% decline and December a 19.8% drop.

The natural aftermath of the panic was severe depression. Factories were shut down, trade at a low ebb, immigration was temporarily replaced by emigration, failures were abnormally numerous. The downward movement of commodity prices continued well into 1908, reaching the lowest point in June. Not until November did volume of trade as measured by outside bank clearings compare favorably with that of the corresponding month of the previous year. In the case of railroad gross earnings this phenomenon occurred in December. Monthly production of pig iron had reached its high point in the panic month of October, 1907. As late as June, 1908, the rate of pig-iron production was still less than half the peak rate, but thereafter recovery was steady. Money rates slowly relaxed after the stringency of the panic and sank to a low level as idle capital began to accumulate and business remained depressed. They then advanced somewhat with the mild business recovery of 1909. This recovery reached its peak as measured by the various indices mentioned about the end of 1909. The prosperity of 1909 was, naturally, a quiet affair compared with the feverish state of activity which prevailed in 1906 and early 1907.

THE STOCK MARKET AND THE PANIC

Having traced the course of a business cycle which is still vividly remembered by all business men past forty it now remains to trace the accompanying cycle of the stock market. The Dow-Jones average of the price of twenty active railroad stocks reached its record high in January, 1906. From that point it reacted mildly to a year's low in May which was only eighteen points under the peak. In view of the tremendous destruction of values by the San Francisco disaster and the necessity imposed on the insurance companies of selling a large part of their marketable securities to pay claims totaling more than $200,000,000 a much greater decline might have been expected. Instead the stock market recovered close to the peak and hovered about that level until December. The high of the railroad average in that month was 137.56, touched on the 11th. Then came a sharp break which carried the average down to 98.27 on March 25. Business, it will be noted, was still booming at that time. A feeble rally occurred in April and the market then turned dull and moved in a narrow range until October. The final smash then occurred which carried the market to its lowest point, 81.41 for the railroad average, in November. It will be seen that by far the greater part of the decline occurred before there was any marked recession in business. The industrial stock average followed substantially the same course as the railroad average. Twenty years ago the bulk of speculative activity was in rails.

From the low level reached in November, 1907, stock prices recovered steadily and fairly rapidly through all of 1908 and the greater part of 1909. There were no interruptions of any consequence to this movement, which carried the railroad average back to within a few points of its record high. The peak of the 1908-09 bull market was reached August 14, 1909, with a railroad average figure of 134.46. The August high of the industrial

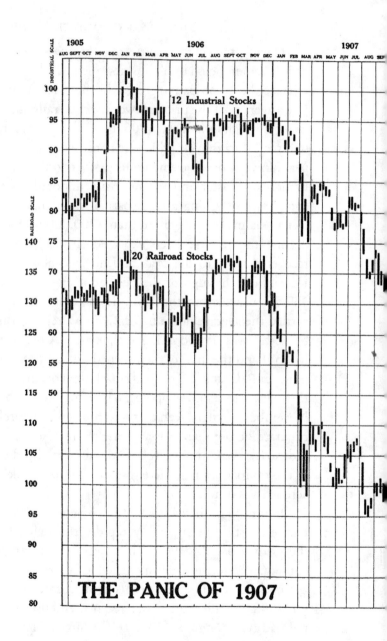

THE PANIC OF 1907

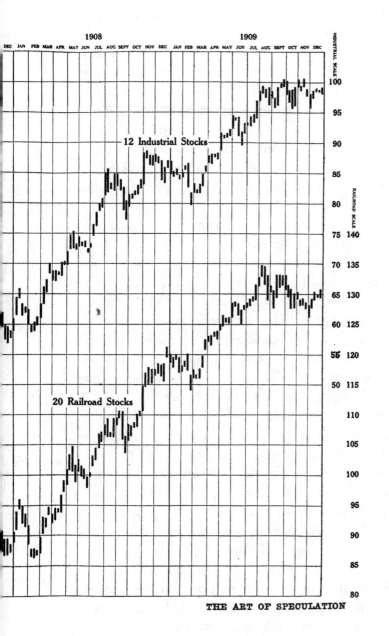

average was 99.26, against a high for the movement of 100.53 reached in November. Since the November railroad average peak was 4.50 points under the August high it seems fair to consider the culmination of the bull market as occurring in August. We have already seen that the high point in business activity came at the close of the year so that once again the turn in the stock market came several months before the turn in business activity.

It is obvious enough upon comparison of the business cycle and the stock market cycle that there is a close relationship between the two. For the purposes of the stock speculator who is seeking some guide to tell him when to buy and when to sell it is somewhat unfortunate that the turn in stocks—accepting the 1906-09 cycle as typical—precedes the turn in business by a number of months. The general state of business thus does not forecast the course of stock prices except in the apparently paradoxical fashion that great prosperity affords an advantageous time for selling stocks, extreme business depression an opportunity for purchase. There have been developed during the past twenty years numerous methods of forecasting general stock market trends on basis of particular indices of business conditions. This subject is broad enough to deserve a chapter by itself.

Study of the long market swings will indicate clearly that the trader who is able to forecast the general trend of the market over its long swings with any degree of accuracy is in a position to make substantial profits as a result. Consider that an investor started in 1904 with enough money to buy outright ten shares of each of the stocks in the railroad average. Suppose further that from that date he correctly forecast each swing of more than twenty-five points in the average, but was a little slow in calling the turns so that he missed the top and the bottom each time by ten points. Add the supposition that our phantom trader kept his money in the bank during bear markets. Finally let us suppose that after 1912 he operated in industrials rather than in rails.

The bottom of the 1903 bear market was reached in September with the railroad average at 88.80. By January the phantom trader would have been convinced that a bull movement was in progress. According to our premise, he would then have bought ten shares of each of the stocks in the average at a cost of $19,760. In April, 1906, the market having then fallen ten points from its peak, he would have sold these stocks for $25,672. He would then have remained out of the market until January, 1908, when his funds would have permitted the purchase of fourteen shares of each stock at an average of 91.41, leaving a cash balance of $77. These shares would finally have been sold in January, 1910, at an average price of 124.46, producing $36,848. A total cash balance of $36,925 would then have reposed in the bank until 1915. During the interim stock market movements were relatively minor in extent.

Phantom Trading

The low point after the Stock Exchange reopened in 1914 was an industrial average figure of 53.17. According to our hypothesis, the phantom trader would then have purchased twenty-nine shares each of the twenty stocks in the industrial average. This would have taken $36,639, leaving $209 in the bank. It is necessary at this point to do a little violence to the facts as the industrial average of twenty stocks did not replace the twelve stock average until the following year. To attempt to allow for this change, however, would unnecessarily complicate the mathematics of the calculation without seriously affecting the final result. The great war bull market culminated in November, 1916, with the industrial average at a peak of 110.15. If the phantom trader's shares were sold ten points lower in the following month, he would receive $58,087 as the proceeds and have a bank balance of $58,296 to carry through the next thirteen months.

The war bear market touched bottom in December, 1917, with the industrial average at 65.95. In the following month the phantom trader would have purchased thirty-eight shares of each of the leading stocks in industrial average, leaving a bank balance of $574. He would have carried these stocks through the creeping upward movement of 1918 and the spectacular advance of 1919. The peak of the latter movement was reached in November with the average at 119.62. According to our premise, the phantom trader's holdings would have been sold within a few days at an average price ten points lower, increasing his bank balance to $83,885. At this point we may conveniently assume that this figment of imagination died and left his small fortune to his phantom heirs. Should they be satisfied with the results of his acumen?

Investor vs. Trader

If $19,760 had been invested at 6%, compounded quarterly, in January, 1904, and the interest consistently added to the principal it would have accumulated by November, 1919, to a total sum of $50,901. During the greater part of the period covered it would as a practical matter have been impossible to obtain a 6% rate on sound investments. In comparing the result of investment and of long-pull speculation over the sixteen-year period an artificial advantage is thus given to investment. This advantage is increased by the fact that no allowance has been made in calculating the result of speculation for dividends on shares held and interest on bank balances. While the stocks comprising the Dow-Jones averages are selected primarily because they are active speculative favorites the majority of them are dividend-payers. If the phantom trader had added his dividends and 2% interest on his bank balances to his fund, it would have been substantially greater than the $83,885 to which it grew by mere market appreciation.

How much acumen did our hypothesis demand of the phantom trader? It did not require him to use any judgment in selecting his stocks. It merely required that he be able to recognize major market movements when they were fairly under way. It required further that he convert that recognition into decision eight times in sixteen years. It is fairly obvious that it is easier to be correct in one's judgment eight times in sixteen years than to be 75% correct in making new decisions every few days as the in-and-out trader must do to make money. Moreover, long-pull speculation such as that of the phantom trader makes no such demand on time and energy as the day-to-day activity of the average speculator.

CHAPTER VI

Forecasting the Major Swings

Primary school arithmetic demonstrates the profits that can be made by the trader who correctly forecasts the major swings of the stock market. The question immediately arises whether it is possible to make such forecasts with any degree of accuracy. In answer to this question, it is not enough to cite the generalization that stocks should be bought when business is depressed and sold when business is prosperous. Economic history never repeats itself exactly. The depression of 1921 differed in many respects from that of 1914. The next depression will differ from that of 1921. Periods of prosperity are also unlike in many respects, differing both in type and in intensity. Business was prosperous in 1905 and had then been prosperous for several years. The speculator who sold his holdings of stocks in the summer of 1905 would nevertheless have suffered the humiliation of seeing the stock market advance for another six months and remain at a high level for ten months after that.

A Depression That Didn't Happen

Examining a more recent stock market cycle, how would the long-pull speculator have fared in 1923 with no other guide than the generalization given? In the early spring of 1923 business was generally prosperous, especially by comparison with conditions two years previously. The trader who sold his stocks at that time would, to be sure, have hit a high spot in the market. If he had then waited for a severe business depression to develop before buying, however, he would have missed entirely the great bull market of 1925. There was no such depression in business in the summer and fall of 1923 as to have suggested purchase of stocks by a long-pull trader who had no other guide than the generalization. Evidently better methods of forecasting the important shifts in market trend are necessary.

The Dow Theory

One of the earliest methods for forecasting the trend of business and incidentally of the stock market itself was formulated by Charles H. Dow, founder of *The Wall Street Journal* and originator of the Dow-Jones averages. The Dow theory has found its ablest exponent in William P. Hamilton, present editor of *The Wall Street Journal,* whose "Stock Market Barometer" should be read by everyone interested in speculation. That publication may speak for itself so that no more than a brief outline of the Dow theory is necessary here.

The theory that the movement of a stock within a narrow range during a considerable period represents either accumulation or distribution and that the action of the stock in breaking out of that range forecasts a movement of considerable extent has already been discussed. Such movements may be the result of unintelligent manipulation or accident. It is clear, however, that the stock market as a whole is too broad to be affected in any important degree by manipulation. An individual or a small group may be able to effect large price movements in individual stocks by shrewd maneuvering and carefully designed publicity under favorable circumstances. To attempt such an operation with the billions of securities listed on the New York Stock Exchange as a group would be utterly beyond human power. A study of the course of business and the course of the stock market over many years also indicates pretty conclusively that the major movements of stock markets are not the result of accident. The correlation is too striking.

A Bear Market Bottom

Manipulation and chance being eliminated, it appears that the action of the market as a whole in "making a line" may be significant. If, for example, during a period of business depression the Dow-Jones or any other representative averages move in a narrow range for a considerable period their action in breaking out of the rut is likely to be significant. Students of the Dow theory regard such action as significant, however, only if the action of the industrials confirms that of the rails, or vice versa. In 1921 we find a typical example of the bottom of a bear market. The trend of the market had been generally downward from November, 1919, through 1920 well into 1921. In the summer of 1921 the market reached the point where liquidation appeared to have exhausted itself. The railroad average made a low of 67.86 in April, a further low of 65.52 in June and a "triple bottom" of 69.87 in August. The high during this period was 75.38. The industrial average made a low of 64.90 in June and a further low of 63.90 in August. In this three months' period its high was 73.51. The two averages were thus both moving in a narrow range following eighteen months of declining prices and at a time when business was extremely depressed. The industrial average was first to break out of the rut, touching 73.93 on October 29 and crossing 75 on November 9. This action was confirmed by the railroad average late in the month, when it reached 76.66. The upward movement thus sluggishly begun carried the averages to a peak in March, 1923. After a moderate decline it was resumed in 1924 and carried the industrial average to a record peak in the winter of 1926.

A Bullish Forecast

This is all very well as hindsight, the reader may remark, but did any observer actually forecast a bull market at that time on the basis of the figures given? The answer is contained in a quotation from an article by Mr. Hamilton in *Barron's* for November 5, 1921:

"I have been challenged to offer proof of the prediction value of the stock market barometer. With the demoralized condition of European finance—all the aftermath of war inflation—with all these things overhanging the business of the country at the present moment, the stock market has acted as if there were better things in sight. It has been saying that the bear market which set in at the end of October and the beginning of November, 1919, saw its low point on June 20, 1921, at 64.90 for the twenty industrials and 65.52 for the twenty railroad stocks."

A MARKET SMASH FORESEEN

The same authority performed the much more difficult feat of calling the turn at the crest of a bull market in an editorial in *Barron's* for January 25, 1926. It read as follows:

"A study of the stock market price movement is enlightening at this time. The conclusions possible are somewhat tentative, but are full of interest after a bull market which has been running since October, 1923. The twenty industrial stocks have displayed the phenomenon of a clearly marked double top. On November 6, 1925, they made the high of the movement, and the highest point on record, at 159.39. From this there was a well marked secondary reaction, with all the characteristic features of such a movement, carrying the price down over eleven points, to 148.18 on November 24. The subsequent rally was to 159.00 and from that the market, on January 21, had reacted to 153.20. "This would be highly significant if the confirmation from the twenty railroad stocks were more nearly parallel. But the railroads did not share the eleven-point reaction in the industrials. They eased off a point or so, but made the high of the present movement on January 7 at 113.12. From that figure there was a reaction of less than five points to 108.26 on January 21. "To indicate a resumption of the major bull market which would be thoroughly dependable on all previous experience, it would be necessary for the industrials to sell above the November high and the railroads to sell above the high of January 7. But as the industrials have already made a significant double top, a recovery of the railroad average to a figure close to, but less than, 113.12, followed by a subsequent reaction, would come near to indicating that the long bull movement had seen its close."

The recovery of the railroad average to a figure close to but less than 113.12 followed by a subsequent reaction occurred in February. The following month was a period of severe declines.

BABSON'S *XY* LINE

One of the earliest exponents of the modern profession of business and stock market forecasting was Roger W. Babson. He has perhaps done more to popularize the conception of business cycles than any other man. The Babson chart of business conditions has become familiar to thousands of business men, bankers and investors. The chart represents a compilation of statistics of bank clearings, business failures, idle freight cars, balance of trade and many other figures. It shows a series of black mountains and valleys bisected by an "*XY* line" which is intended to represent the growth of the country's business. The chart and the Babson forecasting method are based on the theory that physical law—action and reaction are equal and opposite—applies to business and finance. A black area on the Babson chart below the line represents depression, above the line prosperity. These areas are supposed to be equal over any substantial period, a severe depression being balanced by hectic prosperity, a mild period of business activity by correspondingly mild recession. Assuming that the supposition is correct, it is merely necessary to determine when a depression area is equal to half of the preceding prosperity area in order to forecast recovery. This lowest point in the cycle should also furnish an excellent opportunity to buy stocks.

An Unfortunate Selection

The method by which the Babson organization draws its *XY* line has never been satisfactorily explained to the outside public. It has sometimes been unkindly suggested that the direction of the *XY* line is made to fit the action and reaction theory. During the war-inflation period even this method apparently did not suffice to keep the areas in balance. On logical grounds it is difficult to see why the law of action and reaction should be expected to apply to business. If depression and prosperity necessarily counterbalance in human affairs, the appointment of a receiver should be eagerly welcomed, as assuring unusual prosperity to follow. In fact, the action and reaction theory led the Babson organization in 1921 into the error of advising speculative clients to purchase stocks of companies and industries which had been thoroughly "liquidated," in other words, stocks of companies which had lost a lot of money. Accordingly leather and fertilizer stocks were favored in speculative advices while chain-store stocks were neglected. The result was unfortunate.

Watching the Steel Industry

Of the modern students of the stock market perhaps none has made a more thorough study of the relationship between stock market movements and other business phenomena than Col. Leonard P. Ayres, vice-president of the Cleveland Trust Co. In his researches Col. Ayres has discovered a number of such relationships. Doubtless because of his residence in a steel and iron center Col. Ayres was early led to study the relationship between changes in the activity of that industry and stock market cycles. It must be remembered, of course, that the steel and iron industry is the most basic of all our industries. Steel enters into the construction and maintenance of railroads, automobiles, building. The farmer is a user of steel in many forms. There is not a human being who is not constantly riding on steel, walking on steel, working with steel machines. Changes in the activity of the steel and iron industry are thus typical of changes in industrial activity as a whole. They are, however, much more violent. The trend of steel activity thus magnifies greatly a picture of the trend of industry as a whole.

The Blast-Furnace Index

In his studies of the iron and steel industry over a period of many years, the Cleveland statistician discovered that there was a remarkable correlation between the state of blast furnace activity and the trend of the stock market. In a period of increasing prosperity an increase in the number of blast furnaces in blast to the point where 60% of all the furnaces in the country were busy producing pig iron usually marked the peak of an upward movement of the stock market. Conversely a decline of the number of blast furnaces in operation below 60% has usually marked a favorable opportunity for the purchase of stocks. The blast-furnace index has been by no means infallible. Both in

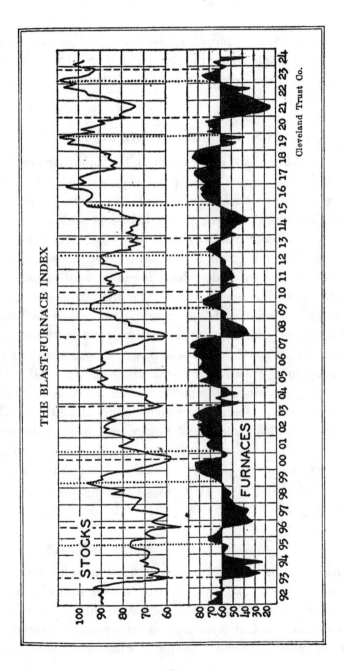

1901 and 1904, for example, it gave the selling signal too soon. On the buying side it gave the signal a little prematurely in 1907 and in 1920. More recently it has been rather more accurate in calling the turn.

How the Index Worked in 1925

The course of blast-furnace activity in 1925 affords an interesting example of its fluctuations. At the end of January increasing activity carried the percentage figure above 60% for the first time in many months. On January 31 the Dow-Jones industrial average was 123.22. Receding activity in the iron trade carried the index below the 60% line at the end of March. The industrial average was then 116.75. The trader who followed the blast-furnace index blindly would thus have got out of the market on the eve of a severe reaction and bought stocks again practically at the bottom of that reaction. The blast-furnace index stayed below 60% for the balance of 1925 and the trader who trusted it would thus have held his stocks during a period of vigorous advances. At the end of 1925 the index again crossed 60% on the way up and suggested the sale of stocks at prices close to the extreme highs which they reached six weeks later. Unfortunately the index went astray at this point, reversing itself at the end of January and suggesting repurchases on the eve of a terrific smash in the market. Two months later it reversed itself again and gave the selling signal when the market was on the verge of a vigorous rally.

Value of Blast-Furnace Index

It is clear that the blast-furnace index alone is not sufficiently reliable to form the basis for profitable trading in stocks. Indeed, because of the smallness of the fluctuations in the index during the past two years Col. Ayres himself has expressed serious doubts as to the continued value of the index. In conjunction with other indices it may still be of value. When the market itself as interpreted by Dow's theory, the blast-furnace index, the condition of general business and other indices to be discussed later, all point to the same conclusion, no trader can afford to disregard the suggestion. The blast-furnace index is particularly useful because it is available monthly early in the month. The steel trade journals publish accurate figures concerning blast-furnace activity each month.

Dividend Yields

In an entirely different direction Col. Ayres has discovered some interesting facts regarding the relationship between stock prices and dividends. Dividing the total price of the stocks used in the Dow-Jones industrial average by the total dividends paid an index results which is in effect their average of yield. In a bull market, of course, stocks sell to yield small returns and in a bear market to give large returns. In the past twenty-five years only one bull market has failed to carry this index above 20 and *no* bear market has failed to carry it under 17. Once the trend of the market is recognized, then, it is possible to set a minimum limit to its extent based on this fact.

It is interesting to note that a chart of this "time line"—total prices equal so many times total dividends—looks rather different from a chart of the average itself. The times line reached its highest point in 1906, when the industrials were selling for more than 26 times aggregate dividends. Measured in this way the bull markets of 1919 and 1925-26 were not such lofty affairs as would appear from a mere consideration of the Dow-Jones averages.

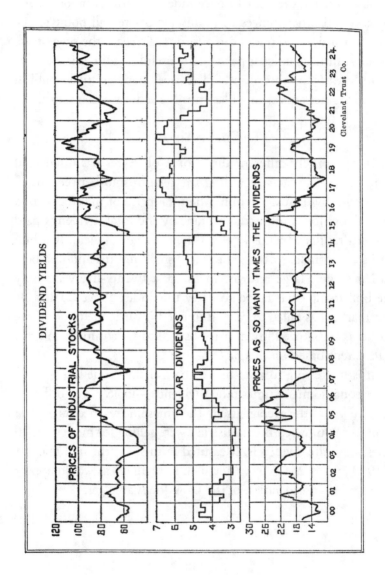

The Fisher Index

Another index of great value to the student of the stock market is the Fisher commodity price index, compiled by Professor Irving Fisher of Yale. There are many indices of commodity prices available, but the Fisher index is perhaps the best. Its great advantage lies in the fact that it is available weekly. Publication of the figure is therefore news and not history. Trade and industry are more profitable on a rising than on a falling market for commodities. The great advance in prices which culminated in May, 1920, produced easy profits for almost every business. On the other hand, the violent decline which almost cut the price level in half during the ensuing twenty months produced a paralysis of trade during which only exceptionally lucky or exceptionally well managed concerns made money.

How Price Movements Affect Business

An overdose of rising prices has the same ultimate effect as an overdose of any stimulant. Business men accordingly do not welcome large and rapid advances in the prices of the goods in which they deal. On the other hand, a moderate upward trend affords them ideal conditions under which to operate. The normal trading profit is then increased slightly by the constant increase in inventory values. In contrast shrinkage in inventory values cuts into the normal trading profit. On a falling market therefore business men buy only for immediate needs, the general business tone is one of hesitancy. When a major decline in commodity prices is nearing its end, as in 1921, a bull market in stocks may get under way, but ordinarily the stock market will not advance vigorously in the face of falling prices nor decline long in a period of rising prices for tangible goods. Even the minor movements of the stock market are frequently influenced by the movement from week to week of the Fisher index.

Some disappointment may be felt by the reader at this point because no infallible rule for calling the turn on the major movements of the stock market has been suggested. A moment's thought will show, however, that if there were any infallible mechanical method of forecasting the major swings of the stock market, there could be no major swings. If every trader knew or could discover by a half-hour's investigation that the stock market was about to go down, there would be no buyers. There never was a time when every possible circumstance favored a rise in security prices nor, on the other hand, a time when every possible circumstance favored a bear market. The most that can ever be said is that the balance of factors favors an upward or a downward movement.

THE BALANCE OF FACTORS

Speculation is no simple business. The amateur cannot take a few thousand dollars' capital, fifteen minutes a day of time, treat it as a side-line and be any more successful than he would be in any other business. Indeed, speculation requires broader knowledge, closer attention, sounder judgment than the average business. Prices on the New York Stock Exchange are affected by French politics, German banking conditions, wars and rumors of wars in the Near East, the Chinese money market, the condition of the wheat crop in The Argentine, the temper of the Mexican Congress as well as by a host of domestic influences. The successful speculator must carefully weigh the effect of all these influences, set down the pros and cons and arrive at a sound conclusion as to the side on which the balance lies. When he has done all this he has made only a beginning. If he concludes that the balance favors an upward movement, he must still decide which stocks he is to buy for maximum profit.

Long-Lived Market Movements

Not only must the trader make a careful analysis of the situation when he first decides that the trend of the market is definitely in a given direction. He must review his position at fairly frequent intervals. Bull markets and bear markets last long enough so that the average trader is likely to forget by the time the climax is approaching that any other sort of movement is possible. His judgment is not assisted by the general temper of business men at such a time. A bull market usually comes to grief when business is generally prosperous with few clouds on the horizon. At such a time many business men are making plans for expansion, business leaders are talking optimistically, the outlook is rosy. Under such conditions it requires real backbone to sell stocks, many of which will still appear to their owner undervalued in comparison to many of the stocks which he does not happen to own. The reverse conditions prevail when a bull market is born. Business is then depressed, failures are numerous, business is apparently going to the dogs. His friends are then likely to question the sanity of a man who indulges in bullish talk or acts upon bullish convictions.

Panic of 1907 Again

It may now be profitable to review briefly the stock market cycle of 1906-09 which has been discussed at length in a previous chapter. The bull market of 1906 got under way in September, 1903, with the railroad average at 88.80. The bulk of speculation was then in railroad rather than industrial stocks. Stimulated by easy money, increasing business prosperity, the bull market swept onward with such momentum that even the San Francisco earthquake could check it only temporarily. The blast-furnace index called the turn prematurely in the early winter of 1904-05. Even then, however, the railroad average had advanced practically two-thirds of its ultimate total. At about the same time that the blast-furnace index gave a bearish indication, dividend-yield figure of the Dow-Jones industrials crossed the level at which the peak of the 1903 bull market had been reached. Money, however, remained very easy for many months longer. The Dow theory, moreover, did not suggest the sale of stocks until 1906. The long-pull trader who sold his stocks when any one of these indices turned bearish would not, after all, have fared very badly.

When Indices Agree

It is usually a much simpler matter to forecast a bull market than to call the turn at its end. Accordingly it is not surprising to find that the various indices were much more nearly in step in suggesting the end of the bear market of 1907. Both the blast-furnace index and the dividend yield of the Dow-Jones industrials suggested purchases prematurely about the middle of the year.

The tight money then prevailing would have prevented any astute trader from entering the market at that time. The convulsive spasm of November would correctly have suggested that the time was ripe for buying. On the Dow theory the averages themselves confirmed the suggestion before the year was out. A study of other cycles would confirm the statement that when the various indices here discussed—and the index of money rates to be discussed more in detail in the next chapter—are in substantial agreement, a trader may safely form a conclusion as to the major trend of the stock market.

CHAPTER VII

The Lifeblood of Speculation

Borrowed money is the lifeblood of speculation. It is possible to speculate without borrowing money, but speculation is usually carried on to a large extent with borrowed money and the profits of successful speculation are greatly increased by operating on borrowed money. The money market is thus a vital factor in speculative operations even for the man who is not himself a borrower.

The mathematical demonstration of the fact that the profits of successful speculation are greatly increased by borrowing money is simple. Suppose a trader buys 100 shares of a stock costing $100 a share, using $2000 of his own money and borrowing $8000. Disregarding commissions and interest, he will make a profit of $2500 on selling it at $125 a share, or 125% on his capital. If he had bought only as much stock as he could pay for outright, he would have had 20 shares and a profit of only 25% on his capital.

PYRAMIDING

Change the supposition a little and visualize a rise in the stock from 100 to 200. Assume further that the trader borrows at intervals to buy more stock so that his equity never much exceeds 20% of the market value. Under this latter supposition he would be able to buy 80 additional shares when the stock reached 125. He would then own 180 shares of stock worth at market $22,500 and owe $18,000. When the stock reached 150 he would buy 120 additional shares costing $18,000, bringing his total holdings up to 300 shares worth $45,000. He would now owe $36,000. At 175 he might buy 140 shares additional costing $24,500, increasing the total value of his holdings to $77,000 and his total borrowings to $60,500. When the stock finally reached 200 he could sell his 440 shares for $88,000. After paying his loans he would then have a balance of $27,500 and a profit of 1275%. If he had borrowed the limit to buy more stock every ten points up, his profits would reach even more startling proportions.

When the Margin Clerk Gets Busy

Needless to say, this process of pyramiding can never be carried out with any such results in actual practice. A broker may be perfectly willing to take a customer's account on a 20% margin, but that does not mean that a trader is secure against any decline of not more than 20%. Long before a reaction in a given stock had reached 20% of its selling price the broker would call for more margin. If it were not forthcoming, he would sell part or all of his customer's holdings to protect himself. This he must do in justice to other customers who rely on the integrity of his capital for the protection of their accounts. The experienced trader prefers a broker who insists on adequate margins to the broker who is too liberal in this respect. Now suppose that our pyramiding trader has carried his operations to the point where his stock is selling at 150 when a fifteen-point reaction occurs in the stock. His 300 shares are now worth $40,500, instead of $50,000, and his equity is only $4500. If he is unable or unwilling to supply additional cash, the broker will need to sell practically 150 shares to bring his equity up to 20% of his total debit balance. A little greater reaction would almost wipe him out. This is exactly what happens to the average margin trader. He may buy stocks consistently in a bull market only to be wiped out by a reaction or by the first sharp drop which marks its termination.

OUTLET FOR BANK SURPLUSES

The fact that the average trader abuses credit is no argument against the use of credit in stock market speculation. For the trader who borrows in moderation, credit is a very useful tool. Loans on listed stocks and bonds are also a most useful outlet for the surplus funds of banks all over the country. Loans aggregating at times more than $3,000,000,000 are extended by the New York banks for their own account and for the account of correspondent banks in the interior. The bulk of these loans are call loans, repayable on demand and in practice renewed by the borrowing brokers from day to day. A country bank in Kansas, for example, with idle funds in its vault may transmit these funds to its New York correspondent to lend on call, earn from 3% to 6% on this balance and be sure of its return on twenty-four hours' notice. Such loans are not only the most liquid form of investment for bank funds but are practically riskless.

Besides the profit which borrowed money enables the speculator to make by carrying from two to five times as many shares on the same capital, there is another sort of profit to be made by borrowing money. If, for example, in a period of depression a seasoned dividend-paying stock is selling to yield 8% while money may be borrowed at 5%, the purchaser may obtain a large return on his capital even though the stock never advances a point. Let us suppose that the stock is selling at 100, paying an 8% dividend rate, and that the trader borrows $7000 from his bank at 5% to buy 100 shares. His dividends will amount to $800 a year, interest on his note will absorb $350 and the balance will be his net income from the stock. It will amount to $450 or 15% on the $3000 of his own capital.

PARTIAL-PAYMENT TRADING

With two powerful incentives encouraging the speculator to use borrowed money, it is not surprising that the average trader is a borrower from his broker. Within the past few years the appeal of stock speculation has been extended to a new class of the population by extensive advertising of the partial-payment plan. The average member firm of the New York Stock Exchange does not welcome accounts involving less than $1000 initial margin. The man with $200 or so has not been neglected, however. A large number of firms not members of the leading Exchange, many of them members of no Exchange, have offered to buy stocks for him on the partial-payment plan—so much down and so much a month. The mystery of how a firm could make money in view of the expensive bookkeeping involved in carrying such small accounts and the fact that Stock Exchange rules would not permit member firms to split even the meager permitted commission with non-member firms has been solved by dozens of failures. Hardly any qualification is necessary in stating that no legitimate profit is possible from such operations. The trader who patronizes a so-called brokerage firm of this nature has only himself to thank when it fails.

Does the Money Market Control the Stock Market ?

Based in part on the obvious relationship between the level of money rates and the profits of the individual speculator, a theory has gained wide belief among students of the stock market that the money market directly controls the stock market. It is usually believed that cheap money encourages a rise in stock prices, high money rates a decline. The authors of a recent book on the subject summarize the orthodox theory by calling it "the doctrine that fluctuations in short-time interest rates are the principal cause of variations in the level of prices of speculative stocks and in the volume of trading on the Stock Exchange." The conclusion of this study (Owens and Hardy, "Interest Rates and Stock Speculation") is that "none of this evidence affords proof that the money market is in any sense a dominant factor in bringing about upswings and downswings in stock prices."

How Stocks May "Carry Themselves"

Since one type of possible profit from the purchase of stocks with borrowed funds depends directly upon the existence of a favorable spread between the rate of dividend received by the speculator and the rate of interest paid on his loan, it would logically follow that the operations of a speculator seeking this profit primarily depend absolutely on the state of the money market. If money rates rise to the point where he cannot buy sound, dividend-paying stocks to yield more than the cost of his money, he will obviously withdraw from the market. It is a question to what extent speculative operations of this type are actually undertaken. There are probably few traders who would borrow money at 5% to buy a sound 8% stock at par merely for the income. The average trader would not buy the stock unless he also believed the probabilities favored an advance in its price. The fact that the stock "carried itself" from the standpoint of incoming dividends and outgoing interest would make him decidedly more certain of his ground, nevertheless, than if outgo exceeded income. When the stock had risen to such a level that its yield would no longer cover interest charges of a new purchaser or when interest rates had risen so far as to accomplish the same result, he would feel much less sure of his ground. A hint that the trend of the market was likely to turn downward would then cause intelligent speculators to consider selling. In the last analysis the sale of their holdings by intelligent speculators has a good deal to do with terminating bull markets.

Cause or Coincidence?

Whatever the interest of the question for theoretical economists the speculator in stocks is not concerned to know whether fluctuations in interest rates cause variations in the level of stock prices. The answer may be in the negative. If the two phenomena are instead the related results of other causes, it is all the same for our purposes. Perhaps the money market does not "bring about" changes in security prices, but if the evidence shows that in the past rising money rates have frequently preceded a down-turn in stock prices, falling money rates an up turn in stock prices, then a study of the money market is essential to the stock speculator.

SEASONAL VARIATIONS

Some comment will now be necessary on two favorite phrases of professional statisticians. They are "seasonal variation" and "secular trend." The former is self-explanatory. Every housewife is familiar with the seasonal variation in the price of fresh eggs. The demand for fresh eggs for the table is a fairly constant phenomenon. Hens show a fine disregard for human appetite, however, and vary the intensity of their efforts with the seasons. The variation in the price of eggs is a natural result. It is not at once so obvious that a seasonal variation in the money market is a natural phenomenon. It is a fact well known to bankers that money rates tend to rise in the late summer and fall, reaching a peak in the last quarter of the year. They then fall abruptly in January, when business men like to pay their debts in order to make their annual statements look as good as possible. In the early spring there is a seasonal rise, culminating in March, followed by a decline to the low of the year in June.

EFFECT OF THE FEDERAL RESERVE SYSTEM

Seasonal variations in money rates were formerly much more pronounced than they are today. Before the establishment of the Federal Reserve System the currency system of the United States was absolutely inelastic. Our money consisted of gold and subsidiary coins, paper certificates issued against deposit of gold and silver, United States notes or greenbacks and banknotes secured dollar for dollar by certain issues of government bonds. The currency could expand only as gold was mined and minted. Bank credit was also necessarily inelastic since the banks were required to maintain certain minimum reserves in legal tender. Under that system the country's currency proved inadequate for expanding business. Every fifteen or twenty years, a panic resulted and money rates literally went out of sight temporarily. This absurd system gave way in 1913 to the Federal Reserve System.

Now twelve regional banks exist which have power to issue federal reserve notes to member banks who pledge the notes of their customers or government bonds as collateral. In this way an elastic currency is provided for the fluctuating business needs of the country. In case prosperity goes to a reckless extreme, over-expansion may be checked to a certain extent by increasing the rediscount rate which is charged borrowing member banks. This not only tends to check speculative borrowing by increasing its cost but also has a tremendous effect upon business sentiment. In general there should now be in theory no seasonal fluctuation in money rates, since our currency may be expected to expand and contract with business needs. Actually there still seems to be a seasonal variation about half as great as that which existed before 1913.

"Secular trend" is a long-range tendency not affected by seasonal factors. If a table of egg production were compiled by months, for example, it would show not only fluctuations with the seasons but a tendency to increase over a period of years with the growth of the hen population and improvements in poultry breeding and husbandry. In drawing charts of business statistics it is necessary to allow for both seasonal variation and secular trend in order to show the true significance of the facts. There are, of course, some sorts of figures not so affected. There is no discernible secular trend in money rates.

CALL MONEY RATES

Offhand it might appear that the class of money rate most important to the speculator would be the call money rate for brokers' loans in the New York market. As it happens this is a very volatile rate which fluctuates widely from day to day with varying conditions. The rate for 60 to 90-day brokers' collateral loans is a still better index of money market conditions. The really important rate as showing the state of the money market, however, is neither of these, but rather the prevailing rate from prime commercial paper maturing in 60 to 90 days. The notes of manufacturers and merchants discounted by note brokers and sold by them in turn to banks which have surplus funds constitute the supply of commercial paper. The rate at which such paper is sold reflects the cost to large borrowers of good credit. It provides the most accurate index of the money market.

CORRELATION

It is now in order to determine whether there is any relationship between interest rates and stock prices. Owens and Hardy, whose work has already been mentioned, have made elaborate studies of this subject. They conclude that the "relationship between stock prices and interest rates is not a random one." By using an abstruse mathematical concept known as the Pearsonian coefficient of correlation it is possible to measure statistically the extent to which two fluctuating indices tend to move together. If their movements synchronize exactly, the coefficient is 1; if there is absolutely no relationship, the coefficient is 0. The degree of correlation may also be tested when one series of data is lagged behind the other a definite interval. In the case at hand the authors found a very small degree of correlation for interest rates and stock prices concurrently. When interest rates were lagged behind stock prices from nine to twelve months a very large degree of correlation was indicated. In less technical language this means that "typically upswings in interest rates are followed in from six to nine months by downswings in stock prices and vice versa. . . . Interest rates turn upward and downward a year or so after similar changes in stock prices."

WHEN STOCKS GO DOWN

In seeking to apply the fact of a high degree of correlation between interest rates and stock prices to the problem of finding the best means of forecasting the movements of the stock market, it will be helpful to assume a casual relationship, Messrs. Owens and Hardy to the contrary notwithstanding. The accepted theory of the relationship between money rates and security prices pictures a cycle starting with business depression. A major recession in business is typically marked by declining interest rates as commercial activity slackens and demand for money declines. Stock prices as we have seen usually begin to decline well in advance of a peak in business activity and thus have receded substantially by the time the decline in business activity is fairly under way. The decline in stock prices, the decline in business activity have now seriously diminished the confidence of investors and speculators. Moreover, the capital of many of them has been curtailed. Over-sanguine business men find themselves compelled to sell some of their stocks to maintain their working capital in the face of shrinking inventory values and possible bad debt losses. Bullish speculators who overstayed the bull market in stocks have automatically been eliminated in large part.

BARGAIN HUNTERS

At such a time there are always a certain number of shrewd individuals with liquid funds. Moreover, capital continues to accumulate despite the slower pace of business. Investors and speculators with funds in hand now find that they can buy sound investments, bonds and the better grade stocks, to yield attractive returns. As both security prices and money rates decline that attractiveness of yields increases doubly fast. If a sound 7% dividend-paying stock is a good purchase at 100 in a 5% money market, it is doubly a better purchase at 90 in a 4½% money market. Accumulation of good securities thus begins early in a period of depression and before long terminates the decline. With confidence at a low ebb, highest grade securities are naturally first purchased, and it is for this reason that bond prices usually turn upward ahead of stocks. Investment stocks for the same reason usually make their lows before more speculative issues.

INCREASING BUSINESS PROFITS

In a period of business depression, with profits in most lines at a minimum or non-existent, purchasers of securities at first pay little attention to prospective business profits and dividends. They are interested in the approximate certainties of continued dividend payment by such concerns as American Telephone, General Electric, Atchison. Investment buying of stocks like these finally stems the downward tide, further declines in money rates make the purchase of stocks continually more attractive, it becomes apparent to close observers that despite occasional outbursts of fresh liquidation in particular stocks or groups of stocks prices in general show no sign of going lower. This stability in itself stimulates confidence and a bull market is soon under way.

Business recovery now begins, occurring earlier in some industries than others. To the attraction of high yields from sound dividend-paying stocks is added the attraction of prospective increases in dividends as business profits expand. Monthly and quarterly statements of earnings by leading companies in many lines give ground for the rumors of "constructive" dividend action which circulate in the financial districts of leading cities, over brokerage wires and in the financial columns of the papers. The general lack of confidence which marked public feeling during the depression period has now given way to the natural optimism of healthy human beings. Action of the market itself is the best advertisement of the brokers. Old customers and new ones, too, are attracted by the bull market and come to reap their share of the general expansion in market values.

A Bull Market Undermines Itself

Speculation for the rise itself ultimately terminates the downward trend of money rates and thereby undermines its own foundation. Then business recovery increases the demand for money and rates begin to rise. The money market has now ceased to be a powerful stimulus of the upward movement of security prices. With the return of prosperity, hopes of increased dividends may nevertheless materialize and thus offset the increasing cost of speculative funds. Furthermore, the rise in security prices has acquired considerable momentum. It will take a powerful brake to stop it. Typically a major market movement runs so far that the amateur in speculation forgets that an opposite trend has ever been known. More than a slight rise in money rates is necessary to kill a real bull market.

Finally such a bull market as we have been describing reaches the point where stocks are selling to yield perhaps half or two-thirds of what they were at the commencement of the upswing. On the relation between actual dividends and money rates they are no longer cheap. Traders long of stocks have ceased buying on prospects of increased earnings or dividends during the next few months and are in many cases discounting the bright prospects of ten years ahead. Here are two pitfalls even for the intelligent trader. First, he has seen stocks of certain groups—the war brides in 1916, the utilities and chain-store stocks in 1925—go so far beyond the prices at which sound judgment would set their maximum possible value that he may become persuaded just on the eve of the decline that ordinary rules of value do not after all apply to certain favored groups. Second, a substantial number of stocks for lack of market sponsorship or some other reason have not kept pace with the general advance and he may embrace the dangerous illusion that the advance cannot terminate until these have had their day.

If money rates are now advancing with the increasing demand for funds from merchants and manufacturers and yields declining with the advance of security prices, speculation on borrowed money is becoming unprofitable at a rapid pace. Business men are now in many cases selling securities in order to get the added capital necessary to do a greater volume. Shrewd speculators are selling stocks which no longer carry themselves. This selling deals the death-blow to the upward movement. Once under way the downward movement tends to gain momentum. Just as speculators are enabled to pyramid in an advancing market, so are the stubborn bulls forced to sell in a declining market. Their margins exhausted by the fall of prices, they are sold out by their brokers. Forced selling brings still lower prices and exhausts the margins of still other speculators. The process continues until yields are again well above the cost of money and bargain-hunters with ready cash once more stem the tide of liquidation.

Wide swings in security prices may occur with moderate swings in money rates without invalidating our theory of the connection between the two. If a bull market goes far enough, carries yields low enough, it must topple of its own weight even though money rates may not have stiffened much. Similarly, if stock prices have gone low enough, even a moderate relaxation in an 8% money market will inaugurate a recovery.

A Harvard Index

A chart of stock prices and money rates clearly enough demonstrates the connection between the two. Studying the figures carefully the economists and statisticians who comprise the Harvard Committee on Economic Research discovered a few years ago that a rise of 1¼% in the monthly average rate of prime commercial-paper, adjusted for seasonal variation, from a distinct low point had almost always marked an opportune time at which to sell stocks. Per contra, a decline of 1¼% from a peak had usually suggested a profitable point at which to buy stocks. Here we have a valuable rule of thumb for forecasting the movement of the stock market. It is not infallible, it has not always "worked," but in connection with other indices it makes a useful tool.

Other Studies of Colonel Ayres

Besides the Harvard Committee, Colonel Ayres has made some useful studies of the relationship between money rates and security prices. He has shown, for example, that in general when rates on 60 to 90 day commercial paper have been above 4½% security prices have tended to fall. When commercial-paper rates have been below 4½% they have tended to rise. The accompanying chart shows the Dow-Jones industrial average with a dotted line when commercial-paper rates—adjusted for seasonal variation—have been above 4½%, and a solid line when below 4½%.

Colonel Ayres has also discovered an interesting relation between short-term and long-term money rates, *i.e.,* between commercial-paper rates and bond prices. Stock prices have usually tended to rise when the 90-day loan rate has been lower than the yield on high-grade bonds and to fall when the 90-day loan rate has been higher than the average bond yield.

All of these mechanical guides to stock market movements would at some time or other have failed the trader who depended upon them in a mechanical way. They offer no royal road to fortune in speculation. Taken in conjunction with other indices, applied with sound common sense, they are an aid of great importance to the formation of a correct decision regarding the market trend. The trader who does not understand the money market is certainly not engaging in a business offering profit to himself. He is a grown-up child playing blind-man's buff.

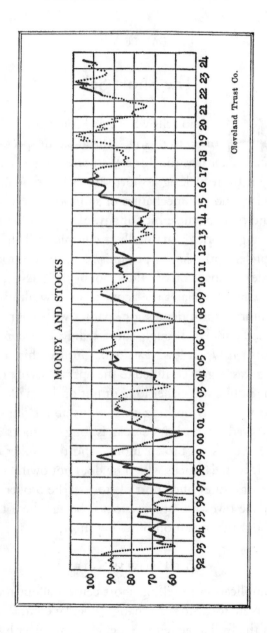

CHAPTER VIII

The Short Sale

"He who sells what isn't his'n must make it good or go to prison." The amateur speculator soon learns this little Wall Street jingle and is often deterred by it from making a short sale. It is essential, however, that he understand the mechanics of short selling, its economic function and perhaps the ethics, if any, of such a transaction.

The average trader is naturally a chronic bull. It is human nature to prefer optimism to pessimism. Moreover, fortunes are usually made by expansion of values, not by their destruction. The man in the street associates the acquisition of wealth with rising markets: failures, ruin, depression, panics with falling markets. Bears are not popular, though short selling is becoming more common than it was a few years ago. Until within a few years short selling was largely confined to the operations of professional traders. The public was either long or out of the market.

In theory there is nothing mysterious about the short sale. The margin trader who buys stocks is long of stocks and short of money. He owes his broker money and the broker owes him the stocks. If he sells stocks which he does not own, however, he is now long of money and short of stocks. The broker owes him money and he owes his broker stocks. So far there is nothing complex about the operation of selling short.

THE DELIVERY RULE

The complication in selling short centers about the delivery rules of the New York Stock Exchange. Regular contracts made on the floor of the Exchange require the seller to deliver his stock by 2.15 p.m. on the following day. Contracts may of course be made for cash, *i.e.,* for delivery on the same day, or for delayed delivery, "seller seven days" meaning that delivery is to be made in seven days. The importance of the delivery rules was illustrated in 1901 during the famous Northern Pacific corner. Arbitrage traders who had bought stock in London and sold it on the floor of the New York Stock Exchange were forced to pay fantastic prices for cash delivery to make good their contracts, even though the certificates they had bought in London might be on the water.

THE BROKER'S POWER

Obviously the trader who sells a stock he does not own in the expectation that he may repurchase it later at a lower price is in no position to make regular delivery. He could, of course, sell the stock "seller thirty days"—probably at a lower price than he would get by selling on regular terms—and hope to be able to buy it in the regular way during the month, but this would be a cumbersome procedure. Instead the trader who goes short of a stock borrows stock in order to make delivery in the regular way. His broker may have the necessary stock in his strong box held for the account of a margin customer who is long of the particular issue or he may borrow it from another broker. In either event a broker who lends stock need not account for it to the customer for whose account it is actually held. A margin trader signs an agreement with his broker on opening an account which gives the broker wide powers, which include the right to lend stock held for his account. A typical agreement signed by the customer of a member house of the New York Stock Exchange reads as follows:

> ". . . any of my securities now or hereafter in your possession for any purpose, other than safekeeping, and any balance of my account at any time with you, shall secure you for, and may at any time be applied upon, any indebtedness from me to you; that any such securities

> may, without notice to me, be loaned by you, or pledged either alone or with any other security, for the payment of any sum irrespective of the extent of my indebtedness to you; that, in case all of my indebtedness to you and/ or all your liability incurred on my account shall not at any time be secured to your satisfaction, you may, without notice to me, sell at any broker's board, or public or private sale any or all security you hold therefor, and/or cover by your purchase any short sale made on my account. . . ."

Having obtained so all-inclusive an agreement from his customers the broker may lend the stocks in their long accounts to his short customers or to other brokers at any time. Suppose that John Smith, a customer of Adams, Jefferson & Co., is carrying 100 shares of United States Steel common in his account. Now suppose that Henry Jones decides that that particular stock is selling too high and gives Adams, Jefferson & Co. an order to sell it short. The broker will then deliver John Smith's stock to the broker to whom Henry Jones's sale has been made. Regular delivery has now been made in accordance with the rules of the Stock Exchange.

Short Sale Accounting

If, as would be most unlikely in the case of a leading issue like Steel common, Adams, Jefferson & Co. did not have the stock in one customer's account to deliver against another customer's short sale, it would be necessary to borrow from another broker. The lending broker upon delivering the stock would be entitled to receive a check for its approximate value to the nearest full point. The amount of cash held by the borrowing broker would be adjusted each day as the stock fluctuated. Since the lender of the stock is a borrower of money, he pays interest. On stocks which are in ample supply the interest rate paid by the lender approximates the ruling call-loan rate. If the stock is somewhat difficult to borrow, the rate is lower. If a given stock is very difficult to borrow, it may loan "flat." In that event the lender of the stock pays no interest on the money he receives for it. In an extreme case he may even collect a premium for lending the stock besides getting the use of the equivalent funds for nothing. On the day this is written, for example, American Woolen preferred is loaning at $\frac{1}{64}$th premium. The trader who is short 100 shares of American Woolen preferred is thus paying $1.56¼ a day for the privilege of maintaining his position, besides putting up the value of the stock without compensation. Finally, the borrower of stock must pay the lender all dividends accruing to the stock during the period of the loan.

Usefulness of the Short Sale

What is the economic function of short selling, or, without using the question-begging terminology of the Street, what is the economic function of speculation for the fall? This is only a part of the larger question: What is the economic function of all speculation as conducted on the organized Exchanges? That question could easily be made the subject of a whole treatise in itself; for present purposes it is sufficient to say that speculation plays an important part in the orderly and convenient marketing of securities and commodities. Without going further into the broader subject, it will be appropriate here to mention some of the valuable functions of speculation for the fall.

The Distant Customer

The machinery of short selling is frequently used when the sale is not a speculation in the ordinary sense and not even a short sale except in a technical sense. Suppose an investor who is traveling in Europe decides to sell some of his Atchison and cables an order to his broker in New York. Or he may be a resident of Florida, or Texas, or California. When the broker sells the stock today he has contracted to deliver it tomorrow at 2.15 p.m.; but his investor-customer may not deliver his certificate to him for a week or a month. The broker is himself in fact short of the stock and makes his delivery by borrowing his stock just as he would have done if his customer had been a speculative short seller, and the effect on the borrowing demand for the stock is the same. A good deal of the short interest in the market at any time is of this character.

Again an important owner of the stock of a company may desire to liquidate some of his holdings. If as he sells, he delivers his own certificates, reports of "inside" selling might demoralize or destroy his market. To avoid this he instructs his broker to borrow stock as needed for deliveries, and supplies his own stock only when his liquidation is completed. In neither of these cases was the principal either a speculator or "short" of the stock at the time of the sale, though the broker was short and might continue to be for a long time.

AN ESSENTIAL OF ODD-LOT MARKET

Turning now to the thorough-going short sale, where at the time of selling the principal does not own the security and where his motive for selling is his expectation of buying later at a lower price, a great and constantly increasing part of the investment business on the floor of the New York Stock Exchange as now transacted is possible only because of the existence of a body of such short sellers. The purchaser of an "odd lot" of stock (*i.e.* less than 100 shares) has his order executed immediately at a small fraction above the last sale of a "round" (100 shares) lot. This is possible because of the activities of the odd-lot brokers who stand ready at all times to sell short, if need be, any odd lots desired at one-eighth above the market for round lots in the case of the principal active stocks, and a larger fraction above the market in other stocks. The odd-lot broker counts on balancing his short sales either by current purchases of offered odd lots at the same fraction below the market or by round lots at the market as necessary.

Maintaining an Orderly Market

Another useful function of short selling is to maintain constant marketability with price stability. An order for the purchase of even a hundred shares in a market bare of liquidating orders in the same stock, might result in an unwarranted advance, were it not for the floor traders who, alert for any temporary discrepancy between demand and supply, are ready to sell short the desired stock at a slight advance, expecting to cover at a modest profit, as soon as offerings preponderate. Short selling is thus a factor of great importance in maintaining an orderly market.

In a larger way the activities of short-selling operators minimize the swings of the stock market. When toward the end of a bull market wild enthusiasm is pyramiding prices to dizzy heights without regard to values, such selling tends to bring the market to its senses, uncover the weak spots, and gives timely warning to investors. When the market has gone to the other extreme, when unwarranted pessimism is rampant, when timid investors delay their purchases for fear of lower prices, the confident buying of such operators in covering their commitments is a powerful and sometimes almost the only stabilizing influence.

Over-the-Counter Difficulties

The usefulness of short selling may best be seen by comparing the listed and the unlisted market. In December, 1925, it became known that the Southern Minnesota Joint Stock Land Bank had an unduly large proportion of delinquent loans and mortgages in process of foreclosure on its books. The institution was one of the largest of its kind and its stock had only a few months previously been distributed to investors as a high-grade issue. Since joint stock land banks as a group were less than ten years old and had attracted the attention of the investing public within only two years, this news was a severe blow to confidence. Whereas in the fall of 1925 bids for joint stock land bank stocks had been more plentiful than offerings with rising prices as a consequence, the situation was now reversed. The new investors in joint stock land bank stocks having lost confidence were obviously not eager to add to their holdings, in the confused situation which existed, salesmen for investment houses could not secure new buyers for the stocks and the investment houses themselves were obviously not in a position to tie up their capital by repurchasing the stocks which they had sold. Bids were thus virtually non-existent and, as a practical matter, there were weeks at a time in the winter of 1925-26 when investors could not sell most joint stock land bank stocks at any price. This is by no means an isolated case of the difficulties which sometimes confront the trader in the unlisted market.

If short selling of joint stock land bank stocks had been possible in the fall and early winter of 1925-26, how would the market have been affected? At the first intimation of unfavorable developments those in close touch with the situation would undoubtedly have sold stock. Many of them would not only have sold their own holdings but would also have sold stock short. When the unfavorable news reached the general public there would have been in all probability just as precipitate a drop as actually occurred, aided by further short selling. As the decline continued, however, traders on the short side would have had a very strong incentive to take profits. They could take profits only by buying stock. There would thus have been at all times buying orders in the market and genuine investors would never have been in the predicament of being absolutely unable to liquidate their holdings.

Ethics of Short Selling

Short selling is sometimes condemned by observers of the stock market—even by some who are close to the machinery—as immoral. Such critics contend that no one has any moral right to sell somebody's else property. This complaint of course ignores the fact that the short seller actually does no such thing. He merely makes a contract to deliver a certain number of shares of stock in the future and thereby places himself under the necessity of acquiring that number of shares at some future date in order to make good his contract. In the ordinary course of business a steel company may make a contract to deliver a certain tonnage of steel rails a few months hence even though the ore from which those rails will actually be made has not been dug from the ground. Nobody would think of saying that the company's sale was immoral, nor would they speak of it as a short sale. The people who believe that there is something immoral about short selling are simply confused by the terminology of the Street which calls what is a contract for the future delivery of securities a "short sale."

The short seller, moreover, is a certain customer for somebody's else property in the future. The position of the bull is much more comfortable because of the existence of the bear, who must some day come to him and seek to buy his holdings than it would be if there were no such assured customer in sight. It must always be borne in mind that the short sale is necessarily an incomplete transaction. A man who buys a stock may sell it again in half an hour or he may lock it in a safe-deposit box for his grandchildren. The short seller has no such choice. Sooner or later he must cover and usually within a comparatively short time. Theoretically he might maintain a short position for years in an active stock. Actually very little short selling is done with the idea in mind of anything more extended than a quick turn. A completed speculative transaction involves entering into two contracts, one to accept, the other to deliver securities, based on the expectation that the price difference will be in favor of the speculator. A little reflection on this will show how absurd is the notion that there is any morality involved in the matter of which contract is entered into first.

BOOTSTRAP LIFTING

Hostile critics of the short seller also condemn the apparent unfairness to the bull trader of the use of his stocks to enable the bear to comply with the delivery rules. Suppose Mr. A. is long 500 shares of North American on margin. He bought it because he thought the stock was going up. His action in purchasing 500 shares in itself affects the price of the stock, tending to make it advance. Mr. B., another customer of the same brokerage house, may be bearish on North American. Accordingly he now sells 500 shares of North American short. The broker delivers Mr. A.'s stock to the trader who has bought from Mr. B. The sale of course tended to depress the market just as the purchase tended to cause it to advance. Now here is an outrage to every instinct of decency, protest the critics of short selling. By the use of his own property the bullish trader has been robbed of the effect which might legitimately be expected as the result of his purchase.

Leaving aside the purely legal argument that the bullish trader in our hypothetical case has signed a formal agreement similar to the one quoted above permitting his broker to make that very use of the property, has he any legitimate complaint? When the time comes when he decides to sell his 500 shares of North American, other things being equal, the depressing effect on the stock of the sale will exactly neutralize the stimulating effect of his purchase.

On the other hand, the depressing effect of the short sale in which the bullish trader's stock played an incidental part is exactly offset by the stimulating effect when the short seller covered. Thus we see that all these influences in the long run cancel. It does not even make any important difference whether the short seller covers before the bullish trader sells or vice versa.

On a moment's thought it is clear that in any event a trader cannot make money by merely buying stocks. If he has a long enough purse, he can put prices up by buying. That is merely lifting himself by his bootstraps, however. If there is no more important reason for the advance than his purchases, the decline when he sells will be equally great and he will be out commissions. Only if other buyers have been attracted in the interim between his purchase and his sale and the floating supply been reduced by substantially more than the amount of his purchases can he make a profit. When this principle is recognized it becomes plain that the bullish trader has been robbed of nothing of value by the use of his stocks to facilitate short selling.

Fear of a Corner

Besides a vague fear there is something unethical about such a transaction, many traders are prevented from selling stocks short by fears of a corner. There have been a few corners in the history of Wall Street in which traders short of the market have been ruined. There have been just enough of them to make the average trader timid about selling short. A corner occurs when buyers of stock take it out of the market and so reduce the floating supply that not enough stock is available to lend to traders short of it. When this occurs the shorts may push up prices to fantastic levels in the effort to get stock to meet their contracts. The famous Northern Pacific corner was the result of a battle between two great railroad geniuses, Hill and Harriman, to secure control of that road. One secured a majority of the common stock, the other a majority of all the stock, preferred included. A compromise was the final outcome of the rivalry, but it was of no use to speculators who had sold the stock short when it began to soar above its intrinsic value and then had to cover regardless of price when they discovered the stock could not be borrowed. Such a contest hardly occurs once in a generation.

An Ill-Fated Corner

In the case of a stock largely concentrated in a few hands, a corner can occur as the result of manipulation. A few years ago the head of a chain grocery system whose stock was listed on the New York Stock Exchange sought to teach Wall Street a lesson. The company was of moderate size, its issue of stock small and not widely held. When the stock reached a level well above anything that the company's assets or earnings justified there was naturally considerable selling of it. The gentleman in question decided that he would "squeeze" the shorts. He refused to lend his own stock and reduced the floating supply practically to zero by buying all stock offered. It was apparently then his intention to dictate terms of settlement to short traders who would be unable to deliver. In this he reckoned without the sweeping powers of the board of governors of the New York Stock Exchange. The rules of the Stock Exchange are drawn with the intention of maintaining a free and open market, not to assist in its strangulation. With the entire issue of stock concentrated in a few hands a free market no longer existed, suspension of trading in the stock was the obvious step to be taken. A reasonable settlement price was then established by negotiation. The fancied Napoleon of finance thus found himself holding most of the stock of his company, largely bought at prices far above its intrinsic value. By his own action he had closed to it the greatest market in the world. Before long he was forced to appeal to the public for financial assistance. Wall Street has long since forgotten him.

Financial Suicide

To corner a stock is obviously to destroy its market. The distribution in the hands of investors which may have required years is replaced by its concentration in the hands of the manipulator. To squeeze a few shorts and force them to buy immunity from fulfilling their contracts the manipulator has been forced to purchase thousands of shares in the open market at prices far above their real value, investment confidence in the stock has been shattered by the wild gyrations in its price, it probably has been stricken from the list of the Stock Exchange and there are now no bidders upon whom the stock may be unloaded. To engineer a corner is the action of a disordered mind, practically equivalent to financial suicide. Since this is known to every intelligent speculator, such incidents occur only at very long intervals.

Short Selling Requires Nerve

It is the fact that a corner is possible though improbable, the fact that the extent of an advance in a stock is unlimited while its decline can do no more than wipe it out, that make short selling generally unsuitable for long-pull operations. It takes a great deal of nerve to cling to a short position in a stock in the face of an advancing market even though the stock may clearly be overvalued. The dramatic collapse of the pool in Devoe & Raynolds "A" stock at the end of the 1924-26 bull market has already been mentioned in a previous chapter. The stock dropped almost vertically from 105 to 35. There were shrewd traders who had gone short of the stock toward the end of its unwarranted advance yet failed to profit by the decline. Persistent strength in such a stock without apparent basis inevitably leads to conjectures of a possible corner or of accumulation of the stock by interests seeking control. "The tape tells the story," says the short trader to himself, and covers at a few points loss. The tape actually may be telling no story except a commonplace one of human folly.

Unprofitable Field for Long-Pull Trader

There are other reasons why the short side of the market does not offer a profitable field of operations for the long-pull trader. Bull markets are almost invariably longer than bear markets. The trader who buys and sells "the averages" or any other diversified group of stocks thus has much more time to make up his mind to take a position in the market, a much better chance of misjudging its end and still making money. For the long-pull trader bull markets thus offer much more certain opportunities for profit based on the time element alone. The long-pull bear is fighting the long-pull upward trend of values. His chances of success are much less than those of the trader who confines himself to bullish operations.

The short sale has a legitimate place in speculation. It is a transaction into which the shrewd trader, however, will enter much less frequently than into purchases. He will recognize that experience has demonstrated that human nature is such that few people are so constituted that they can take a short position in any extensive way and keep their heads. In selecting his mediums he will not only assure himself that the stock is clearly over-priced but he will make sure that there will be no difficulty in procuring stock for delivery, which means that he will select only stocks of large capitalization of which there is always an ample well distributed supply on the Street. And if the amateur finally decides to leave short selling to those who make speculation their business, it is likely to be profitable decision.

CHAPTER IX.

What Is a Bull Market?

Most useful and most dangerous are the stock market averages, most useful in revealing the general trend of the market, most dangerous if they mislead the trader into forgetting that after all his profits depend on the movements of the individual stocks in which he deals.

The twenty stocks used in the Dow-Jones industrial average give as good a picture of the general trend of the market as would an average composed of fifty or one hundred stocks. The demonstration of this fact involves a tedious computation. Suffice it to say that it has been done. The dependability of the averages as criteria of market movements may be tested in another way, by determining how many stocks move counter to the general trend as shown by the averages, how many industrial stocks, for example, were higher when the industrial average was at its last distinct low point than when it was at the previous peak. Testing a number of major market movements in this way, the student will find that in each case only a handful of issues move counter to the trend.

MOVEMENT OF SEVENTY STOCKS

The fact that an overwhelming majority of stocks will be lower when the averages are at their lows than when the averages are at their highs tends to obscure the fact that individual stocks move in widely different paths. The accompanying chart shows the result of an investigation of the action of seventy industrial common stocks in 1921, a year notable for the occurrence of the nadir of a great bear market. The seventy stocks were chosen at

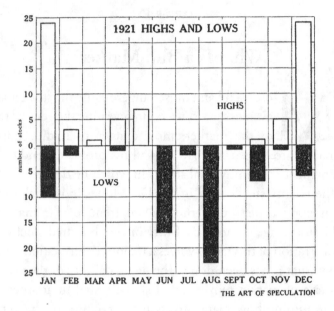

random by taking all the industrial common stocks of companies whose names began with A, B, C, D, E and F listed on the New York Stock Exchange in which there were transactions for each month of the year. The chart shows the number of these stocks making their highs and lows during each month of the year. Thus in January twenty-four stocks sold at what later proved to be their high prices for the year and nine at what later proved to be their low points. This is graphically shown by a vertical rectangle whose height above the horizontal line on the chart represents twenty-four units, its depth below the line nine units. There were two months in which no stock made its low for the year, four in which no stock made its high for the year.

A Chart of Highs and Lows

The chart clearly corresponds to the movement of the Dow-Jones industrial average, which touched bottom in August. In

January, when twenty-four stocks made their highs for the year, the market was on its way down. At the close of the year the market was in the early stages of the 1921-23 bull market. The bottom of the bear market is clearly depicted by the figures for August, when twenty-three stocks out of the seventy made their lows for the year and none made its high.

More interesting are the divergences from the course of the averages shown by individual stocks. Of the seventy issues studied eleven made their highs during the first quarter of the year and continued to decline after the general market had turned, not reaching their lowest quotations until the last three months. In contrast, thirteen issues reached their lows well ahead of the general market, in April or earlier, and were well started on the upward course while the general market was still declining. These thirteen stocks made their highs for the year in the final quarter. The two lists follow:

High in first quarter *Low in last quarter*	*Low in first quarter* *High in last quarter*
Advance-Rumely	Am. Bank Note
Ajax Rubber	Am. Ice
Am. Beet Sugar	Am. Radiator
Am. Chicle	Am. Snuff
Am. Sugar Ref.	Am. Tel. & Tel.
Assets Realization	Am. Woolen
Atlantic Fruit	Assoc. Dry Goods
Am. Sumatra Tob.	Brooklyn Union Gas
Cuba Cane Sugar	Butterick
Cuban-Am. Sugar	California Pet.
Emerson-Brantingham	Coca-Cola
	Cons. Gas N. Y.
	Endicott-Johnson

Speculative and Investment Stocks

Further instructive lessons may be drawn from an analysis of these two lists. The first list contains stocks for the most part of a highly speculative nature. Only three of the stocks were on a dividend basis and all later cut or passed. Five of the companies whose stocks appear in the list have since passed through voluntary or involuntary reorganizations. In a number of cases the stocks were lower at the peak of the 1923-26 bull market than at the high point of the bear year 1921. In contrast the second list is distinctly a group of investment stocks. All but one of these stocks were on a dividend basis in 1921. With few exceptions these stocks scored notable advances in the bull markets of 1921-23 and 1923-26.

The conclusion may be drawn tentatively from these examples that investment stocks tend to reach their lows early in bear markets, that they offer more certain profits and in general larger profits than more highly speculative low-priced non-dividend-paying issues. This conclusion would be supported by a more exhaustive analysis, which it would merely be tedious to reproduce here.

Divergent Trends

A more important conclusion is suggested by the chart and the data from which it was compiled. Individual stocks may obviously pursue courses widely dissimilar. Advance-Rumely sank from a high of 19¾ in January to a low of 10⅛ in December. Between those same months American Ice rose from a low of 42 to a high of 83½ As between two old-time investment favorites, American Sugar Refining and American Telephone, the former fell from a high of 96 in January to a low of 47⅝ in October, the latter rose from 95¾ in January to 119½ in October. Many similar examples might be adduced, but these will probably suffice. It is clear that a correct judgment of the trend of the general market would not have been enough to make profits in these stocks. The trader who refused to buy American Ice or American Telephone in January, because he thought the bear market had not reached its lowest point, lost money by waiting. Similarly a purchase of Advance-Rumely or American Sugar in August did not relieve him of concern when those stocks touched still lower levels later in the year.

MOVEMENT OF GROUPS

A further study of the behavior of seventy stocks in 1921 suggests another approach to the problem of profitable speculation. It may be noted that among the eleven stocks which made their highs in the first quarter of the year and their lows in the last quarter were four sugar stocks. On the other hand, there were no sugar stocks among the thirteen issues which behaved in a contrary manner. This is hardly a coincidence. It suggests the possibility that the outlook for a given industry is the important factor in a speculator's calculations. In the sugar industry 1921 was a year of severe price declines, Cuban raw sugar reaching a low point of two cents a pound, as contrasted with twenty cents a pound in the previous year. With raw sugar declining no refinery could possibly be operated at a profit. The refiner's margin of profit is narrow at best, refined sugar prices quickly adjust themselves to raw sugar prices. If raw sugar constantly declined as little as an eighth of a cent between the time a cargo of raw sugar was purchased and the time the refined sugar was ready for the market, losses were inevitable. At two cents a pound, moreover, no producer of raw sugar in the world could make a profit. Sugar stocks thus naturally declined in a falling raw sugar market. Until raw sugar had clearly touched bottom no holder of sugar stocks could be sure that his dividends were safe, or even that his company could survive the crisis.

Reason for Group Movements

Many other companies besides sugar companies are affected alike by special conditions. The trend of the beef-cattle and hog markets affects all the packers in the same way. The swings in the market for crude rubber affect all the rubber manufacturers, who must keep large stocks of the raw material on hand owing to the 9,000 miles distance which separates them from the source of supply. An unfavorable rate structure in the Northwest cripples the earning power of all the railroads operating in that territory. If the boll weevil is particularly ravenous in a certain year, all cotton mills suffer from the effect of a short cotton crop. To a very large extent stocks may be grouped in this way, the stocks in a given group responding to conditions affecting that industry and not the general trend of the stock market.

A Striking Contrast

Many instances might be adduced to show in what a contrary manner particular groups of stocks may behave. The accompanying chart of the Dow-Jones industrial average, the average of two leading ten-cent store stocks and the average of three fertilizer stocks, is strikingly suggestive of the necessity for going deeper than a mere forecast of the trend of the general market in speculation. The average of the price of Woolworth and Kresge is adjusted to allow for stock dividends and the average composed of American Agricultural Chemical, International Agricultural Corp. and Virginia-Carolina Chemical is similarly adjusted to allow for capital readjustments.

In 1922 Virginia-Carolina's capital structure was readjusted. For each four shares of common stock, a holder received in addition one share of class "B" common. The figure taken into the average thereafter was the price of one share of common plus one-fourth the price of class "B" stock.

SIMULTANEOUS BULL AND BEAR MARKETS

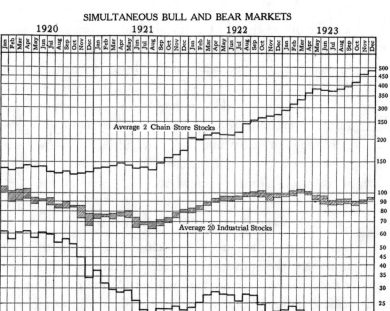

THE ART OF SPECULATION

The scale of the chart is technically known as a logarithmic scale. It is based on the theory that an advance from 10 to 12 is as great a percentage advance as an advance from 100 to 120. Such a chart has the great advantage of presenting movements over a very wide range without distortion. On an ordinary chart the movement of the chain-store stocks from the 1920 low of 128¾ to the 1923 high of 482 would completely dwarf the movement of the other two averages. By the use of the logarithmic scale, all three are shown in proper perspective.

CHAIN STORES VS. FERTILIZERS

Examination of the chart will disclose that, during the four years it covers, the industrial average indicates a major bear market succeeded by a major bull market. At the trough of the bear market, however, the average of the chain-store stocks was only five points below the 1920 high. The advance from that time was steady. Moreover, it took no note of the culmination of the upswing in other industrials in March, 1923. At the end of 1923 the chain-store stocks were 50% above their March level. In contrast, the fertilizer stocks behaved in orthodox fashion during the bear market which culminated in August, 1921. From the beginning of 1920 to that date they declined about 67%. However, the bull market of 1922-1923 almost passed them by completely. In March, 1923, the average of the fertilizer stocks was only 2⅛ points above the 1921 low. At the end of 1923 they were selling at practically the lowest level of the whole four-year period. During the whole of this period, then, the ten-cent store stocks were enjoying a bull market of their own; during the whole of it the fertilizer stocks were passing through a bear market on their own account.

Fashion in the Stock Market

Fashions play their part in the stock market as in other affairs of life. For some years after the introduction of Woolworth and Kresge to trading on the New York Stock Exchange, the investing and trading public was skeptical of the continued growth of those enterprises. Moreover, they did not participate in the war prosperity conferred on many industrial concerns by munitions and shipbuilding contracts. They merely continued to open new stores, sell more goods in the old stores, make more money, year after year. By 1920 the public had begun to realize the remarkable possibilities of a business which showed uninterrupted growth month after month regardless of business conditions. As this growth continued throughout 1920 and 1921 there was naturally no tendency for stocks which were cheap on an investment basis at the beginning of the period, which were not widely scattered in the hands of small traders and investors, to decline with the general market. When the general market turned, therefore, Woolworth and Kresge were in a far stronger position than the average stock to advance. They became popular stocks in which to trade for several years thereafter.

Public Utility Popularity

A similar change in public sentiment occurred in the case of the public utilities a little later. Troubles of the tractions, failure to profit by the after-war boom in commodity prices in 1919 and 1920 had obscured the remarkable record of the electric light and power industry and diverted the attention of the public from it. By 1923 growth of business had far more than caught up with the market for public utility securities. The public then awoke to the merits of the utilities, they became popular stocks and in the 1923-26 bull market were among the most generously exploited issues. Here we have one of the difficulties of the speculator. A group of stocks having distinct merit may remain out of favor for months and even years. The alert analyst of values may buy such issues and hold them for a long and discouraging period when everything else is going up without making a profit. Eventually his patience will be rewarded, but it may be subjected to a severe strain by the vagaries of speculative sentiment.

Sentiment played its part also in the decline of the fertilizer stocks. Until 1920 American Agricultural Chemical and Virginia-Carolina Chemical ranked as semi-investment stocks. The public was slow to appreciate the magnitude of the misfortune which had overtaken those companies with the agricultural depression of 1921. Viewing the heights from which these stocks had fallen there were many short-sighted traders ready to buy the stocks on the faintest signs of an improvement. It thus happened that they participated to a moderate extent in the early stages of the 1921-23 bull market without any real justification for such a movement in their earnings or financial condition.

THE FACTOR OF MANAGEMENT

It is clear that the intelligent speculator must have due regard in his operations not only to the trend of the general market but also to the position of particular groups of stocks. Must he go still further and place his emphasis on the analysis of individual issues? What are the prospects that the course of a given stock will diverge from the course of a group average? Logically it would seem that we must take this final step. Our groups are never homogeneous. Traders speak of the rubber stocks as one group, including stocks of companies making tires exclusively, with stocks of companies making more rubber footwear and mechanical rubber goods than tires. Both types of company are affected by fluctuations in the market for the raw material. In many other respects they are affected by different factors. Even two companies in a still more homogeneous group may fare very differently. As between two Cuban sugar producers with properties at opposite ends of the island one may suffer from strikes and a drought while the other is raising a bumper crop under peaceful conditions.

To consider stocks by groups rather than by individual companies is further to ignore the vital factor of management. Getting back to first principles, consider two competing retail grocers. The one may be a surly individual running a store with fly-specked windows and mouldy cereals on his shelves; the other an alert merchant with a pleasant smile, a spotless store and a fresh stock. Will the banker whose customers they are base his treatment of their applications for credit on statistics of the position of the retail grocery trade?

SUCCESS AND FAILURE IN FRUIT

Taking an extreme case, it is apparent that the stock of a company headed for receivership will respond but feebly to the forces producing a bull market and, on the contrary, will tend to sink out of sight despite the general trend. Some years ago an ambitious attempt was made to create a rival for the phenomenally successful United Fruit Co. Under the sponsorship of a distinguished group of directors the Atlantic Fruit Co. began in 1920 a program of expansion, issuing at first $10,000,000 debentures and later $6,000,000 more bonds to finance it. Despite its distinguished sponsorship, the company was never a success and when the stock dropped from its 1920 high of 20¼ to below $2 a share in 1921 no bargain was thereby offered to the speculative public. The stock made no recovery in 1922 and eventually faded out completely. In contrast the stock of the United Fruit Co. was hardly affected at all by the 1921 bear market. The stock reached a record high in December, 1920, at 224⅞ just before the declaration of a 100% stock dividend. "Ex" that stock dividend the lowest it ever sold was 95¾ in the following year or the equivalent of 191½ for the old stock. The difference was hardly more than a reaction in a bull market. From this low point the stock advanced almost steadily to another record high of 297 in February, 1926, just on the eve of another stock split-up, this time of 2½ for one, and in November sold at equivalent of 315. The trader who called the turns correctly on the general market would not have been conspicuously successful in trading in either United Fruit or Atlantic Fruit.

THE PRINCE AND PAUPER INDUSTRY

If these appear to be extreme cases, consider the case of the two leading factors in the most basic industry. Bethlehem Steel and United States Steel are the two largest manufacturers of steel in the country. Their stocks are among the most active industrial issues on the New York Stock Exchange. The steel industry has long been known as the "prince and pauper" industry because of the breadth of the swings between prosperity and depression. For this reason steel stocks are also subject to rather wide price fluctuations. In a genuine bear market it is pretty nearly a certainty that an active steel stock will decline. We might accordingly expect that the movement of the stocks of the two leading steel companies over a considerable period would synchronize closely. Examination of the chart shown below discloses an interesting divergence. At their 1920 highs both stocks were selling above par and less than eight points apart. From that level both dropped sharply with the development of the bear market which culminated in 1921. In the case of Bethlehem Steel, however, the decline was much more abrupt than in the case of the larger company. While the two stocks made their 1921 lows in the same month, June, the low point in the one case was 41½ in the other 70¼.

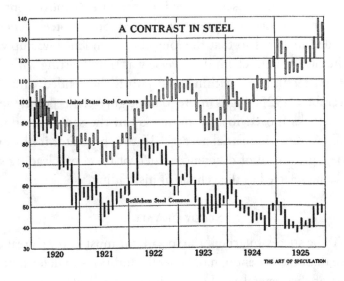

A CONTRAST IN STEEL

THE ART OF SPECULATION

A WIDENING SPREAD

Following the bear market of 1921 both Bethlehem and United States Steel recovered, but Bethlehem exhausted its upward possibilities early, reaching a peak of 82¼ in May, 1922. The advance in United States Steel continued until the stock reached a peak of 111½ in October of that year. During the balance of 1922 and half of 1923 the trend of both stocks was downward, Bethlehem reaching its bottom in June, United States Steel in July, at 41¾ and 85½ respectively. It will be noted that whereas the two stocks had started at the same level, at this turning point they were over 43 points apart. A mild bull market developed in the latter part of 1923 and culminated for both stocks in February, 1924. At this point they were 46⅞ points apart.

It would be tedious to trace the further movement of these stocks, which is clearly depicted on the chart. The lesson is obvious. While the two stocks were for the greater part of the time moving in the same direction, the rate of movement was different. The gains scored by United States Steel generally exceeded its losses so that the long-range tendency was upward. In the case of Bethlehem the reverse was true. Starting with their January, 1920, highs within seven points they ended with their November, 1925, highs more than eighty-eight points apart. Both stocks moved for the most part in the same direction as the Dow-Jones industrial average. To the speculator it obviously made a great deal of difference which of these two leading steel stocks he selected as the vehicle of his trading.

STUDY OF VALUES

To be successful, then, the speculator must know a great deal more than merely enough of general conditions to determine the trend of the general market. He must be a student of values in individual securities. To appraise values in individual securities he must know something about a great many different businesses. He must know in a general way the trade practices in the rubber industry, understand the colono system in the sugar industry, be familiar with depreciation practices among the public utilities, appreciate the significance of ton-miles and many other technicalities of railroading. Above all he must know something of accounting. He must study financial statements as intently as the banker does those of the applicant for credit, though from a different view-point. The question of ascertaining trend of the market is important to the speculator, but it should not rank any higher in importance than the question of intelligent selection of his vehicles.

Chapter X

How to Read a Balance Sheet

Finance has its anatomy and its physiology. The former is studied through the medium of balance sheets, the latter through income statements.

A balance sheet is a statement of the condition of a business enterprise at a given moment. It lists the assets and the liabilities of the business as at that moment. Usually the chosen moment is the close of business on the day which ends a fiscal year or shorter fiscal period. Practically every business closes its books at least once a year —to do less is to violate the income tax law. Progressive businessmen usually like to know where they stand at more frequent intervals, quarterly or monthly. Since months are of variable length, some business executives divide their years into thirteen four-week periods. While reports of business condition are often available to business executives at frequent intervals, the investing public is not often privileged to examine the condition of a business more frequently than quarterly and in the case even of many large corporations balance sheets are available only once a year.

Why a Balance Sheet Balances

The most striking thing about the balance sheet is that its two sides, assets and liabilities, always balance. The balance is the result of the conception that the business enterprise owes its proprietors the equivalent of that portion of its assets not required to meet the claims of outside creditors. This difference between assets and indebtedness to outside creditors is the net worth of the business. If the business is incorporated, it is represented primarily by capital stock of one or more classes. This stock may or may not have a nominal or par value, supposed to represent the amount originally invested by the stockholders. If the original investment has been increased by prudent management out of earnings, there is another item in the net worth account, which may be known as profit and loss, undivided profits or surplus.

The balance sheet of the United Shoe Machinery Corp. as of February 27, 1926, lies before the writer and will serve as well as any for an example. The net worth accounts in this case are three, preferred stock $10,594,375, common stock $48,534,891, profit and loss $24,303,786. Par value of both classes of stock is $25. The net worth belonging to the holders of the 423,775 shares of preferred and 1,941,395 and 16/25 shares of common stock is the sum of these three figures, or $83,433,052. In the event the corporation were dissolved as of February 27, 1926, there would theoretically be this sum left after all debts had been paid, for division among the stockholders.

What Happens on Dissolution

In the event of dissolution the two classes of stockholders would not share alike. By agreement the preferred stock has certain prior but limited rights. Its holders are entitled to $35 a share plus accumulated unpaid dividends in liquidation before anything is paid on the common. This $35 a share is equal to $14,832,125. If the assets of United Shoe actually brought as much on liquidation as the book values at which they were carried on February 27, 1926, there would then be left $69,600,927 for division among the common stockholders. This would amount to $35.43 a share. Here we have the theoretical book value of the common stock. Parenthetically it may be remarked that on February 27, 1926, United Shoe common sold at $51 a share, thereby suggesting a doubt as to the practical value of our computation.

The United Shoe Machinery balance sheet is not so complete as would be desirable for analysis. Accordingly we choose another statement almost at random and give the following statement of the Davison Chemical Co. as of December 31, 1925, for a specimen:

Assets

Land, plant, etc...	$11,968,068
Cuban property...	8,056,262
Advs. to other companies	448,637
Investments...	2,000
Investment in affiliated companies................	3,323,700
Sinking fund	774,000
Cash..	706,767
Notes and accts. receivable	415,306
Advances..	853,471
Accruals...	253,025
Inventories	656,164
	$27,457,400

Liabilities

Capital stock (235,000 no-par shares)	$9,057,107
Funded debt..	774,000
Debentures..	3,000,000
Reserve for depreciation	
Other reserves	3,065,002
Notes payable..	*1530,366*
Accounts payable	
Capital surplus	9,166,153
Profit and loss surplus..................................	1,864,772
	$27,457,400

Net worth in this case is $20,088,032, equal to $85.50 a share for the 235,000 no par shares of capital stock. The highest price at which Davison Chemical sold on December 31, 1925, was 40¾, a further indication that book value and market value are not necessarily related.

The first two items on the Davison Chemical balance sheet are so-called "fixed" assets. They might have been lumped together as "real estate, machinery and equipment" or any one of a dozen other designations. It is useful, however, to have them in detail. If it were reported in the press, for example, that the company planned to sell its Cuban property it would be very desirable to have some inkling as to how important such a transaction would be.

UNCERTAIN VALUE OF FIXED ASSETS

It will be noted that in the Davison Chemical statement the fixed assets are in themselves almost equal to the company's net worth. Here we have an obvious reason for the discrepancy between book and market value. The fixed assets may be relatively unproductive. A company may find it necessary to invest large sums in a source of raw material, for example, which may not be required in its business for years to come. More commonly the book value of fixed assets may represent plants at their cost or even at their reproduction value which are equipped with obsolete machinery and unable to compete with other concerns. An old factory of a concern which has gone out of business is usually an asset of very uncertain value. New England cotton mills, which it would cost millions of dollars to reproduce, have long been valued in the stock market at zero. The explanation lies in the fact that investors who had those millions of dollars in cash would never think of reproducing cotton mills which in many instances have shown their owners no profits for years.

WHEN FIXED ASSETS ARE IMPORTANT

Sometimes fixed assets are worth very much more than their book value. Some of the fertilizer companies were able to sell

Florida land from which they had stripped its phosphate beds at fancy prices during the land boom in that state in 1925. Conservatively managed industrial companies usually understate substantially the value of the plants in which they produce goods at generous profits. In the case of public utility companies subject to public regulation of rates it is well settled by law that they are entitled to such rates as will permit them with competent management to earn a fair return on capital investment. The railroads of the country as a whole are theoretically entitled under the Transportation Act to earn 5¾% on their capital investment. If they earn more, the excess is subject to "recapture" by the same law. In the case of railroads and public utilities, therefore, the value of fixed assets is an important factor in estimating the value of their securities. The reverse is the case with industrial companies, the book value of whose fixed assets is relatively a matter of small concern.

Following the fixed assets on the Davison Chemical balance sheet is an item "advances to other companies." This doubtless represents loans to companies affiliated with Davison. If these companies had strong credit of their own, it would probably not be necessary for them to borrow from the related enterprise. A doubt accordingly arises as to the value of this item in the event of liquidation. It would certainly be conservative to treat it as of doubtful value.

INVESTMENTS: GILT-EDGED AND OTHERWISE

The next item is trivial in amount. So far as Davison Chemical is concerned it would not be worth while to spend much time on the "investments" of $2,000. In many balance sheets, however, the name of the account is followed by a figure of substantial size. In such cases it is very important, though usually very difficult, to have some idea what the investments really are. They may consist of shares in a subsidiary company which could not readily be sold. On the other hand, they may consist of United States government bonds or other marketable securities. If they are investments of the latter type, the management is deceiving its stockholders and the public by not calling them "marketable securities" or some similarly descriptive term. If they are of the former type, the management is equally open to censure for an apparent desire to make the item appear more valuable than is actually the case. Lacking definite information the analyst is justified in discounting an item of investments very heavily.

"Investment in affiliated companies" is an honest way of describing an asset which may or may not be of substantial value. It sometimes happens that the stock of a subsidiary has a market of its own by which some light may be thrown on the value of the stock held by the parent company. More often such an investment item in a balance sheet must likewise be discounted rather heavily.

How Funded Debt May Be Paid

"Sinking fund" is a partial offset to funded debt. The indenture of a bond issue frequently provides that the company must set aside certain sums annually or oftener for the ultimate repayment of the issue. These sums form a sinking fund. They may be invested in marketable securities or in the company's own bonds. The latter is the sounder procedure. Sometimes bonds so acquired are canceled, sometimes they are held alive in the sinking fund. If this procedure is adopted, interest on the sinking-fund bonds remains a charge against the income of the corporation and the amount available for bond purchase or redemption increases annually. In the case of Davison Chemical it will be noted that "sinking fund" and "funded debt" are equal, indicating that the entire bond issue is held in the treasury of the company.

The equation of assets and liabilities would not be changed if both items were eliminated from the balance sheet.

The last five items on the asset side of the Davison Chemical balance sheet consist of what are known as "current," "quick" or "liquid" assets. Theoretically they can all be converted into cash within a short period.

Even Cash is Not Always Good

First of the current-asset items is cash. This consists of bank deposits and petty cash in the office safe. A great corporation may have deposits in dozens of banks throughout the country. The small corporation carries its account in one or two banks. It is usually a good asset to the extent of 100 cents on the dollar. In the case of a corporation whose credit standing is not very good there may be strings on its bank accounts so that they are by no means 100% liquid. The investor or speculator relying upon published statements will have no means of knowing whether this is the case, and if the rest of the statement is satisfactory he need have no hesitancy in considering the cash item perfectly good.

Credit to Customers

Below the cash item in the Davison Chemical balance sheet are two items lumped in one, "notes receivable" and "accounts receivable." It would be better if they were reported separately. Accounts receivable are the amounts due a company from its customers. Goods are not sold to any great extent by manufacturers, wholesalers or even retailers for cash on delivery, but are sold for the most part on credit. A manufacturer selling to a wholesaler will ordinarily make the sale on some such terms as "2% ten days, net thirty days." This means that his customer may save 2% of the amount of the invoice by paying for the goods within ten days and is expected to pay for them net thereafter and within thirty days. Accounts not over thirty days old due from customers who have always paid their bills promptly in the past are sound assets to the extent of nearly 100 cents on the dollar. For accounts older than thirty days a reserve should be set up and deducted from the amount of the accounts receivable before publishing the statement. If past-due accounts are included, the item is obviously less liquid than if proper charge-offs have been made. Scanning the published statement the trader has no means of knowing whether the accounts receivable item is conservatively stated or not. If on comparison with previous balance sheets it shows a tendency to increase faster than the growth of the business, he may question it.

A QUESTION OF TRADE PRACTICES

"Notes receivable" represents sums owing to a corporation for which it holds notes. It is the custom in certain trades to take notes on the sale of goods rather than allowing the debt to stand as a book account. Farmers, for example, have long been accustomed to give notes for fertilizer and farm implements purchased. Where it is not the trade practice to take notes when goods are sold, notes receivable usually represent accounts which there has been some difficulty in collecting. When a debtor is pressed under such circumstances he will often give a note as evidence of his good intentions. Such notes are obviously not as good security as accounts owed by good customers. Notes receivable may also represent advances to officers and employees of a corporation. If the corporation gets into a tight place, it will be very difficult to collect from its employees. Such notes are therefore not a very liquid asset.

"Advances" may represent sums advanced to suppliers of raw materials for materials to be furnished. In the Cuban sugar industry much of the cane is grown by colonos who contract to supply it to the nearest mill on a sliding-scale price basis. Many of the colonos are financed by the mills and "advances to colonos" is usually a prominent item on the balance sheet of a Cuban sugar producer. Similar practices prevail to some extent in other industries. It is a question how great weight should be given to such an item.

"Accruals" represent prepaid taxes, insurance premiums and similar expense items. If a five year premium on a fire insurance policy was paid December 1, for example, it is clear that on December 31 only one-sixtieth of the protection paid for has been received. Accordingly 59/60 may theoretically be considered an asset. Since such assets are not realizable unless the concern goes out of business, it is a very questionable practice to consider them current assets. Another name for accruals is "deferred charges."

The Inventory Account

The final item on the Davison Chemical statement is "inventories." This is typically the most important on an industrial balance sheet, though it does not happen to bulk large on this particular statement. A synonym for inventory is "merchandise." A detailed balance sheet of a manufacturing concern would show raw material, goods in process and finished goods, but such detailed information is seldom vouchsafed the general public.

The inventory account is always stated by conservatively managed corporations at "cost or market, whichever is lower." If the market for the raw material which a company uses has been advancing over a considerable period, a balance sheet may thus understate substantially the real value of the asset. Some companies follow an even more conservative practice and value their raw materials at an arbitrary price well under the actual market. Some New England mills have made it a practice, for example, to carry their cotton at two cents a pound. The National

Lead Co. follows a similar policy in valuing its lead inventory at a constant figure well under the lowest market of recent years. It is clear that there may sometimes be a substantial "hidden asset" in the inventory item on a balance sheet.

UPS AND DOWNS OF COMMODITY MARKET

It is usually a mistake to count too heavily on appreciation in a corporation's inventories as a bullish factor in the stock market. If a raw material rises because of a temporary shortage in the supply, the usual sequel is a corresponding drop in price which wipes out the extra profits resulting from the advance. The 1925 advance in crude rubber from under 40 cents to $1.20 a pound did the rubber manufacturers no real good. Prices of finished rubber goods did not keep pace with the advance in the raw material and the reverse movement in the rubber market in 1926 more than offset the temporary extra profits of 1925. Business is best done on stable markets.

If a speculator should not place too much weight on possible appreciation in inventories, it follows that he should make due allowance for possible depreciation. Here enter not only the factor of market changes but also the factor of accumulation of "shopworn" goods. If a business is managed in slipshod fashion, it is quite possible that obsolete, out-of-style or shopworn goods may accumulate. When a leading wholesale dry-goods house whose name was synonymous with strength in banking circles failed a few years ago, it was discovered that it had on its shelves goods which had been out of style and practically unsalable for years. There is thus a distinct possibility that inventory may be worth less than book value not only as a result of depreciation in a raw material market but also through accumulation of unsalable material.

Importance of Balanced Inventories

In the case of a manufacturing concern there is still a further possible cause for shrinkage in the real value of the inventory item. Suppose that the manufacturing process is so extremely simple as to involve merely the assembling of four parts which we may designate A, B, C and D in the ratio of 2A, 1B, 5C and 1D. Suppose further that A is valued at 39 cents for inventory purposes, B at $1.18, C at 42 cents and D at 68 cents. Obviously these various parts are of little value in themselves. They must be combined to be salable. If the management of the concern in question is efficient, its stock of parts on hand will be in close correspondence with the ratio in which the parts are used. The management may be inefficient, however, and have, for example, 200 A, 300 B, 500 C and 400 D. The inventory may then be valued at $914.00, whereas actually only 100 articles with a value in their parts of $267.00 may be manufactured from it. As it stands, the rest of the inventory is practically worthless and can become valuable only if a substantial sum is spent for additional parts in the proper proportion. It is clear that for a number of reasons the book value of inventory may be subject to heavy shrinkage. Without the detailed analysis which the average speculator cannot give, it is impossible to tell just how liquid an inventory may be. In prudence a substantial allowance must be made on this account in analyzing the value of a stock.

The liabilities items on the Davison Chemical balance sheet require briefer treatment (see pages 142-143). The first is one of the net-worth items already considered. The second and third would ordinarily be lumped as "funded debt" in one item. In this instance the segregation is useful as indicating by the correspondence with the "sinking fund" item on the asset side that one issue of bonds is held wholly in the treasury.

THE DAVISON CHEMICAL COMPANY
(Incorporated under the Laws of Maryland)
DAVISON SULPHUR & PHOSPHATE COMPANY *Condensed*
Consolidated Balance Sheet, December 31, 1925

After Giving Effect to Appraisal of Property in Maryland and to Proposed Sale of $3,000,000, 5 Year, 6¹/₂%, Gold Debentures, and Application of the Proceeds Therefrom in Liquidation of Current Liabilities and in Providing a Fund for Retirement of Outstanding Bonds of Davison Sulphur & Phosphate Company

ASSETS

LAND, BUILDINGS, MACHINERY, EQUIPMENT, ETC., IN MARYLAND—AT REPLACEMENT VALUE PER APPRAISAL OP DWIGHT P.. ROBINSON & COMPANY, INCORPORATED, AS OF JANUARY 1, 1926		$11,410,750.00
EXPENDITURES FOR PHOSPHATE ROCK PROPERTY IN FLORIDA		557,317.85
CUBAN PROPERTY:		
Expenditures for property, mining rights, prospecting, developing, etc., less proceeds of sales of certain equipment	$ 3,632,489.38	
Value of ore blocked out, based on appraisal of Pope Yeatman, as of February 22, 1919	4,423,772.43	8,056,261.81
CURTIS BAY RAILROAD COMPANY—ADVANCES		448,637.23
PREFERRED STOCK OF MERCHANTS AND MANUFACTURERS ASSOCIATION BUILDING, INC.—AT PAR		2,000.00
VOTING TRUST CERTIFICATES REPRESENTING 184,650 SHARES OF COMMON CAPITAL STOCK OF THE SILICA GEL CORPORATION WITHOUT PAR VALUE—AT $18.00 PER SHARES		3,323,700.00
INSURANCE, TAXES', INTEREST, DISCOUNT, AND OTHER EXPENSES PREPAID		253,024.93
CASH FUND FOR RETIREMENT OF DAVISON SULPHUR & PHOSPHATE COMPANY BONDS		774,000.00
CASH		706,767.44
		415,306.22
ACCOUNTS RECEIVABLE—TRADE DEBTORS AND OTHERS		853,471.49
CURRENT ADVANCES—THE SILICA GEL CORPORATION		
INVENTORIES—BOOK VALUE		656,163.70
TOTAL		$27,457,400.67

LIABILITIES

THE DAVISON CHEMICAL COMPANY—5-YEAR, 6$\frac{1}{2}$%, GOLD
DEBENTURES, DUE JANUARY 1, 1931 $ 3,000,000.00

DAVISON SULPHUR & PHOSPHATE COMPANY, 10-YEAR,
FIRST MORTGAGE, 6%, GOLD BONDS, DUE MARCH 1, 1927 (see cash
fund for retirement contra)   774,000.00

NOTES, ACCEPTANCES AND ACCOUNTS PAYABLE   530,366.11

RESERVES:
Depreciation:
           Property in Maryland—per appraisal of Dwight
           P. Robinson & Company, Incorporated, as of
           January 1, 1926, plus transfer of
           $1(813,440.32 by company from capital Surplus

                                       $ 2,502,777.32

Property In Cuba   216,894.42

Contingencies   345,330.24   3,065,001.98

SHAREHOLDERS' ACCOUNTS:
CapitalStock—23 5,000 shares without par value $ 9,057,107.72
Capital surplus from appraisal of property in Maryland and ore blocked
out in Cuba, and excess of book value over cost of 184,650 shares of
The Silica Gel Corporation stock (less transfer of
           $1,813,440.32 to reserve for depreciation of
           property in Maryland)

                                     9,166,152.82

Profit and loss surplus   1,864,772.04   20,088,032.58

                         TOTAL $27,457,400.67

NOTE: *There were contingent liabilities amounting to $98,291.59 at December 31 , 1925, on account of trade notes receivable discounted.*

CERTIFICATE OF AUDIT

We have made a general audit of the accounts of The Davison Chemical Company and Davison Sulphur & Phosphate Company for the year ended December 31, 1925, and, subject to the net value of the Cuban property as reflected by the above statement.

WE HEREBY CERTIFY that, in our opinion, the above Condensed Consolidated Balance Sheet, December 31, 1925, after giving effect to appraisal of property in Maryland and to proposed sale and application of proceeds of $3,000,000.00. 5-year, 6$\frac{1}{2}$%, Gold Debentures, is correct.

HASKINS & SELLS. *Baltimore, April 27,1926.*

DEPRECIATION: AN IMPORTANT FIGURE

"Reserve for depreciation" is really a deduction from the fixed assets. These might have been shown as a net figure after deducting reserve for depreciation. It is useful to know what allowance has been made for depreciation, however, and to check the fluctuations in the item from year to year. If sound accounting methods were followed, fixed assets might originally be placed on the books at cost. As buildings and machinery grew older, provision would have to be made for their replacement. This would be done by setting aside reasonable sums each year to the reserve for depreciation. Cost of replacements of major items would be charged against this reserve. If a company charged $500,000 to depreciation in a given year, for example, and spent $300,000 for replacements of machinery, the reserve for depreciation would actually be increased by $200,000-plus the scrap value of the discarded machinery. Unless the company spent money for permanent improvements—not replacements—during that year the $200,000 plus would appear elsewhere in the balance sheet either as an increase among the current assets or as a decrease among the items of indebtednesss.

If a company makes insufficient allowance for depreciation, it will ultimately find itself with old buildings and worn-out machinery, unable to compete with more progressive rivals. On the other hand, a company may build up substantial "hidden assets" by taking too much depreciation. The figures for this account are among those which a speculator should study with care. By comparison of the practice of various companies in the same type of industry he may be able to evolve certain standards which will be helpful.

OTHER RESERVES

Besides a reserve for depreciation a company may set up other reserves for numerous purposes. If a high market level for a raw material appears unstable, it may be prudent to establish a "reserve for contingencies" to meet any threatened shrinkage in inventory values. This reserve may either be set up as a liability or deducted directly from the inventory account. In the latter event the fact should be clearly stated. A company which has widely scattered plants may find it good economy to carry its own fire insurance or liability insurance and set up reserves for this purpose. A pension system for employees necessitates still another kind of reserve. If the management desires to conceal unusual prosperity from casual inspection, other reserves may be set up without any special designation merely for good luck. A reserve account may thus represent an offset against an asset which would otherwise be overstated, a contingent or future liability or a hidden net-worth account.

One reserve is always a debt of inescapable character. Taxes, local and federal, have a preferred claim on the assets of an enterprise. A reserve for taxes should properly be set up out of earnings before payment is actually due. On the balance sheet it represents a debt quite as much as an item of notes payable to banks.

WHAT ARE CURRENT LIABILITIES?

Debts which are definitely payable within a year are known as current liabilities. In this class are reserve for taxes, notes payable, accounts payable, accrued wages, and occasionally other items. Notes payable represent borrowings from banks or others due ordinarily in from 60 days to six months. Accounts payable represent sums owing for purchases of materials and supplies. Accrued wages explains itself. Occasionally other items may be found among current liabilities, as saving deposits made by an employee with his employer.

A balance sheet is the picture of a moment. The analyst must not forget that a statement as of a certain date might look very different if it were taken a few weeks later. Of course intelligent businessmen are well aware of this fact and more or less "window-dressing" in order to make a favorable statement is the natural result. It also happens frequently that a company adopts a fiscal year differing from the calendar year so that the end of the fiscal year shall fall in a period of normally dull business. A food-canning company, for example, may adopt a fiscal year ending late in the winter when the bulk of its pack has been sold. At such a time its bank borrowings will be at a minimum, its cash and receivables at a maximum.

There is another reason for adopting such a fiscal period. It is physically easier to check inventory when it is light than when it is heavy and the possible error is also less in the off season.

The Current Ratio

The old-fashioned banker presented with a balance sheet by an applicant for a loan first compared two items, the sum of the current assets and the sum of the current liabilities. If the ratio between them was two to one or better, he would probably make the loan. The reason for adopting this standard is not far to seek. In varying degrees the current assets are subject to shrinkage in the event of forced liquidation, the current liabilities may be shrunk only by bankruptcy. If the current assets were twice the current liabilities, the margin of safety was presumably sufficient. Modern thought and research have greatly elaborated this simple test of a company's condition. Obviously it makes a great deal of difference what proportions cash, accounts receivable and inventories bear to one another. In 1924 the Virginia-Carolina Chemical Co. went into receivership despite the fact that its working-capital ratio was 1.88 to 1. In that particular case notes receivable from farmers, which were anything but a readily realizable asset, constituted the greater part of current assets.

How "Window-Dressing" May Be Accomplished

There are other weaknesses in the current ratio as a test of strength. Suppose that a company has $10,000,000 inventories, $4,000,000 accounts receivable and $1,000,000 cash while its current liabilities amount to $10,000,000. Here we have a 1½ to 1 current ratio. A few months later the company may have sold $5,000,000 of its inventory and received the cash for it. If the cash had been applied to the payment of debts there would now be $10,000,000 current assets and $5,000,000 current liabilities. It will be noted that the ratio has changed merely by subtracting the same amount from both sides of the balance sheet. There has even been no allowance for the profit ordinarily to be expected in converting mechandise into cash or accounts receivable. This is why a company can make the best showing merely by closing its fiscal period at a season of the year when business is normally dull and inventories at a minimum. The same result can be accomplished in a less ethical manner by selling part of the accounts receivable for cash to a discount company or by secretly hypothecating part of the inventory or accounts and failing to disclose the obligation to take them back on the books.

Working-Capital Requirements Differ

The current ratio is unsatisfactory for still other reasons. In some lines of business, large working capital is not necessary. A chain of restaurants, for example, doing a cash business and carrying only a few days' supply of food on hand does not need the large working capital required by a company selling on credit and forced by conditions beyond its control to carry several months' supplies of raw material or to manufacture several months ahead for a seasonal demand. Companies with a large fixed investment and stable earning power also do not require large working capital. A public utility company planning a $10,000,000 construction program, for example, would be very foolish to sell bonds or preferred stock at the outset to raise the necessary funds. So long as the company's earnings are satisfactory and its credit good, it is much cheaper to borrow at the banks as the work progresses and fund the entire indebtedness when it is completed. The current-ratio or working-capital position is of no great consequence in analyzing a prosperous railroad or utility; it becomes of great importance when earning power falls and the possibility of raising permanent capital disappears.

INTERNAL COMPOSITION

Clearly the internal composition of the current-assets item is vitally important. To take an extreme case, suppose a company with $1,000,000 cash, $300,000 accounts receivable and $200,000 inventory to cover $1,000,000 current debts. Clearly this 1½ to 1 ratio is better than the position of a company with $200,000 cash, $500,000 accounts receivable, $1,300,000 inventory and the same indebtedness, even though the latter is a conventional two-to-one statement.

Allusion has been made to the factor of profits in converting merchandise into receivables. If $1,500,000 inventory is sold at a 33⅓% profit and there is no other change in the balance sheet, clearly the current ratio has improved by the addition of $500,000 to the current assets with no diminution of the current liabilities. On the other hand, merchandise may have increased and accounts receivable diminished between two successive balance sheets, resulting in an impairment of the current ratio. At certain stages of the business cycle such a change would by no means indicate an unhealthy development in the business. The ratio between receivables and inventory should be watched in the light of these facts.

Owner and Creditor

Another ratio which is of great importance to the speculator or investor is the ratio between owned and borrowed capital. If current liabilities plus funded debt equal net worth, then creditors have as much at risk in the business as the owners. If the ratio between debts and net worth is two to one, the creditors have much more at stake than the owners. Unless earning power is very stable, such a condition is dangerous to the owners. If debts and net worth are seriously disproportionate, creditors really dominate the business, management does not have a free rein and in a crisis reorganization is the probable outcome. The market value of the net worth rather than its book value is the important figure in this type of analysis. A serious disproportion between debts and owner's capital or between debts plus preferred stock and common stock is a danger signal to the investor-holder of the senior security; under certain circumstances it may spell opportunity to the speculator. If a company in such a condition begins to enjoy improvement in earnings, the effect in relation to market value of the equity is greatly multiplied. A classic example is furnished by American Water Works & Electric Co., whose 100,000 shares at the low point of 1921 were valued at $400,000 in contrast with more than $150,000,000 of senior securities. It did not take any startling increase in earning power to put the stock from four to the equivalent of 380 within four years.

There are many ratios besides those already mentioned which are useful to the balance-sheet analyst. Most of them are related to the income statement and will be considered in the following chapter.

Chapter XI

How to Read an Income Statement

If a balance sheet is the picture of a moment, two balance sheets show the beginning and end of a period. The income statement bridges the gap and informs the analyst what hapened to the business during the period. Even if no income statement is furnished, he can obtain a great deal of information by comparing the two balance sheets. The first statement at hand will serve as an example. It depicts the condition of a shoe-manufacturing concern selling its product in a chain of its own retail stores.

Assets

	1925	1924
Real estate, equipment, etc......	$676,384	$633,594
Good will.............................	2,500,000	2,500,000
Prepaid items	27,613	......
Mortgage note receivable........	138,000	144,500
Accts. and notes receivable	39,721	45,616
Inventories.............................	1,278,633	1,274,882
Cash.......................................	646,470	558,340
Advertising expenses	38,094	70,642
Life insurance policies	83,472	78,317
	$5,428,387	$5,305,891

Liabilities

Common stock	$2,000,000	$2,000,000
Preferred stock	2,029,800	2,029,800
Dividends payable Jan. 2........	35,521	35,521
Accounts payable....................	80,677	63,725
Reserve for federal taxes..........	16,592	96,000
Accrued items	145,631	129,465
Surplus...................................	1,120,166	951,380
	$5,428,387	$5,305,891

Perhaps the first thing the analyst would look for in these statements would be the change in the net-worth accounts. Common and preferred stock outstanding did not change during the year, but surplus increased $168,786. This increase in surplus could have occurred in only one or two ways, by retention of profits earned during the period in the business or by revaluing assets or releasing a portion of accumulated reserves. The only increases in assets are moderate in amount and such as would be expected in a healthily growing business. The only reserve item is reserve for federal taxes, which shows a substantial decline, suggesting the possibility that a portion of an unnecessarily large reserve may have been transferred to surplus. The chances are, however, that the bulk of the $168,786 increase in surplus came from profits.

It will be noted that we have no way of knowing what the total profits of the business were and can merely estimate that portion not paid to the stockholders in dividends. It is possible to deduce the fact that preferred dividends were regularly paid at the rate of 7%. The item of "dividends payable January 2" is equal to exactly 1¾% of the amount of preferred stock outstanding.

Valuing Good-Will

There are one or two items on the balance sheets reproduced above which were not explained in the previous article and a few words regarding them are accordingly in order. Good-will is a purely intangible asset with an artificial valuation. It is conservative practice to value good-will, trade-marks, patent rights and similar intangibles at a nominal figure, frequently $1, but if the stockholders of a company are happier in seeing a generous figure for such an item, it is after all their affair. The analyst either disregards intangibles or considers a generous estimate of their value by the company as an unfavorable indication. "Mortgage note receivable" presumably represents a mortgage taken by the company on sale of some of its fixed property. "Advertising expenses" is merely a prepaid item. "Life insurance policies" represents the cash surrender value of life insurance policies covering executives of the company and payable to it as beneficiary.

An Impression of Strength

Despite the good-will item this particular pair of statements gives an impression of strength and prosperity. Ratio of current assets to current liabilities improved from 5.77 to 1 to 7.07 to 1. Moreover, composition of current assets improved. A trifling increase in inventories and a drop in accounts and notes receivable were more than offset by a substantial increase in cash. Ratio of cash alone to all debts increased from 1.72 to 1 to 2.32 to 1. Slight reduction in the mortgage notes receivable item suggests that the mortgagor is making installment payments on his note and that it is thus probably a good, though not a current, asset.

Real Income Statement Valuable

If this comparison of balance sheets has told us a good deal about the business of the shoe company in question during 1925, it is still true that there are many things which could be learned only from a real income statement. The sales of the company, operating expenses, non-operating or other income, taxes, amount appropriated for depreciation, interest on loans, net income and its disposition are all matters of interest to the speculator or investor. Many companies which publish annual statements confine themselves to balance sheets and many even of those publishing income statements omit many details. It is nevertheless essential that the student of values be familiar with income statements. The following detailed statement is taken from the listing statement published in connection with the listing of the Belding Hemingway Co. convertible 6s, 1936. It covers the operations of the company for the calendar year 1923:

Gross sales		$5,864,177
Discounts and allowances		93,838
Net sales		$5,770,339
Cost of sales		4,431,118
Gross profit		$1,339,221
Selling expenses	$526,842	
General and administrative expenses	418,617	945,459
Net operating income		$393,762
Other income:		
Interest	$16,772	
Purchase discount	91,569	
Profit on sale capital assets..	1,446	109,787
Balance		$503,549
Deductions:		
Depreciation	$66,977	
Federal taxes	64,557	131,534
Net profit		$372,015
Dividends paid		258,252
Balance to surplus		$113,763

The first figure in an income statement is that of gross sales, gross receipts, gross revenues, as the case may be. This is the total sum of cash receipts or charges to customers on the company's books for goods sold or service rendered. It may be itemized in certain cases. If a company manufactured rubber footwear, tires and mechanical rubber goods, for example, it would be of interest to know what proportions of its total output these items constituted. Railroads always divide their revenues into freight, passenger and other. Sometimes the "other" is divided into mail, express, and so on.

Trade Discounts

In the typical case chosen the second item is "discounts and allowances." This covers the discounts given customers for prompt payment and the allowances for goods returned. It will be noted that under the heading "other income" is an item covering discount on goods purchased which substantially offsets the discounts and allowances given customers. Well-managed concerns always take their trade discounts, which constitute a substantial addition to profits in most lines of business. After deducting discounts and allowances given from gross sales there is left the item of net sales, the net proceeds of goods sold to customers during the year.

Costs of sales is the total of raw materials, labor, power and other items used in manufacturing the goods sold to customers. After the goods have been made they must be sold, the general supervision of the business requires an expensive organization. These two necessities are covered by the items "selling expenses" and "general and administrative expense." Deducting total operating expenses from net sales there is a residue of "net operating income."

The next group of items on the income statement is headed "other income." This includes all items of income not directly attributable to the regular operations of the business. Interest and dividends on securities held for investment, rent for portions of property leased to outside concerns, incidental profits of various sorts comprise the other income group of items.

Charges Against Income

Final group of deductions from income consists of interest on bonds and on short-term borrowings, depreciation charges and federal taxes. Since local taxes are assessed on property values regardless of the result of operating the property, they are an operating charge like labor costs and the cost of raw material. Federal taxes are levied on net income, however, and thus constitute a charge ranking after direct operating expenses. Depreciation is a bookkeeping item, though a very important one. If a company has made more than sufficient depreciation charges against its property in the past, it can, perhaps, afford to skimp a little in a poor year in order to make a better final showing. Interest on temporary or funded borrowings is another charge not directly related to operations. The adequacy of the capital supplied by the owners will determine the size of this charge. After all charges have been met which either must be paid to meet the company's obligations or to maintain its reserves in accordance with sound managerial policy, the remaining balance is surplus income for the period. It may either be retained by the company as surplus or distributed to the shareholders. Conservatively managed companies usually retain at least a substantial portion of it for reinvestment in the business.

The Trend of Sales

There are many points at which an income statement may be analyzed. Starting at the beginning the item of sales first engages attention. Taken by itself this is an interesting figure. A well-managed company should do a larger volume of business year after year. There are few lines of business in which it is reasonable to expect that each year shall show a gain over the preceding one, but the trend should be consistently upward. If the figures are somewhat erratic in their fluctuations, there is a simple method of determining the trend by comparing the weighted average with the arithmetic average. Suppose that over a five-year period a given company has reported sales as follows: first year, $38,350,000; second year, $29,700,000; third year, $48,200,000; fourth year, $56,150,000; fifth year, $36,800,000. At a glance it is a little difficult to tell whether the trend of sales is upward or not. A weighted average of sales will tell the story. It is obtained by multiplying the sales of the fifth year by 5, fourth year by 4, third year by 3, and so on. Now divide the total of these weighted sales by the sum of 5, 4, 3, 2, 1 or 15. The result is a weighted average of $43,396,667. It compares with an actual average of $41,840,000, showing an upward trend.

Allowing for Elastic Dollars

In estimating the trend of sales it is important to take account of price fluctuations. If the sales of a department store in 1920 were $20,000,000, against $10,000,000 in 1913, there was no real gain in volume of business. The general increase in prices during the war accounted for the gain. Wherever possible it is important to get the figures of sales in physical units as well as in dollars. If this is not possible, an estimate may sometimes be made based on known price fluctuations in the goods in which a given company deals. Unofficial statements as to physical volume are frequently made in such reliable financial publications as *The Wall Street Journal, Boston News Bureau* and *Barron's,* and these are also a dependable source of information.

Turnover

The sales figure in an income statement has many other uses. Foremost among them in analyzing many types of corporations is the determination of the merchandise turnover. The more rapidly a corporation can turn its inventory into cash and accounts receivable and replace it with a fresh stock, the greater its percentage of profit, the less the risk of loss through market fluctuations and other causes. The corner grocer with a $5,000 stock of goods and a 5% margin of profit will make $3,000 a year if he turns his stock monthly, and only $1,500 if he is able to turn it but six times a year. In the latter case his losses from spoilage will be greater, he is more likely to lose customers by selling them stale goods. The margin of profit will in all probability not be the same at the two turnover rates. It will be greater for the merchant with the faster turnover. This same principle applies to every business, great or small, which is concerned in the distribution of goods.

Notions and Heavy Machinery

The ratio sales/merchandise varies widely between different types of business. A chain of ten-cent stores can turn its inventory much oftener than a manufacturer of heavy machinery. The fact that F. W. Woolworth reported sales of $239,000,000 in 1925 with an inventory of $26,295,000 at the end of the period while General Electric with sales of $290,000,000 had $87,324,000 inventory is no reflection on the management of the latter concern. In seeking to determine the character of the management in a given case, the sales/merchandise ratio must be compared with the similar ratio for other leading concerns doing approximately the same type of business. The fluctuations in the ratio from year to year may also be useful indications of the trend of managerial efficiency. In this connection it is important to note that there are normal seasonal variations in the ratio. If the sales/merchandise ratio as of December 31 compares unfavorably with that as of June 30, the fact may be of no consequence. Ratios should be compared as of the same date in consecutive years. A declining ratio may be justified in a period of rising prices, when goods increase in value on their owners' shelves; on a falling market the salvation of the merchant or manufacturer is to speed up his turnover.

The Credit Policy

Sales/receivables is another interesting ratio. Its fluctuations throw some light on the credit policy of a corporation. If a company shows a constantly larger proportion of receivables to sales, the suspicion is inevitable that the company is relaxing its credit standards, that possibly a growing amount of bad accounts are being treated as current on its statements. In a period of business depression and falling prices some relaxation of credit terms may be desirable, accounts receivable being a better asset than inventories in such a period. With improvement in general business the credit department should hold a tighter rein.

SOME LIGHT ON DEPRECIATION

A story of efficiency or conservatism may be read from a progressive increase in the ratio sales/fixed assets. The following table gives the sales billed by General Electric Co. for the seven-year period 1919-25, inclusive, book value of plants at the end of those years and ratio of the two figures:

Year		Sales	Fixed Assets	Ratio
1925	....	$290,300,000	$57,500,000	5.05
1924	....	299,200,000	57,700,000	5.17
1923	....	271,300,000	59,600,000	4.55
1922	....	200,200,000	65,000,000	3.08
1921	....	221,000,000	68,700,000	2.84
1920	....	275,800,000	67,900,000	4.05
1919	....	230,000,000	51,500,000	4.47

The average ratio for the period was 4.17. The weighted average, giving the greatest weight to the most recent figure, was 4.38. The trend of the ratio was therefore distinctly upward. This indicates either that the company was getting greater efficiency in the use of its plants at the close of the period under analysis or that plants were being written down well under their real value by an ultra-conservative depreciation policy. The impression of efficiency and conservatism is strengthened when it is remembered that the general trend of commodity prices was downward during the seven-year period so that sales in tons probably increased much more than sales in dollars.

The Profit Margin

Besides the various ratios between sales and balance-sheet items, there is one ratio involving sales and another income statement item which is significant. This is the ratio net operating income/ sales or the margin of profit. A declining trend in the margin of profit may indicate declining efficiency of management, increasing competition in the industry or increasing difficulties arising out of conditions over which the management has no control. It is possible for a whole industry to be so beset by troubles that profit margins for most companies may be wiped out for years at a time. On the other hand, an increasing trend to the profit margin cannot be maintained for very long without attracting competition which will restore the normal balance. From the speculator's standpoint, the ideal condition is one of stability. Due allowance should be made, of course, for the progress of the business cycle. A decline in the profit margin in 1921 was not an alarming symptom; a concern had to be either very lucky or very well managed to show any profit at all in that year.

Other income is an important item with many corporations. The size of this item may throw some light on the value of an item of "investments" on a balance sheet. It is not often that it is given in such great detail as on the Belding-Hemingway statement and in many cases it is lumped with gross revenues from normal operations.

Depreciation Is Vital

Depreciation is perhaps the most important item on an income statement in many respects. All other items are to a greater or less extent beyond the control of management, but depreciation is an

159

accounting item determined to the last dollar by the management. If earnings are poor, the appropriation to depreciation reserves can be cut in order to make a better final showing. If earnings are exceptionally large and the management wishes to accumulate some "fat" with a minimum of disturbance resulting from a clamor for larger dividends, the depreciation reserve can be swelled in generous fashion. The speculator will, therefore, examine the depreciation figure closely to see whether it appears inadequate, reasonable or excessive. No hard-and-fast rule can be laid down for the determination of this point. The Treasury Department under normal conditions allows taxpayers to charge 4% per annum as the rate of depreciation on frame-wooden buildings, 2% on concrete and steel buildings, 10% on machinery, 20% on automobiles. The fixed assets of a manufacturing company will probably include all these kinds of property as well as the land on which its plants stand. The land, of course, is not subject to depreciation. If the analyst cannot determine more than roughly what would be the proper charge in a given case, he can at least note whether the ratio of depreciation charged to fixed assets varies much from year to year and what is the trend.

Uniform Railroad Accounting

So far discussion has been confined to industrial statements. Income statements of railroad and public utility companies superficially appear somewhat different, are analyzed somewhat differently. They are of even more importance to the speculator because they are more readily available. All the railroads of the country are under the jurisdiction of the Interstate Commerce Commission, which requires them to keep their accounts in a uniform manner and to report their income regularly. Monthly income statements of leading railroads are easily to be had. Similarly most public utility companies report their income at regular intervals to the various state regulatory bodies, though there is not the same country-wide uniformity of accounting methods as in the case of the railroads. The following somewhat condensed income statement of the Colorado & Southern Railway for 1925 will serve as a sample:

Freight revenues	19,598,517
Passenger revenues	4,140,562
Other revenues	1,915,076
Total operating revenues	$25,654,155
Maintenance of way and structures	$2,888,666
Maintenance of equipment	4,934,683
Traffic	348,603
Transportation	8,461,550
Miscellaneous operation	203,689
General	958,266
Transportation for investment-Credit	44,830
Total operating expenses	17,750,628
Net operating revenue	$7,903,527
Railway tax accruals	$1,637,703
Uncollectible railway rev.	6,992
Deductions from net operating revenue	1,644,695
Railway operating income	$6,258,832
Hire of equipment	$378,164
Joint facility rent income	98,193
Miscellaneous rent income	95,261
Dividends and misc. int	596,012
Miscellaneous income	2,945
Total non-operating income	1,170,575
Gross income	$7,429,407

		COLORADO AND SOUTHERN LINES		
		COMPARATIVE STATEMENT OF INCOME, YEARS ENDED DECEMBER 31		
Percent of Ry. Oper. Rev.	1925	RAILWAY OPERATING REVENUES	1924	Percent of Ry. Oper. Rev.
76.40	$ 19,598.517.62	Freight	$ 19,694,843.42	75.90
16.14	4,140,562.10	Passenger	4,415,840.05	17.02
1.59	408,040.43	Mail	404,527.87	1.56
1.99	510,614.49	Express	474,000.55	1.83
2.26	579,358.62	All other transportatio	625,781.98	2.41
1.35	347,178.90	Incidental	297,183.38	1.14
.27	69,882.59	Joint facility	34,553.54	.14
100.00	$ 25.654,154.75	Total railway operating revenues	$ 25,946,730.79	100.00
		RAILWAY OPERATING EXPENSES		
11.26	$ 2,888,666.33	Maintenance of way and stuctures	$ 2,844,059.39	10.96
19.23	4,934,682.89	Maintenance of equipments	5.015,677.61	19.33
1.36	348,603.41	Traffic	337,844.24	1.30
32.98	8,461,550.13	Transportation	8,478,912.80	32.69
.79	203,688.94	Miscellaneous operations	166.692.02	.64
3.74	958,266.44	general	955,001.39	3.68
.17 Cr.	44,829.91	Transportation for investments - Cr.	28,018.36	Cr..ll
69.19	$ 17,750,628.23	Total railway operating expenses	$ 17,770,169.09	68.49
30.81	$ 7,903.526.52	Net revenue from railway operations	$ 8,176,561.70	31.51
	$ 1,637,702.52	Railway tax accruals	$ 1,512,347.14	
	6,992.52	Uncollectible railway revenue	9,828.48	
	$ 6,258.831.48	Railway operating income	$ 6,654,386.08	
		NON-OPERATING" INCOME		
	$ 378,163.82	Hire of equipments	$ 281,456.02	
	98,192.69	Joint facility rent income	61,014.39	
	95,260.94	Miscellaneous rent income	89,091.25	
	596,011.96	Dividends and miscellaneous interest	617,954.26	
	2.945.87	Miscellaneous income	1,708.92	
	$ 1.170,575.28	Total non-operating income	$ 1,051,224.84	
	$ 7,429,406.76	Gross income	$ 7,705,610.92	
		DEDUCTIONS FROM CROSS INCOME		
	$ 909,588.67	Hire of equipements	$ 668,198.77	
	164,116.24	Joint facility rents	107,894.26	
	7,121.02	Miscellaneous rents	21,072.44	
	2,551,365.45	Interest on funded debt	2,698,054.61	
	7,859.66	Interest on unfunded debt	9,365.19	
	32,157.44	Amortization of discount on funded debt	32,926.00	
	91,259.22	Miscellaneous income charges	112.128.61	
	$ 3,763,467.70	Total deductions from gross income	$ 3,649,639.88	
	$ 5.661.483.08	Net railway operating income	$ 6,220,763.46	
	$ 3,665,939.06	Net income	$ 4,055,971.04	
		DISPOSITION OF NET INCOME		
	$ 680.311.04	Dividends	$ 680.311.04	
	$ 680,311.04	Total appropreastion of income	$ 680.311.04	
	$ 2,985,628.02	Income balance	$ 3.375.660.00	

Hire of equipment............................	$909,589
Joint facility rents............................	164,116
Interest on funded debt	2,551,365
Other deductions	138,398
Total deductions from gross income	3,763,468
Net income	$3,665,939

The analysis of a railroad report will be discussed at greater length in another chapter, but the high spots may properly be pointed out here. The ratio of operating expenses to operating revenues is known as the operating ratio. Before the war it was somewhere in the neighborhood of 70% on a normally prosperous road. An upward trend of the operating ratio over a period of years is obviously a serious threat to earning power. The ratio of maintenance to operating revenues often provides a clue to the condition of the property. It is normally somewhere between 30% and 35%. If it appears abnormally high, the suspicion arises that the management is concealing earnings by making improvements to the property and charging them to maintenance. If it appears low, the analyst is led to fear that the management is letting the property deteriorate in order to maintain dividends or interest payments. This uneasiness would be increased, if apparent skimping on maintenance were followed by an increase in the proportionate cost of hauling freight and passengers, *i. e.,* the ratio of transportation expense to operating revenues. On the other hand, abnormally high maintenance charges should be followed, if the condition of the property has really improved, by a declining transportation ratio.

RAILROAD PROPERTY DEPRECIATES SLOWLY

Depreciation does not have the prominent role in a railroad income statement that it plays in an industrial statement. To an extraordinary degree railroads are permanent properties. The right of way is not subject to depreciation, renewals of rails, ties, switches, signals are charged to operating expenses as maintenance. The same is true of most items of railway property except the locomotives and cars. Depreciation reserves are set up for their replacement, appropriations being charged to maintenance of equipment. In the Colorado & Southern statement used as a sample $439,711 was so charged.

Income statements of a public utility company also differ greatly from those of an industrial concern. The following statement of the Detroit Edison Co. for 1922 is typical:

Gross revenues	$26,408,159
Operating expense, maintenance, taxes	16,823,614
Net operating revenue	$9,584,545
Renewal, replacement and contingent reserve	2,415,000
Net income	$7,169,545
Interest on funded and unfunded debt	3,556,381
Balance for dividends and surplus	$3,613,164

Perhaps the most interesting figure in this very brief statement is the appropriation to "renewal, replacement and contingent reserve." This is another name for depreciation. Public utility companies usually charge from 6% to 10% of their gross revenues to such reserves. Since a public utility company ordinarily has $5 in fixed assets for every dollar of gross revenues such a charge is equivalent to 1.2% to 2% of property value. A good many companies still do not report their depreciation separately, but leave it as a deduction from surplus after dividends. In this case the balance after payment of interest charges would be labeled "balance for dividends, depreciation and surplus." Since it is considered by most authorities to be just as necessary to accumulate reserves to take care of major property replacements as to meet interest charges it is obvious that in such cases the analyst is justified in making his own allowance in calculating balance available for the stock.

The Auditor's Certificate

A portion of the conventional annual corporation report which is seldom read by stockholders is the auditor's statement. The following certification by a leading firm of accountants of the Westinghouse Electric report for 1915 is a sample of an unusually detailed certificate:

"We have made an audit, for the year ended March 31, 1915, of the books and accounts of the Westinghouse Electric & Manufacturing Company, and the following subsidiary companies, viz.: . . .

"We have verified the Stocks and Bonds owned, the Cash and the Notes Receivable, by count or by proper certificate from the depositaries. The Stocks and Bonds owned are stated at the book value, which is considerably less than the aggregate cost.

"We have examined the Accounts Receivable and in our opinion the reserves created therefor are sufficient to cover probable losses. "The inventories of Raw Materials and Supplies, Finished Parts and Completed Apparatus, and Work in Progress were taken under our general supervision and valued at cost or less, and

"WE HEREBY CERTIFY that, in our opinion, the accompanying Consolidated General Balance Sheet, March 31, 1915, of the Westinghouse Electric & Manufacturing

Company and subsidiary companies named above, properly presents the financial condition on that date; that the accompanying Consolidated Statement of Income and Profit and Loss for the year ended March 31, 1915, correctly states the result of operations for that period, and that the books of the companies are in agreement with these statements."

A Naive Official

There is no "hedge clause" in this certificate and the auditors obviously went much deeper into the affairs of the company than a mere taking of a trial balance. Many companies still do not include an auditor's certificate in their annual reports. It is apparent that there should be some independent check at regular intervals of the books of any corporation and that holders of its securities are entitled to know that a responsible firm of accountants vouches for the accuracy of statements submitted. It is not very often that serious defalcations occur in large corporations, but this is one of the minor risks of speculation. The discovery some time ago that the treasurer of an important cotton mill had padded the inventory account to make a better showing led the president to make the naive comment that "the stockholders had not lost anything, they merely did not own as much property as they thought they had." This was cold comfort for investors whose stock shrank in value from around $40 a share to about $1 a share as the result of the disclosures.

CHAPTER XII

Rails and Utilities—Victims or Beneficiaries of Regulation?

A certain well known brand of canned and pickled foods is celebrated for the fact that it is available in 57 varieties. This number looks small beside the 167 or so varieties of regular reports which the railroads of the country must make weekly or monthly or quarterly to the Interstate Commerce Commission. The kind of safety appliances they may use, the rates they may charge their customers, the terms on which they may issue new securities, whether or not they may build proposed extensions to their lines, are subject to the regulation of the Interstate Commerce Commission. The relations of the railroads and their employees are subject to regulation by still another governmental agency. Besides this, the railroads are in most states subject to local regulation by state public utility or railroad commissions.

STATE REGULATION OF UTILITIES

Public utility companies—gas, electric light and power, traction and water companies—are not as yet subject to regulation by any federal agency. Practically every state in the union, however, has a public utility commission or some similar body which supervises the operations of the utility companies within its jurisdiction. If a peppery citizen thinks his gas bill is too large, he airs his grievance before the commission. If an increase in rates is necessary to give an adequate return on property investment, a whole community may be agitated by the suggestion.

What chance is there for initiative in such a field? How can business be successfully transacted in a field so encumbered with red tape and regulation? Granted that the energetic and intelligent manager of an industrial enterprise can increase its value many fold, what hope is there that the value of a public service enterprise can be similarly increased in the face of the restrictions that surround it?

PUBLIC UTILITY STOCKS DO FLUCTUATE WIDELY

The answer is, of course, found in the facts. Stocks of public service corporations have shown market fluctuations quite comparable in breadth to those experienced by industrial issues. Seaboard Air Line Railway common advanced from 6¼ in 1924 to a high of 54¼ in the following year. American Water Works & Electric common rose from a low of four in 1921 to the equivalent of 381¼ in1925. Such spectacular movements can hardly be matched in the industrial field.

Restrictive regulation it appears, is just that. A government agency may say "Thou shalt not" do thus and so. It never takes the place of management. Commissioners and inspectors on the civil-service payroll may audit and examine, check and inspect, forbid and criticize. They never take the initiative. When they have finished with their negatives there is still a broad field left in which the management elected by the stockholders may seek to get additional business and to cut costs of handling the business already obtained, just as the industrial manager must succeed in solving the problem of getting business and transacting it at minimum cost. In a public service corporation bad management may curtail profits or produce losses, good management may turn a weak corporation into a strong one. The speculator need not avoid the rails and utilities merely because such companies are subject to a larger degree of regulation of their affairs by public authorities than industrials.

ADVANTAGES OF PUBLIC REGULATION

Public regulation, on the other hand, has distinct advantages to the speculator. It assures to him a vast amount of detailed information about the companies in which he is interested that might not otherwise be available. In the case of the railroads, detailed figures of earnings are available monthly and a large amount of other information at frequent intervals. Moreover, this information is standardized in form. The analyst does not have to stop and wonder what a given account really is. He knows that it is exactly the same thing as the account of the same name in the statements of fifty other roads. There is not the same wealth of information or uniformity of accounts in the case of public utilities, which are subject in varying degrees to the regulation of forty-nine different jurisdictions rather than to one central body, but on the whole more adequate information is obtainable regarding utilities than is the case with industrial companies.

ETHICS OF BIG BUSINESS

Radical critics of the social order frequently consider that great fortunes can be made only dishonestly, that crookedness and big business are inseparable companions. This is of course a very ignorant and prejudiced view of the business world, yet it is undeniably true that on rare occasions transactions take place which cannot be defended by the believer in strict ethical standards. By such departures from a stern moral code, small stockholders, investors or speculators are sometimes the losers. Obviously crooked transactions can occur only under shelter of darkness. Full and constant publicity regarding its affairs makes it impossible that any dishonest deal could be engineered in connection with a large corporation. Such full and constant publicity is assured in greater degree in the case of public service corporations than in the case of industrials. Moreover, a certain type of politician is constantly seeking weak spots in the armor of the public service corporation and would seize upon any such occurrence with unholy glee. Big business is undoubtedly 99% honestly conducted. In the field of the public service corporation the pressure to keep on the straight and narrow path is even greater than it is in the case of an industrial corporation.

TRADING ON THE EQUITY

One factor largely responsible for the possibility of wide price swings in public service corporation stocks is the policy of "trading on the equity" in setting up the capital structure of such companies. The ideal capital structure for an industrial company comprises no bonds, no preferred stock, one class of capital stock. In the public utility or railroad field such a capital structure is almost unknown. Thanks to the permanent character of their fixed assets, the relative stability of their earning power, railroads and utilities can and customarily do obtain a large part of their permanent capital by selling bonds or senior issues of stock. More than half the capitalization of the American railroads consists of bonds and of the balance a substantial portion consists of preferred stock entitled to a limited rate of dividend. In the case of public utilities the common stock in many instances represents an even smaller proportion of the total capitalization than is normally the case with the railroads. This is particularly true of the holding companies which control scattered properties through ownership of all or a majority of their common stocks. It is not at all unusual for $10,000,000 of common stock in such cases to control $100,000,000 of property.

A CONCRETE CASE

The principle of trading on the equity may easily be explained by taking such a case as an example. Suppose that a public utility holding company system has $60,000,000 of 5% bonds, $30,000,000 of 7% preferred and $10,000,000 of common stock outstanding. If the public service commission of the jurisdiction in which the company operates fixes rates at such a level that under competent management the company can earn 8% on its investment, income of $8,000,000 will be possible. The bondholders will get $3,000,000, preferred stockholders $2,100,000 and there will be $2,900,000 left for the common stock, or $29 a share. Now if the rates are inadequate, the management less than competent or for some other reason earnings amount to only 6% on property value, the balance for the common will be only $9 a share. In other words, a 25% decrease in earnings per dollar of property will produce a 69% decrease in earnings per share. Under the conditions assumed a 36% cut in earnings per dollar will wipe out the balance for the common. If the effects of comparatively small fluctuations in the rate of earnings per dollar of investment are so striking, the results in the stock market are likely to be even more remarkable. If a group of public utility properties are earning so small a return on their property value as to leave little or no balance for the common stock, the market value of that stock may be anywhere from $5 to $20 a share. A slight decrease in operating expenses, an increase in gross or an improvement in the rate structure may yield a slightly larger return on the investment and a balance of $10 a share or more for the common. In a bull market in stocks such earning power would make the common worth from $100 to $150 a share.

Sensational Stock Market Movements

The two examples cited of sensational movements in the stocks of public service corporations bear out the theory that such movements are primarily to be expected in stocks of companies with topheavy capital structures. On December 31, 1924, Seaboard Air Line had $151,700,000 funded debt and $23,900,000 preferred stock ahead of only 370,191 shares of common stock. In 1923 the road had earned 17 cents a share on the common following a long series of deficits. It is not surprising that the stock sold under $10 a share. A substantial increase in gross earnings resulting from the development of Florida rapidly increased net earnings and it is quite as natural that an equity in a $200,000,000 property valued by the market at only about $2,000,000 should have rapidly increased in value nearly ten-fold. In 1922 American Water Works was another $200,000,000 company. Its capital structure was even more top-heavy, $170,000,000 of bonds and preferred stock being senior to 100,000 shares of common stock valued at the 1921 low at only $400,000. Incredible as it may seem the company earned almost as much in 1921 on the common stock as the lowest price at which it sold. At that time utility stocks were distinctly out of favor with the investment and speculative public. It took only a slight change in sentiment and a small improvement in earnings to start American Water Works on its spectacular upward march.

WHERE INVESTOR AND SPECULATOR PART COMPANY

Broad price fluctuations are much less likely to occur in the stocks of soundly capitalized public service corporations. The Pennsylvania Railroad is an example. At the end of 1925 capital stock outstanding of $499,000,000, compared with $598,000,000 funded debt. It requires a relatively large change in earnings per dollar invested to produce much change in earnings per share where the equity is so broad. Stability of earnings is the natural accompaniment of such a capital structure. The Pennsylvania has paid dividends every year since 1856. Its stock is an investment issue which fluctuates within narrow limits. The disastrous effect of the war and federal control on all the railroads caused a cut in the Pennsylvania's dividend rate in 1921 and the stock sold down to 32¼. From this level it recovered to 55⅜ in

1925, a sizeable advance in itself, but small in comparison with that of the Seaboard, for example.

A Soundly Financed Utility

In the utility field, Brooklyn Edison is an example of a soundly capitalized company, $74,000,000 stock being junior to only $45,000,000 bonds at the end of 1925. The company had remarkable growth in the period 1919-25, gross revenues very nearly trebling in this period. If the company had been financed principally by bonds and preferred stock, the value of a small equity would have shown astounding increase under such circumstances. As it happens, the company was conservatively financed by the sale of additional stock and from its low in this period to its high, the stock did not double. Such advance as it did enjoy was the result of the general decline in yields on investment securities rather than any increase in earnings per share. It is obvious that a public service corporation, which must ordinarily increase its capital investment heavily in order to obtain an increase in gross revenues, can maintain a conservative financial structure only at the expense of any possibility of a sensational advance for its stock. Moreover, it appears that in this field the investor and the speculator very definitely part company. The capital structure which is ideal from the investor's standpoint greatly diminishes the likelihood of those wide price swings which spell opportunity to the speculator.

Of course large market movements are not impossible in the case of the stock of a company whose capital structure approximates the ideal. The New Haven structure of 1913 consisted of $180,000,000 of stock and $200,000,000 of bonds, but that fact alone did not prevent the stock from dropping from its 1913 high of 129⅞ to a 1923 low of 9⅝. The Pere Marquette in 1922 had an ideal capital structure with $42,000,000 funded debt,

$23,000,000 preferred and $45,000,000 common stock, but the latter issue nevertheless rose from 19 in that year to a high of 122 in 1926. A sound enterprise whose stock is an investment may fall upon evil days, one which is a mediocre success may become really prosperous as the result of hard work on the part of the management. Market movements resulting from such changes are nevertheless likely to be less rapid than those which occur when changes in fortune affect a thin equity.

Allowing for Seasonal Variation

To the extent that the movements of railroad shares depend on individual factors rather than on the trend of the general market, it is important to the speculator to know how to analyze railroad accounts. In the case of all railroads of any size, he will find monthly reports of earnings in the financial press as soon as the figures are received by the Interstate Commerce Commission. A month is a short period and the earnings of a single month may be very much less or very much more than one-twelfth of the earnings for the full year. Roads with heavy grain traffic may not earn their fixed charges in the spring months, yet show a handsome surplus for the full year. The Florida roads, on the other hand, enjoy their heaviest traffic in the winter and early spring. By taking the average of a number of years, it is possible to calculate the percentage of a year's gross revenues and net operating revenue ordinarily earned in a given month on a particular road. With these figures, which are readily available in a number of statistical compilations, it is a simple matter to calculate the year's earnings of a railroad with a considerable degree of accuracy when the results of the first four or five months are in. The detailed monthly figures also show whether there is any tendency to curtail maintenance expenditures, whether the proportionate cost of conducting transportation is being reduced or is rising.

THE RAILROAD YARDSTICK

Besides the dollars and cents figures of the income account, there are important details of the operating statement ordinarily available annually and expressed in terms of tons and miles. From year to year the volume of traffic is best shown by the figures of ton-miles—number of tons of freight moved one mile. This figure should show a distinct upward trend over a period of years. The average haul in miles is another important figure. Since terminal costs are a major part of the cost of moving freight, long-haul traffic is the most profitable to a railroad. The roads which carry a large volume of perishable fruit and vegetables at high rates from California to the Mississippi river crossings or Florida to the north are fortunately situated. If the average haul of a railroad tends to increase over a period of years, its business is probably becoming more profitable. Classification of freight is another important detail of a railroad report. A tendency toward a larger proportion of manufactures and miscellaneous freight and products of agriculture and a smaller proportion of products of mines and products of forests, less valuable and carrying lower rates, indicates increasingly profitable traffic. On most roads passenger traffic is much less important than freight, but there is money in long hauls.

TRAIN-LOADING FIGURES

Efficiency of operation of a railroad is most frequently measured by the weight of an average train-load. The greater the number of tons that can be handled with a single train-crew, the more fully freight cars can be loaded, the smaller the direct operating cost. The aim of every operating railroad man is to get better car-loading and train-loading. One way to do this is to reduce the movement of empties. This is a serious problem with many roads whose heavy traffic moves principally in one direction, as from mines to tidewater in the case of the soft-coal roads. The heavy movement of empty cars in the reverse direction naturally cuts sharply into the average train-loading figure. Success in stimulating a movement of traffic to counterbalance the ore-dominant movement will accordingly be reflected in the train-load figure. A well managed road's average train-load will thus tend to increase over a period of years. It is not possible satisfactorily to compare the train-load of one road with that of another. A railroad handling principally coal may succeed in getting an average train-load of 800 or 900 tons. Another road with lighter traffic may handle only 300 or 400 tons in the average train. The train-load figure is nevertheless an important one for the railroad analyst.

ATCHISON EFFICIENCY

Apply these tests to one of the country's strongest railroads, the Atchison, Topeka & Santa Fe. In 1913 the company hauled 25,062,000 tons of freight; in 1925, 42,782,000 tons. The increase in ton-miles was slightly greater, from 7,802,000,000 to 13,862,000,000. A simple process of arithmetic will indicate that the average haul thus increased slightly, from 311 miles to 324 miles. As a result of the loss of short-haul traffic to private automobiles and buses, the number of passengers carried decreased more than 50%, but average haul increased from 90 miles to 209 miles.

On most roads the war resulted in a great increase in the operating ratio. Compared with 1913 the majority of roads spend a greater proportion of their gross revenues for maintenance and transportation. Atchison's 1925 showing is remarkable in the close approximation of these ratios to the 1913 levels. Maintenance took 32% of gross in 1913, only 34.3% in 1925. Transportation expense consumed 30% of gross in 1913, only 30.8% in 1925. The impression of efficiency thus given is borne out by figures of train-loading. The average train-load was 425 tons in 1913, it increased to 670 tons in 1925. This was exceptionally good performance for a road which does not handle principally coal. In 1925 over 32% of freight carried consisted of manufactures, merchandise and miscellaneous, against less than 25% for these classifications in 1913.

St. Paul's Troubles

A comparison of the figures for the Chicago, Milwaukee & St. Paul in 1913 and in 1924, the year before the road went into receivership, may also be enlightening. Increase in freight tonnage handled was substantially less than in the case of the Atchison and average haul actually declined. St. Paul's proportionate transportation expense increased and in each year was substantially greater than that of the Atchison. Ratio of maintenance to gross was far lower than Atchison's in 1913 and only slightly higher in 1924, suggesting a doubt as to adequacy of expenditures. The St. Paul made a slightly better gain in train-loading than Atchison during the period. A distinct retrogression was shown, however, by the change in the character of its freight traffic. In 1913 a trifle more than 30% of freight handled consisted of merchandise, manufactures and miscellaneous, in 1924 less than 23%.

Another interesting contrast between the Atchison and the St. Paul is the treatment of depreciation of equipment. Unfortunately St. Paul does not segregate road and equipment in its annual balance sheets. The total, however, on December 31, 1923, was $689,000,000, against $824,000,000 for Atchison on the same date. Of the latter figure $191,000,000 represented equipment. The stronger company carried in its reserves on the same date an item of $76,000,000 accrued depreciation of equipment. The same item on the St. Paul balance sheet of the same date was only $25,000,000. Even allowing for a moderate difference in size of the two systems, it nevertheless appears that there were then grounds for suspecting that St. Paul's expense figures included inadequate provision for maintenance. It should be remembered, of course, that the depreciation figures are a part of maintenance expenditures in a railroad report. In the face of this reasonable suspicion and the showing of 30 cents a share earnings on the preferred in 1923, St. Paul preferred actually sold at 32⅛ in 1924.

Kilowatts and Kilowatt Hours

If the ton and the ton-mile are the typical figures of a railroad operating report, the kilowatt and the kilowatt-hour are the important units in connection with an electric-power and light company. The kilowatt is a unit of power, much more commonly used by engineers than horsepower. One kilowatt is equal to approximately 1-⅓ horsepower. An electric company sells its product by the kilowatt-hour. Sales of the very largest companies passed the billion-kilowatt-hour mark in 1925, New York Edison selling 1,216,000,000 kilowatt-hours, for example, in that year. Of this total the company generated 967,000,000 in its own stations and purchased the balance. The company had generating capacity of 416,000 kilowatts. If every generator had run 24 hours a day throughout the year, the output of electricity would have been 3,640,000,000 kilowatt-hours. To have produced and sold this amount of energy would have been 100% theoretical efficiency. The ratio of actual theoretical maximum output is known as the load factor. Every utility executive is eagerly seeking to get classes of business which will take current at normally slack hours or seasons and thus improve the load factor. In practice it is never possible to get very close to a 100% load factor.

In comparing railroads it is not necessary to make very large allowances for points of unlike-ness between two companies; in the public utility field the disparity is likely to be much greater. One company may generate power at various water-power developments and sell current wholesale to a few large customers, another may have no generating station of its own, but merely buy current wholesale and distribute it to retail consumers in its territory, still another may both generate and distribute electricity. The company which generates current wholly or principally in hydro-electric plants will show a very different sort of income statement from that of a company which generates wholly by steam.

SLOW TURNOVER OF CAPITAL

In general one of the most important things for an analyst to remember regarding public utilities is the fact that they turn their fixed capital very slowly. It usually requires $5 or more of fixed assets to produce $1 of annual gross revenue. The ratio is much higher in the case of a hydroelectric company, which must invest from $100 to $300 per kilowatt in generating stations to say nothing of long transmission lines and a distribution system. At the end of 1925 the Montana Power Co. carried its fixed assets at $95,000,000 or more than eleven times its 1925 gross revenues of $8,438,000. On the other hand, operating expenses of a hydro-electric plant are very small. Cost of a little lubricant and the wages of a handful of men comprise direct operating costs. In 1925 operating expenses of the Washington Water Power Co. consumed only 29% of its gross revenues. The company depending wholly or principally on steam for generation will have a higher operating ratio than a hydro-electric company, but substantially lower capital costs. A rough-and-ready rule of thumb for valuing a company which generates the greater part of its current by steam and distributes it at retail is to consider that it is worth five times a year's gross revenues. If this figure, minus bonds and preferred at par, is much in excess of the market value of the common stock, there is some ground for considering that the stock may be undervalued, and vice versa.

Depreciation allowance of a public utility company should normally amount to 6% to 10% of gross revenues. If the accumulated reserve, however, is equal to 10% or more of property value, a company may reasonably reduce its appropriations to depreciation reserves somewhat. The indentures of public utility bond issues frequently require the issuing company to set aside specified sums for maintenance and depreciation. A common provision binds the company to "pay the trustee annually an amount equal to at least 12½% of the gross operating revenues, less the amount expended during the preceding year on unfunded improvements, betterments, additions, maintenance, repairs, renewals and replacements." Of such an appropriation about half would ordinarily be required for maintenance and the balance would be added to depreciation reserves, an equivalent amount being thereby provided for improvements and additions to the property.

A SUGGESTIVE ANALYSIS

On April 13, 1925, *Barron's* published an article on Latin-American utility companies in which the remarkable depreciation policy of Havana Electric Railway, Light & Power Co. was discussed. It was shown that in 1923 the company had charged 24.9% of its gross revenues to reserves for depreciation and contingencies. If it had charged only a normal 10% to reserve, balance for the common would have been $21.94 a share instead of the $8.57 actually reported. The stock was then selling around 102, actually sold below par within the next few weeks, but crossed 250 within a year. Such opportunities are rare, but they demonstrate that the depreciation figures are worth investigating.

Artificial gas companies are much fewer in number and smaller in importance than electric light and power companies. In many important cities, including New York, Baltimore, Denver, San Francisco, the same company supplies both gas and electricity. For such companies and for holding-company systems whose subsidiaries supply both gas and electricity the same ratios may be used in analysis as for electric companies. There are a few important gas companies, Brooklyn Union, Massachusetts, Laclede of St. Louis, Peoples of Chicago. It is usually considered that gas companies need charge slightly lower rates of depreciation than electric companies.

Troubles of the Tractions

Traction companies are, of course, a specialized sort of railroad and the ratios used in analyzing railroads may readily be adapted to tractions. A distinction should be made between interurban lines, which are particularly vulnerable to the competition of busses and private automobiles, and systems affording mass transportation service to great cities which could not exist without surface, subway and elevated lines. The financial difficulties which began to afflict the tractions during the war, when they found difficulty in overcoming public opposition to a fare level higher than the conventional five cents a ride, and were later intensified by the increasing competition of private automobiles and busses, gradually lost the tractions most of their friends among the investing and speculating public. As this is written, the elimination of weak tractions by receivership and abandonment of mileage is not yet at an end. Companies serving the larger cities of the country are nevertheless showing gains in traffic and in earnings in some instances. Even the situation of the interurban lines is not hopeless. Weak as most of them are they are usually in better condition to finance bus operations than independent operators. Cut-throat competition of bus lines among themselves and with the interurbans will eventually be ended by financial exhaustion of the weaker participants and by legislative and court action to insure safe and adequate public service. When that day comes a real bull market in traction securities is by no means inconceivable.

The stocks of public service corporations—railroads, electric, gas and traction companies—offer the speculator a broad field in which to operate and one possessing many advantages to him. Information about them is more complete and more reliable than that to be obtained in the case of industrial, mining and oil companies, much better and more detailed standards of analysis are available.

CHAPTER XIII

The Analysis of Industrial Stocks

Over the doors of many stores in our great cities are signs in brilliant red, formed of glass tubes containing the rare gas neon, which becomes red when an electric current is passed through it. The sale of neon to the makers of these signs is one of the minor activities of an important industrial corporation whose shares are listed on the New York Stock Exchange. This is but one example of the multitude of activities carried on today which were undreamed of a generation ago. Besides the production of a host of new commodities, the industrial corporations of today manufacture the familiar goods of past generations on a tremendous scale. The factory of a generation ago was a small affair with a few hundred employees at the outside owned by an individual or a limited group. Today manufacturing is on a vastly greater scale and the capital of a given enterprise must be supplied by thousands of individuals instead of a handful.

RISE OF THE TRUSTS

The speculator of the generation between the Civil War and the Spanish War had practically no industrial stocks as vehicles for trading. In the '90s then occurred the creation of "trusts" by merger of competing companies in many lines, steel, sugar, paper, rubber and others. There thus began the introduction of industrial securities to the trading public, a process which has continued to this day. Where once the railroad stocks were the principal media of speculation, they are now far outnumbered by industrial stocks representing the most varied sort of activities. Taking the record of Stock Exchange transactions on a recent day it appears that the first ten companies alphabetically represented the following range of activities: supplying armored-car service to banks, manufacture of farm machinery, mining of lead, extraction of the atmospheric gases, manufacture of tires, manufacture of heavy chemicals and dyestuffs, manufacture of turbines and other heavy machinery, production of fertilizer, engraving of bank notes and production of beet sugar.

WHY STOCKS TENDED TO MOVE TOGETHER

As late as the first few years of the twentieth century the number of industrial stocks available for the speculator's operations was distinctly limited. United States Steel, American Sugar, a few coppers, representatives of some of the other "trusts" were about the only stocks in which there was an active market. The result was that speculative attention was focused on this limited group and there was a strong tendency for stocks to move together. A decided movement in one direction by a single stock attracted much more attention than a similar movement by one of the hundreds of stocks now listed would today. Moreover, the country as a whole was far less diversified industrially than it is now, so that unfavorable conditions affecting a single industry adversely affected other industries sympathetically to a much greater degree. With both the stock market and the industrial fabric of the country now broadly diversified, there is now much wider latitude for individual movements within the general movement of the stock market than there was formerly.

DEPRESSION AND PROSPERITY SIDE BY SIDE

It is now possible for a considerable number of industries to suffer severe depression while the country as a whole is prosperous. During the period 1923-26, for example, the leather manufacturers, makers of book and writing papers, fertilizer manufacturers, packers, producers of most lines of textiles, soft-coal mines suffered depression in varying degrees. Securities of companies in those industries were affected by the condition of their industries as well as by the state of the money market and the course of the stock market in general.

In a previous article attention has been called to the fact that even within the same industry stocks may move in diverse directions or in the same direction at widely varying rates. It thus appears that the speculator must not only determine whether general market conditions favor a purchase or a sale but also whether conditions in a particular industry favor a purchase or a sale of securities of companies in that industry and finally whether the condition of a particular company favors the purchase or sale of its stock. Since industrial stocks afford him the broadest field for his operations the analysis of industrial stocks will consume an important share of his attention.

ANALYZING THE TOBACCOS

Hindsight is easier than foresight. It would be a simple matter at this writing to analyze the position of an industrial stock as it was several years ago and show how the intelligent speculator should have known that it was destined to behave as it did in fact later do. Instead let us see how an analysis actually made in the past turned out. On May 5, 1924, *Barron's* published an exhaustive article discussing the history of the four leading tobacco companies from the dissolution of the American Tobacco Co. in 1911 and their position at the time the article appeared. It will be remembered that the tobacco "trust" was dissolved by order of the Supreme Court in 1911 and succeeded by four principal manufacturers of chewing and smoking tobacco and cigarettes and by a number of less important manufacturers of snuff, licorice and allied products. The four major successor corporations—American Tobacco, Liggett & Myers, P. Lorillard and R. J. Reynolds—entered on a period of active competition. All prospered, in large part due to the tremendous growth in the consumption of cigarettes. Reynolds concentrated its activities largely on a single brand of cigarettes, "Camels," and achieved a conspicuous success, becoming the largest of the four companies in volume of profits in 1924 instead of the smallest as in 1912. American Tobacco continued to produce a broad line of cigarettes and other tobacco products, enjoyed sustained prosperity, but grew much more slowly than Reynolds. Liggett & Myers pursued the same general policy as American Tobacco, but grew somewhat more rapidly. Lorillard concentrated its attention on the relatively high-priced Turkish brands of cigarettes. Its principal attempt to popularize a low-priced, blended cigarette up to 1924 had been a failure. Just before the article in question was published, the management of Lorillard had changed.

FORECAST AND RESULT

Comments of the article on the four stocks in the concluding paragraphs were as follows:

American Tobacco—"The record of earnings is a consistent one and would seem to entitle the stock to investment rating. Altogether the stock has decided attractions."

Liggett & Myers—"Earned per share practically as much last year as Reynolds. The company has not the same past record of growth as Reynolds, but the yield on the stock is more attractive, the future prospects bright."

Lorillard—"Until 1923 the record was good, but it remains to be seen whether that slump was more than temporary."

Reynolds—"Should be able to maintain its commanding position in the industry. The current market for the stock would seem, however, to have discounted favorable developments for a long time ahead."

The industry—"Cigarette manufacturers look forward to an ultimate consumption in this country of 1,000 cigarettes per person annually. Thus all four of the companies should enjoy continued prosperity."

In the light of these comments a table showing the market for these four stocks on May 5, 1924, and December 30, 1926, is of interest:

	Dec. 30.'26	May 5,'24	Advance
American Tobacco "B"	†21	*140	73
Liggett & Myers "B"	100⅝	50	121
Lorillard	32	35¾	(a) 10
R. J. Reynolds "B"	120⅛	65¾	81

*$100 par. †$50 par. ‡Allowing for 10% stock dividend. (a) Decline.

PRODUCTS AND POLICIES

The favorable comments on American Tobacco and Liggett & Myers were fully justified by the advance which occurred in the next thirty-one months. As it turned out, the comment on Reynolds was much too conservative. The cautious tone of the remark about Lorillard appears to have been entirely sound in the light of the dormant market which existed in that stock during the period under review.

The tobacco stocks lent themselves particularly well to analysis when the article in question was written. Every one of the four companies had had a prosperous career in the twelve years following dissolution. Each of them had made a profit in every year of the period and in each case the tendency of profits had been upward. All four companies were soundly capitalized and all of them were amply supplied with working capital. No particularly detailed scrutiny of financial statements was accordingly necessary and the analyst had merely to analyze the products and the sales policies of the four companies.

Opportunity for a New Management

The position of Lorillard was and is at this writing of especial interest. Total income available for bond interest was only $35,000 greater in 1923 than in 1919 though the company's three principal competitors increased their business and earnings largely in that period. Lorillard's 1923 showing was by no means a poor one. Earnings were equal to 14.01% on the $30,305,000 common outstanding. Current assets of $51,896,000 at the end of the year contrasted with current liabilities of $4,948,000. Net working capital of $46,948,000 was $11,868,000 greater than at the end of 1919. Of this increase about $6,000,000 had come from the sale of additional stock at par and the balance from earnings. As previously noted, a new management took the reins early in 1924. This new management undertook direction of a company which could cover the 12% dividend on its common stock by a narrow margin on the smoking and chewing tobacco and Turkish cigarette business, a company with a notably strong treasury.

An Advertising Venture

Within a few months after the new regime took command, a large increase in the volume of advertising of Lorillard products was noticeable—particular attention being given to the two leading brands of Turkish cigarettes. Earnings increased slightly in 1924 and again in 1925 over the 1923 level. Working-capital position was fully maintained. Finally, just a few weeks before this article was written, the Lorillard management took the obvious step of making another attempt to introduce a blended cigarette, backing the attempt with lavish advertising expenditures. At this writing it is impossible to tell how much of a factor "Old Gold" cigarettes are likely to be in the country's cigarette business. From a speculative standpoint, however, it would appear that a purchaser of Lorillard common has much to gain if the new brand should be a success, and little to lose if the venture on the part of the company should not turn out so well.

BETHLEHEM STEEL'S POLICY

The diverse market action of two leading steel stocks in recent years has already been the subject of comment in a previous chapter. In this connection a comment published in *Barron's* on October 22, 1923, is of interest. In reply to a correspondent who was looking for a bargain and tentatively considered Bethlehem Steel common selling under 50 as such as it was said: "Perhaps the $5 dividend is not seriously in danger, but doubt as to its permanency is sufficiently great to raise the question whether an otherwise attractive yield may not prove illusory." Within a year the dividend was passed. At the time the comment was published Bethlehem was earning its $5 dividend by a narrow margin, but was spending money freely on a program of improvements to its plants. A program of cutting costs by spending money on plant improvements was obviously good business, it was equally obvious that results in the way of greatly increased earning power would not be obtained in a few months. Under these circumstances the speculator had to ask himself the same question that the directors faced. Was it better policy for Bethlehem to deplete its working capital to make the improvements contemplated, to finance their cost with bonds or preferred stock thus adding to the charges ahead of common dividends or to make them out of earnings even though it might be necessary to pass the common dividend?

COMPARING TWO INDUSTRIAL GIANTS

The fact that Bethlehem Steel's working capital, in proportion to its size, was considerably smaller than that of its chief competitor at the end of 1923 obviously had some bearing on the dividend policy. In comparing steel producers, the unit of size is the ingot ton of annual capacity. Steel plants make sheets, bars, rails, plates, rods, tubes, billets. Some companies make a very much greater diversity of products than others. The greatest common denominator is the ingot ton. Capacity of the whole country at the end of 1923 was about 50,000,000 ingot tons of capacity. United States Steel had a capacity of 22,000,000 tons, Bethlehem 7,600,000 tons. At that same date Bethlehem Steel had $119,724,000 net working capital, United States Steel $451,192,000. Reduced to a comparable basis of dollars of working capital per ton of capacity, the figures were $15.75 for the smaller company, $20.51 for the giant of the industry. The difference in favor of the larger company was substantial.

Comparison of United States Steel and Bethlehem on the basis of capitalization might also have been made. The former company had $527,160,000 funded debt, $360,281,000 preferred stock, $508,302,000 common stock, against $212,884,000 funded debt, $58,776,000 preferred and $180,152,000 common stock for Bethlehem. The comparison per ton follows:

	Bethlehem	United States
Funded debt	$28.01	$23.96
Preferred stock	7.73	16.37
Common stock	3.70	23.10
Total capitalization	$59.44	$63.43
Working capital	15.75	20.51
Net capitalization	$43.69	$42.92

The differential in favor of United States Steel was more substantial than appeared on the surface. The great corporation owned thousands of miles of railroad, great cement plants and other assets which Bethlehem could not boast. Its diversity of output was likewise greater. The ingot ton as a unit fell considerably short of telling the whole story.

USE OF PHYSICAL UNITS

In analyzing stocks, industrial or otherwise, the speculator must constantly bear in mind that no two companies are strictly comparable. He must always be prepared to make due allowance for points of unlikeness. One raw-sugar producer may own its own refinery, another be a sugar producer and nothing else. One leather company may make sole leather, another upper leather, another belting. Even such apparently similar concerns as Woolworth and Kresge are not fully comparable. One holds to the 10-cent limit in pricing its merchandise, the other carries more expensive articles in many of its stores. The procedure of comparing companies on the basis of physical units, valuable though it is, is of limited applicability for still other reasons. Many concerns are so diversified that no single unit covers their activities. Allied Chemical & Dye makes roofing and pharmaceutical chemicals. It would be impossible to compare this company with any other chemical company on the basis, for example, of tonnage output. Congoleum-Nairn and Big-low-Hartford Carpet both make floor coverings, but comparison on the basis of capitalization per square yard of output would be ridiculous.

COST OF PRODUCTION VITAL

Another fact must never be forgotten in seeking to arrive at a fair conclusion by comparison of two or more properties. The vital thing in connection with a security is earning power. Two properties with the same reproduction value, book value or outstanding capital may differ widely in earning power. Thus two cement companies may have the same annual capacity in barrels, but the properties of one may be much more favorably located both with respect to raw materials and in relation to markets than the other. An estimate of security value based solely on capitalization per barrel of capacity would thus be wholly misleading. The statement is frequently made, and seems well founded, that the Steel Corporation can make steel fifty cents a ton cheaper than any of its competitors. If capitalization and working capital per ingot-ton of steel capacity were then exactly the same for Bethlehem Steel and United States Steel, there would still be sound reason for a wide differential between the prices of their stocks.

While he must make comparisons cautiously the speculator should nevertheless learn as much as possible about the business of the company in which he is interested. The price trend of its principal raw material or principal product may be information of the greatest importance. Stocks of Cuban sugar companies fluctuate to a very large degree in sympathy with the market for raw sugar. Oil stocks are very sensitive to the trend of oil prices. Figures of weekly production of crude oil are also an important factor in the market for active oil stocks. In both instances the figures are readily available to every speculator. The financial press publishes raw sugar quotations daily, oil quotations whenever they change, oil production figures weekly. Prices of other commodities are not always so easy to obtain. The speculator who has several thousand dollars ventured on a commitment in United States Industrial Alcohol would nevertheless find it worth while to take some pains to follow the fluctuations of the industrial-alcohol market.

IMPORTANT FACTORS IN ANALYSIS

From the foregoing brief analyses of well known industrial stocks, it is possible to make an outline of the factors which the speculator consciously or unconsciously considers in arriving at a conclusion regarding the intrinsic value of an industrial stock.

He will estimate:
    (1) The outlook for the industry
        (a) Prospects for long-range growth
        (b) Prospects for immediate trend of profits
           i. Probable price movement of principal commodities
           ii. State of competition
    (2) Position of the company in the industry
        (a) Relative size in comparison with competitors
        (b) Relative rate of growth in comparison with competitors
    (3) Condition of the company
        (a) Record of earnings and trend
        (b) Working-capital position and trend
        (c) Capital structure

PROSPEROUS INDUSTRIES

Studying first the industry in which the company he is investigating is engaged, he will wish to know whether it is generally prosperous or not. According to orthodox economics, competition tends to keep the return on capital at a fairly constant level. If the retail grocery business is notably prosperous, according to theory, new capital will flow into it until competition has reduced profits to a normal level. If shoe manufacturers can barely make ends meet, enough of them will desert the field for more prosperous enterprises to restore the normal balance. The theory is sound enough, but it assumes that capital can readily move from one field to another. This premise is unsound. The shoe manufacturer cannot readily liquidate his business when it is not prosperous. Instead of suffering heavy losses by so doing he is much more likely to hang on as long as possible, hoping for a turn for the better. This natural tendency is increased by the fact that he knows all about the involved technique of manufacturing and selling shoes and probably nothing about the involved technique of another industry which is exceptionally prosperous at the time. The readjustments which economic theory postulates are thus likely to be a matter of very slow development.

AVOIDING CHRONIC DEPRESSION

Other things being equal, the speculator will wish to avoid industries which are chronically depressed and stick to industries which are unusually and consistently prosperous. On the short side of the market, of course, his attitude would be the reverse. It is matter of casual observation that industries differ widely in profitability. Despite the gallant efforts of the tanners to convince themselves and the consuming public that "Nothing takes the place of leather" it is apparent that the leather industry has not expanded in recent years with the growth of the country, that profits in the industry have been few and far between. On the other hand cigarette manufacturers have enjoyed a growth in demand for their products much more rapid than the country's growth in population and wealth. Their operations have as a result been highly and consistently profitable. The speculator must look for such differences and estimate the probable future trend as well as possible.

The immediate outlook for an industry is also of particular interest to a speculator. Here the price trend of the commodities in which the company deals is particularly important. It is the more so when the manufacturing process involves an unusual amount of time or the sale of the product is concentrated largely in a given season, so that for either reason the company has a small turnover of its inventory. The state of competition in an industry is less easily susceptible of analysis, but it should be estimated as well as possible. Politics and the prospects for tariff revision, new inventions, the entrance of new interests into a given field all have their bearing on this point.

LEADERSHIP SELDOM ACCIDENTAL

The position of a company in its industry has an important bearing on the intrinsic value of its stock. The leading company has probably not attained its position by accident, but by superior skill of management. It is not, moreover, likely to be a "one-man" company as may be the case with a prosperous company of smaller size. The large company undoubtedly has an efficient team of executives who can carry on successfully even after the loss of one or more of their number. Moreover, sheer momentum favors the continued prosperity of a large company with a successful record to an even greater degree than a small company. The large company which is the recent product of a consolidation engineered by bankers looking for securities to sell may of course be an entirely different story. In general mere size gives the large company a certain advantage over its smaller competitors.

COMPARING RELATIVE GROWTH

Where the figures are available it is useful to compare companies in the same industry to note their relative growth in sales, profits, financial strength. It is no indictment of a great corporation to say that it has not maintained its position in percentage of the total business done in that line. Such strong leaders of their fields as United States Steel and Standard Oil of New Jersey, for example, do not today produce the same proportion of the country's output of steel and refined oils respectively as they did twenty years ago. They are still far ahead of any competitor. With the growth of the country there is a natural tendency for its business to be divided among a larger number of factors. If, however, as between the two leading companies in an industry, one is obviously gaining on the other, that is an important fact for the trader's consideration.

VALUE OF SUPERABUNDANT CASH

The analysis of income statements and balance sheets has already been discussed in a previous article. The speculator will hardly be bullish on the stock of a company which has not shown a distinct upward trend in earnings over a period of years, unless some marked change in its affairs has occurred which leads him to believe that a sharp upward turn is at hand. He will similarly desire to see a fairly constant improvement in its working capital position. It sometimes seems to the novice that a company which has millions in cash and government securities has a surplus of working capital, that it might well increase its dividend or declare a large extra. He should remember that a large reserve of cash not ordinarily needed assures the management absolute control of the business. If depression in the trade affords an opportunity to make an exceptionally advantageous purchase of raw materials or even of the business of a distressed competitor, the wherewithal is ready. No banker can veto the sound expansion plans of such a company under those circumstances.

The principle of trading on the equity applies to industrial as well as to public service corporations, but not with the same force. An industrial enterprise which is wholly owned by one class of stock may nevertheless show spectacular growth in earnings per share under favorable conditions. Many types of industrial enterprise are ordinarily able to finance expansion out of earnings. Occasionally an industrial whose business requires very heavy fixed investment in proportion to sales and profits may have a capital structure which would be typical of a public service corporation. In such a case the principle that a small gain in total earnings is greatly magnified in reckoning earnings per share on the small equity issue is fully applicable.

Advantages of Small Capitalization

From a strictly market standpoint a small capitalization is distinctly advantageous. The stock of a company with 100,000 shares outstanding will ordinarily "move" much more rapidly than the stock of a company with 5,000,000 shares outstanding. In stock market language it "takes a ton of dynamite to move" the latter issue. If a speculative pool is looking for a suitable vehicle for its operations, it will take the former rather than the latter stock, other things being equal. By the same token, such a stock is much more likely to go to absurdly unjustified heights in the excesses which mark the termination of a typical bull market. The in-and-out trader will get more "action" in a stock of this character than in such a stock as Steel, the student of values will probably prefer a stock of the latter type. The factor of capital structure nevertheless plays a rather important part in his calculations.

Chapter XIV

The Romance of Buried Treasure

Victims of the financial underworld, the proverbial widows and orphans who place their funds in worthless securities, are prone to select mining and oil stocks as the vehicles of their misfortunes. There is undeniably a certain glamor about the adventure of extracting its mineral wealth from the earth's crust. A desolate arid waste, an arctic tundra, a remote mountain, may carry below its surface vast wealth in the form of a deposit of gold, silver, copper, lead, zinc, tin or some other mineral or of that "liquid gold," petroleum. The average man cannot participate directly in the supposedly romantic career of the prospector, but he can share vicariously in the search for mineral wealth by the purchase of mining and oil shares whose vendors assure him that there is every prospect of a tremendous increase in value.

Cupidity is, of course, a primary factor in making it easy for high-pressure salesmen to distribute worthless mining and oil stocks. Every human being has heard more or less authenticated tales of the fortunes won by lucky prospectors or by lucky purchasers of shares in mining prospects. In a western city lives a wealthy man of affairs who was a Y. M. C. A. physical instructor thirty years ago. He joined in the rush to the Klondike and was one of the few to come out with a fortune. To many thousands who know of him by name at least he is a living example of the fact that fortunes in mining may come quickly.

An Historic Fortune

For decades Calumet & Hecla was a name to conjure with. Every mining stock salesman for fifty years has used Calumet

& Hecla as an example of the possibilities involved in the transformation of a mining prospect into a producing bonanza. A distinguished scientist became a millionaire and made his family one of the wealthiest in a rich old city as a result of his discovery of this great copper mine. In the early stages of development Agassiz and his associates were forced to put every cent they could raise into the mine and at times were so hard pressed that they were compelled to offer their servants and tradesmen stock in the mine in place of cash in settlement of their obligations. Those who accepted netted small fortunes as a reward for their faith. It may be noted that while a little stock was distributed in this way the Agassizs did not create an elaborate stock-selling organization or employ salesmen to go from door to door to sell their stock. This fact, however, is not called to the attention of prospects by salesmen of speculative mining stock today.

AN ORE DEPOSIT PLUS

One fact often forgotten by the credulous is that a mine is a great deal more than a deposit of mineral matter. The occurrence of the precious or the baser metals is not an uncommon phenomenon. There is gold dissolved in the waters of the sea; there is gold in the bricks of which the older portions of Philadelphia were built; the baser metals occur very widely throughout the world. A mine, however, is a deposit of mineral ore plus equipment in the matter of underground workings, mill, smelter and other surface equipment, transportation facilities, a technical and a laboring staff. If it is to be a successful mine, the amount, grade and character of ore, the design, quality and adequacy of equipment, the cost of transportation of supplies and product, the character of the staff must all contribute to the extraction and sale of the metal or metals sought at a profit.

A Great Failure

An ore-body may contain 5,000,000 ounces of gold each of which can be exchanged at the United States Mint for $20.67 in United States coin, but if it will cost on the average $20.75 to extract each ounce from the earth no mine can be developed. The history of the Alaska Gold Mines Co. almost exactly parallels this suppositious case. The company owned a large body of low-grade ore near Juneau, Alaska. Reputable mining engineers estimated that it contained 75,000,000 to 100,000,000 tons of ore having a recoverable value of $1.50 per ton. It was expected that mining and milling costs would average about a dollar a ton. The company was financed with $3,000,000 convertible debentures and 750,000 shares of stock, sold by reputable banking houses. In 1915 at the commencement of operations the stock sold as high as $40 a share.

In actual operation Alaska Gold proved to be an engineering marvel. Cost of getting a ton of ore out of the ground and running it through the mill was cut below 80 cents a ton. Despite this extraordinary performance the mine was a failure. In actual operation it turned out that the recoverable value of the gold per ton of ore was not $1.50 but less than half as much. The gap between gold recovered and cost of its extraction was on the wrong side of the ledger. The mine was finally abandoned and its security holders entirely wiped out.

How Prospects Are Financed

So far discussion has centered about prospects and mines in the development stage. A prospect is merely a tract of ground believed on more or less good authority to contain ore in paying quantities. To turn it into a producing mine it must be opened up and equipped, a process which may require heavy capital expenditures and a great deal of time. In the case of a big mine millions of dollars and years of effort may be necessary to turn a prospect into a producing mine. Comparatively few mines have rich enough surface ore to pay their own development costs. The discoverer of a prospect must finance development in one of three ways: sell it to a big exploration company, perhaps retaining a royalty interest, find a wealthy individual or small syndicate to back him or organize a company whose securities will be given broad public distribution. If he chooses the latter alternative, there is a good chance that he may fall into the hands of financial pirates, interested only in a generous commission on the sale of stock. Thus a potentially valuable property may be used as the mere vehicle of a swindling crew, who make no real attempt to develop it. If the property has real merit, however, it is much more likely that it will be financed by an exploration company or a small but wealthy syndicate than that it will be made the vehicle for the broad distribution of stock to the public in its early stages.

The greatest possibilities for profit and the greatest risk of loss naturally exist in the stock of a mine in the prospect stage. A barren tract of ground which would otherwise have value only as pasturage for a few goats may prove on development to be worth millions of dollars.

The speculator who buys mining shares in the prospect stage may reasonably expect to share in the profits of development on some such tremendous scale. The risks of loss are almost equally great, as is indicated by the fact that hardly one in a hundred of the prospects offered to the great exploration companies— American Metals, American Smelting & Refining, United States Smelting—each year is accepted. The ordinary man should leave stocks in such mines strictly alone.

RISKS DURING DEVELOPMENT

Beyond the prospect stage is the development stage, when mining experts have endorsed a mine, strong interests have sponsored its securities and the work of opening the mine and equipping it is in progress. It was in this stage that Alaska Gold bonds and shares were offered to the public. Estimates of ore values, percentage and cost of recovery of the gold in the ore were made by reputable engineers, the project was sponsored by financiers who had made fortunes for themselves and their customers in mining securities. On the basis of the estimates high prices for Alaska Gold shares were fully justified. The estimates were unfortunately too optimistic and the venture was a complete failure. Even stock of a mine being developed under the most favorable auspices carries a substantial risk.

DEVELOPMENT MAY BE SLOW

The speculator interested in a mine in the development stage is prone to underestimate the time necessary to bring it to profitable production. The history of the Chile Copper Co. emphasizes this point. In 1910 and 1911 a Boston mining man took options on an extensive property in the mountains of northern Chile. In 1912 the Guggenheim family became interested and drilling to establish the extent of the ore body was begun. The purchase and development of the mine were financed in part by the sale of $15,000,000 convertible 7s, 1923. Later $35,000,000 convertible 6s were sold. It was not until 1915 that production of copper was really begun and in the following year 41,000,000 pounds of copper were produced. This contrasted with 360,000,000 pounds a year production recommended by the engineers in charge of development. In 1915 the 3,800,000 shares of capital stock were listed on the New York Stock Exchange, where they ranged between 23⅜ and 26⅜.

Chile Copper reached the 100,000,000-mark in output in 1918, crossed the 200,000,000-pound mark in 1923. In that latter year cost of production before bond interest was cut to less than eight cents a pound and the stock was placed on a $2.50 dividend basis. In that same year the Guggenheims sold a majority of the stock to the Anaconda Copper Co. for $35 a share, but not until 1924 did the stock sell as high in the open market.

Speculators who bought the stock in the development stage in 1915 had to wait eight years for dividends and a moderate profit on their funds. Yet Chile Copper may properly be considered one of the outstanding mining successes of the world.

VALUATION BY FORMULA

The bulk of the mining companies whose stocks are listed on the New York Stock Exchange are producing properties. The value of a producing mine may be determined by mathematical calculations involving three factors—the life of the mine, the cost of production, the market value of its product. Those mining engineers who have made fortunes in mining stocks have done so by applying simple mathematics to the valuation of mining stocks. Obviously these three factors can never be known with absolute accuracy, excepting only that the product of a gold-mining company is always worth exactly $20.67 an ounce. The geology of a given mine may make it impracticable to estimate its life with any certainty. In the case of a deep-vein mine with a complex geological structure it might be ruinously expensive to block out its ore reserves more than a year or so ahead. In most cases, however, a reasonable estimate of the mine's ore reserves is available. The tonnage of ore reserves divided by the tons mined annually equals the life of the mine in years. In the case of a producing property, figures of production cost are also available. This cost will vary somewhat with changes at the mines and with changing commodity price levels, but unless there is some reason to expect a drastic change the current value of a mining stock will have a certain relation to current production costs. Price of the metal produced is another fluctuating quantity, except gold, but here again the market for mining stocks tends to fluctuate with the metal market so that the speculator seeking undervalued issues may usually take the current market for the metal in his calculations.

An Example of Valuation

An industrial or public service corporation may and theoretically will continue in business forever. If it can pay $2 a share in dividends and sells at 20, the speculator is getting a 10% yield by purchasing it. The life of a mining company is limited. If a mine has a ten-year probable life and can pay $2 in dividends annually until the ore is exhausted, the purchaser at 20 is not even getting a 6% yield. This is the reason mining stocks must sell on what superficially appears to be a high-yield basis in order to give their holders a fair return. Tables are available which show the present value of an annual dividend of $1, allowing for the replacement of capital by reinvestment of an annual sum at 4%. Suppose such a table were applied to the stock of the Hecla Mining Co. early in 1923. Hecla is an Idaho silver-lead producer which produced in 1922, 42,490,000 pounds of lead and 1,178,000 ounces of silver. At that rate of production, ore reserves at the end of 1922 were sufficient for eight years of operation. With lead at six cents and silver at 70 cents, gross revenues would be $3,375,000 on production at the 1922 rate. Costs in 1922 were $4.30 per ton of ore handled or slightly over $1,000,000 for 237,000 tons. Net before depreciation and depletion would then be about $2,350,000 or $2.35 a share for the 1,000,000 shares outstanding. Allowing for adequate depreciation balance of $2 a share would theoretically be available for dividends. Turning to a table of present values it is seen that a dividend of $1 for eight years on a 10% basis is worth $4.79. Double that figure is $9.58 as the theoretical value of the stock.

As a matter of actual fact, Hecla's costs in 1923 were substantially greater than in 1922 and net income fell far short of $2,350,000. The company continued to expand output capacity, however, lead rose to better than nine cents a pound and in 1925 new ore discoveries added some thirteen years to the prospective life of the mine. As a result of these favorable developments, the stock sold as high as 18⅛ in 1925.

Mining Consolidations

The modern tendency toward expansion in the size of corporate units has not omitted the mining field. Many mines are owned and operated by large exploration companies, such as American Smelting and United States Smelting. Companies of this type are always in the market for promising mining properties. American Smelting, for example, owns a large number of copper, lead and zinc smelters and refineries in the United States, Mexico and Chile as well as mines in this country, Mexico and Peru. A company of this type derives a steady income from its smelting and refining operations as well as its mining profits. It is rather an industrial than a mining enterprise. Another great group of properties is the Anaconda group. Originally Anaconda was merely the leading mining property in Butte, Montana. Today it has not merely these properties and a smelter and refinery but controls the International Smelting Co., with smelters in other states, the great Chile Copper Co., the Andes Copper Co., the American Brass Co., leading producer of brass products in the world, and other subsidiaries. This company is also quite as much an industrial as a mining enterprise. Kennecott owns its own copper mine in Alaska, a majority interest in the Mother Lode mine in Alaska, a 99% interest in the Braden mine in Chile and a 95% interest in the rich Utah Copper Co. More and more mining companies are thus extending their interests and tending to prolong their lives almost indefinitely. The analysis of such large units is much more difficult than the analysis of a company owning a single mine, but the general principles are the same and diversification of interests greatly reduces the risks inevitably involved in mining.

IMPORTANCE OF DEPLETION

Depletion and depreciation are two deductions in the income account of a mining company with which the speculator need not concern himself seriously. If he is intelligent, he realizes that his dividends represent a return of capital as well as income. He does not expect the mining company to try to accumulate in cash out of its profits a fund which will repay the par value of its shares when the mine is exhausted. On the other hand, the government does recognize that from an income tax standpoint it would be unjust not to permit a deduction from earnings theoretically sufficient to accumulate a fund which would ultimately repay the stockholders for the cost of acquiring, opening up and equipping the property. In computing the company's taxable earnings, it is thus proper to make appropriations to reserves for depletion—of the ore body—and for depreciation—of the equipment. It is no affair of the government what the company does with these reserves and it may and usually does distribute the greater part of them in dividends. That portion of a mining company's dividends taken from depletion reserves rather than from surplus is exempt from income tax.

In keeping its books on the most favorable basis from an income tax standpoint it may very well happen that a mining company will apparently pay in dividends more than it earns for years. The speculator is not interested, however, in the showing of net income after depreciation and depletion nor in the bookkeeping deficit resulting from generous appropriations to those reserves. If net income before depreciation and depletion more than covers dividend requirements, if the net quick assets of the company are maintained, he is satisfied.

TECHNICAL BARRIERS TO MINING SPECULATION

A discussion of mining stocks would hardly be complete without some use of the terms stope, crosscut, lens, porphyry, tailings, flotation, hanging wall, amygdaloid, gangue, drift, refractory, and so on. These and many other technical terms must be familiar to the speculator before he will be able to read a mining report intelligently. If he wishes to study economic geology, he will find it a fascinating subject, a necessary preliminary to any extensive speculation in mining stocks which is to have hope of success. The average speculator will perhaps not devote any great amount of attention to mining stocks. The technicalities necessary to a comprehension of the merits and demerits of industrial and public service corporation stocks are a broad field of study in themselves and the opportunities for profit in such securities are at least as great as in mining stocks. An occasional excursion into mining convertible bonds, into the stocks of well known producing mines when the metal market outlook is favorable and into the stocks of the great exploration companies will probably suffice for most speculators.

YOUTH OF OIL INDUSTRY

Within the memory of men now living, the oil industry of the world was founded when oil was discovered in Pennsylvania in 1859. Today it is one of the greatest of industries, supplying the fuel for 20,000,000 automobiles in the United States alone, the fuel for a great part of the world's shipping, lighting the less civilized portions of the world where gas and electricity are unknown, supplying the lubricants without which no machine could run five minutes. So far as the extraction of crude petroleum from the ground is concerned, the oil industry has much in common with mining. The location of underground deposits is still largely a matter of luck, their profitable extraction a hazardous venture. In the case of oil, the work of transporting, refining and distributing is of far greater relative importance than in the case of mineral products. Because it is a liquid crude oil requires special equipment, tank cars, tank steamers and pipe lines, for its transportation, and a large part of the billions of dollars invested in the oil industry is in this form of equipment, for which there is no counterpart in mining. Again the distribution of refined-oil products involves a very heavy investment for which there is little counterpart in mining.

Production, Transportation, Refining, Distribution

There are very few oil companies in which the intelligent speculator is likely to be interested, which confine their activities to the extraction of crude oil from the ground, selling it in the crude state in wholesale lots. Those companies of any importance which do confine their activities to the extraction of crude oil from the ground usually have properties in a number of fields so that the hazards of this branch of the industry are somewhat reduced. The proverbial wildcat oil stock which has such a fascination for the unsophisticated, on the contrary, represents merely fractional ownership in a single tract of ground in which there may or may not be oil in paying quantities. The risks in such a development, even assuming honest and competent management, are very large. Not only are there few important oil companies which are mere producers of crude but there are also many important companies which are not at all interested in crude oil production. Until within a comparatively few years it was traditional Standard Oil policy to let the "other fellow" assume the risk of drilling for oil. For years Standard Oil confined its attention to refining and distribution to consumers. To assure an adequate and uninterrupted supply of crude oil for costly refineries it has become necessary for most leading oil companies in recent years to go into the producing end of the business. There are still some, however, which buy all or a considerable part of their crude from outside sources.

PIPE-LINE DIFFICULTIES

There are a number of companies which confine themselves to the transportation end of the industry. These are mostly former Standard Oil subsidiaries operating pipe lines or tank car lines. The pipe-line companies suffer a serious disadvantage. Like lumber railroads they handle traffic which will ultimately dwindle away to an un-profitably small volume. In striking contrast to the history of most of the companies which were split off from Standard Oil of New Jersey, as a result of the dissolution decree of 1912, the pipeline companies declined in prosperity in the following fourteen years. Most of them operated short lines serving fields of limited extent or sections of the great trunk line from the midcontinent to eastern seaboard refineries which ultimately found it cheaper to get their crude by water. The big tank-car subsidiary, on the contrary, constantly grew in strength and earning power.

WIDE RANGE OF ACTIVITIES

The typical large oil company of today covers the whole range of the business. Its crude oil may be obtained from its own wells, not only in many different fields—but from fields scattered over several continents. Its own pipe lines and tank ships may transport this crude to its refineries and its refined products to market. The refineries distill gasoline and other products from the crude oil. Of these products gasoline is the chief in point of dollars. Kerosene, once the principal distillate of crude petroleum, is now a minor factor in commerce in comparison with gasoline, although it still enjoys a good market in the Far East and in other remote portions of the world. Lubricants are extremely important as an essential commodity for which there is no substitute. Some important companies concentrate their energies on the production of lubricants, notably Vacuum Oil. Fuel oil is another important product of the oil refinery. Usually it is the product of a low-grade crude oil and is perhaps the output of a refinery which is equipped merely to distill a small fraction of gasoline leaving the bulk of the crude as fuel oil. Refiners are making constant progress in the technique of the industry, however, and constantly increasing the proportion of gasoline and other valuable products obtained from each barrel of crude. The output of the refineries of a large company is no longer sold exclusively at wholesale, but is now largely distributed at retail through the company's own filling stations.

Oils Resemble Industrials

The analysis of oil stocks is comparable to the analysis of industrial stocks rather than to that of mining stocks. The factor of depletion does to be sure enter into the accounting of oil companies, but in the case of the large companies it is not so vitally important an item. Their holdings of oil lands are ordinarily so scattered that the speculator does not need to worry about exhaustion of supply, an element of great importance in the analysis of a mining stock. In calculating the earnings of an oil company available for dividends income before depletion— but after a reasonable appropriation for depreciation of plants —may properly be used as giving the correct figure. As in the case of any other type of company, evidence of excessive reserves for depreciation may suggest that a given stock is undervalued, or vice versa.

Statistics Readily Available

The general level of oil stocks fluctuates in close sympathy with fluctuations in the price and quantity in storage of crude oil. If an oil pool is discovered underneath ground whose ownership is scattered, a race to get the oil out necessarily follows. Any land owner who did not immediately drill for oil would simply be permitting his neighbors to drain the oil from under his land without compensation to him. Since there is always wildcatting in progress, it frequently happens that the supply of oil in storage above ground is greatly augmented in the face of a falling market for the product. Under such circumstances an advance in the oil stocks would hardly be likely. On the other hand, wildcatters may for many months discover no new oil pools of consequence. With falling production from old wells, no new production in sight, consumption steadily increasing the price of crude oil would naturally rise and the prices of active oil stocks would probably follow suit. Figures of production and oil in storage are available weekly and changes in the price level of crude oil and of gasoline receive wide publicity.

An Attractive Field for Speculation

The speculator will find many promising vehicles for his operations among the oil stocks. The group covers a broad range from companies owning little except land which may contain oil to companies owning widely scattered producing wells and all the facilities for transforming their product into marketable form and getting it to the consumer, from companies operating principally in politically unstable regions like Mexico to companies operating almost exclusively in the United States. In general he will find ample information about leading oil companies and about the state of the industry in the financial press. Thanks to the glamor of the word "oil," he will have plenty of company in his operations and thus be assured always of a good market on which to buy or sell leading issues.

CHAPTER XV

Profits in Financial Surgery

An operation by a skilled surgeon often transforms a dying man into a convalescent, whose life will soon recover its value to himself and to society. In finance as in medicine there are surgeons. A business enterprise with a large volume of business, extensive assets and a great staff of employees may be unprofitable for no more serious reason than an unbalanced capital structure, or lack of working capital. With earning power lacking, however, it is probable that the corporation will be unable to finance itself in a normal way by the sale of bonds or additional stock. A readjustment of the capital structure may be necessary. Here is a job for a financial surgeon by whose efforts a weak enterprise may be transformed into a strong one, with corresponding benefit to creditors and shareholders.

SUCCESS: A MATTER OF MANAGEMENT

Such drastic measures as a voluntary or involuntary reorganization may not be necessary. Perhaps a mere change of management will suffice. Business success is largely a matter of management. Methods of doing business are constantly changing. The management of an enterprise must be alert to sense these changes, to adopt those which are improvements over old methods. It is not enough that a concern shall be rich in assets, possess a well known name, carry the accounts of a host of customers. Despite the advantages of size, wealth, a good name and a long tradition a large enterprise will cease to be profitable if the men at the head get hardening of the arteries or atrophy of the brain tissue or if their heirs prove unequal to inherited responsibilities. Momentum alone will not carry a business forward under such circumstances. Some younger and more aggressive group will assume the leadership of the industry.

KEENNESS PLUS EXPERIENCE

Age alone constitutes no indictment of a business leader. An Elbert H. Gary or a George F. Baker may be younger mentally, more receptive to new ideas, possess sounder judgment when in the eighties than any but the exceptional executive of fifty. The thirty years' additional business experience and accumulated knowledge give the older man a decided advantage. It sometimes happens, however, that a business man does not maintain his mental alertness, his receptiveness to new ideas, the soundness of his judgment as his years increase. The company whose management is dominated by such a man will very possibly show a declining rate of earnings. A change in management may be the only tonic needed to restore it to a position of leadership.

An enterprise which is a going concern with an established business and plenty of fixed assets is obviously in a strong position when a reorganization or a change in management injects new life into it. Such a change in its position must necessarily be of great interest to the speculator since the change in security values following the dethronement of a mediocre and the inauguration of an aggressive management or following the successful consummation of a drastic reorganization is likely to be far greater in extent than the normal growth in value of the stock of a normally successful company. The very word reorganization scares away the average investor, the quality of a new management is always somewhat an unknown factor. As a result, the investor usually leaves the securities of companies which have just emerged from the hands of the financial surgeon severely alone. This fact spells opportunity for the speculator.

Voluntary and Involuntary Reorganizations

When a company becomes financially involved so that its working-capital position is impaired, its credit rating diminished, its access to ordinary means of financing destroyed, its financial position may be restored in one of two ways, by voluntary reorganization without receivership or by forced reorganization following receivership. Since the appointment of a receiver by the courts takes control of the property away from the stockholders, entails heavy legal costs, occasions unfavorable publicity and shakes the confidence of customers the attempt is frequently made to achieve the desired end by a voluntary reorganization without recourse to receivership. Since a voluntary reorganization requires practically the unanimous agreement as to terms of all concerned, including creditors and shareholders with diverse interests, it is a very difficult type of readjustment to achieve. When it is successfully consummated it often happens that the terms have been so lenient to security holders that the surgical job has not been a thorough one. The speculator prefers a decidedly drastic readjustment as the recovery is likely to be more rapid, the accompanying rise in price of the new securities more extensive.

Receivership and Bankruptcy

Ordinarily reorganization follows receivership. This is the administration of a property by an official appointed by a federal court following judicial establishment of the fact that the corporation is unable to pay its debts when due. It should be noted that receivership and bankruptcy are not synonymous. The latter is applicable only when debts exceed assets, while a receivership usually occurs when assets are still substantially in excess of debts. It is probable, however, that many of the assets are fixed and could be realized only after considerable delay. If then the creditors are pressing their claims vigorously, an attempt by the corporation to pay them would quickly strip it of all its current assets and disrupt its other properties. For the protection of all concerned, the court may in such circumstances (and upon petition of a creditor) appoint a receiver. It is the duty of this official to conserve the assets to the end that all the creditors may receive equitable treatment. In the case of a public service corporation or an industrial of any size, the receiver will also be directed to operate the property. Ordinarily the president of the company will be one of the receivers, perhaps with some prominent attorney as co-receiver.

The Receiver Protects the Creditors

The primary object of a receivership is to preserve the value of the property for the benefit of creditors. The receivership will terminate when the business has been restored to sound financial condition. Very rarely this may occur through a sudden shift in the fortunes of the distressed company without raising any new money. The outbreak of the World War in 1914 forced the International Mercantile Marine Co., whose earnings record for many years had been disappointing, into receivership. The war, which at first seemed a calamity, turned out to be the source of extraordinary profits for shipping companies. In 1916 the company emerged from receivership not only without having raised any new money by the sale of securities but actually with the achievement to its credit of being able to pay off a substantial part of the principal of its funded debt. This was an extraordinary case. The termination of a receivership usually involves sacrifices on the part of the security holders, frequently payment of an assessment by the stockholders.

Restoration of Earning Power

Before a successful plan of reorganization of a corporation in receivership can be formulated earning power of the patient must be restored. This is quite likely to be a slow process and may require years. The receiver does not have to bother about paying interest on the company's obligations, except possibly underlying liens which are likely to be left undisturbed in reorganization, but may devote such earnings as are available to the improvement of the properties in his control. Perhaps maintenance was neglected prior to receivership in an effort to avoid receivership by bolstering up the cash account at the expense of fixed assets. The receiver will reverse this policy and make heavy expenditures for maintenance, perhaps actually charging improvements to maintenance. With the court's permission he may borrow money on receiver's certificates, which will enjoy a lien on the property prior to that of outstanding obligations. When he has put the property in good shape he must next develop earning power which will encourage shareholders to participate in a reorganization. All this may require considerable time. The Second Avenue Railroad Co., operating a surface traction line in New York, went into receivership in 1908. As this is written, in 1927, it is just in process of reorganization.

PRIORITY OF CLAIMS

Theoretically the reorganization of a company in receivership should be a simple process. Take, for example, a fairly complicated capital structure and suppose a company with three issues of bonds, two issues of preferred stock and common stock. Suppose further that the bonds consist of first mortgage bonds, first and refunding mortgage bonds—actually second mortgage bonds for all practical purposes—and debentures, that the two issues of preferred stock are first preferred stock, entitled to par and accrued dividends in liquidation before anything is paid on any other issue, and second preferred stock, entitled to par and accrued dividends in liquidation before anything is paid on the common. In theory the property will be sold to satisfy the claims of creditors, the first mortgage bonds will be paid off in full and any balance applied to paying the first and refunding mortgage bonds. If this balance suffices to pay them off in full, a further balance will be applied to the debentures. If this balance should take care of the debentures, anything left will go to the first preferred stockholders, and so on.

THEORY AND PRACTICE

In finance as in other fields: theory and practice sometimes differ. Actually a large company in receivership would not be liquidated in any such fashion as that described. In the first place the assets in the hands of the receiver will be very largely fixed assets. If there were plenty of current assets, there would probably be no receiver. The fixed assets may stand on the books of the corporation at many millions of dollars; they may have cost an even greater sum and the cost to reproduce them would be still larger. The fact remains that these assets have not produced profits, or, again, there would probably be no receiver. Under the circumstances it is not likely that any outside group would care to raise any substantial sum with which to purchase them. As junk they are worth only a small fraction of their going concern value. The only alternative to junking the assets, a procedure which would probably wipe out all the junior security holders, is for the security holders to organize a new company to purchase the assets in effect from themselves.

In its simplest terms this constitutes a reorganization of a company in receivership, the organization of a new company to acquire the properties of the old company, security holders of the old company acquiring the securities of the new company on various terms. The bondholders because of their senior claim on the property are in a strong position in the course of the negotiations which fix the terms of reorganization. Their position is not invulnerable, however, except perhaps in the case of one or two underlying issues. In the first place they are usually scattered and concerted action is difficult to obtain. Secondly, they are by inclination creditors and not owners, they desire a fixed return and their money back rather than the risks and profits of ownership. Third, they are usually unwilling to put up the additional money which must be provided to put the company on its feet. Fourth, they did not choose the management and they are probably not in position to provide a new management.

Strength of Stockholders' Position

Despite their theoretically weak position, the stockholders have certain advantages in the bargaining which precedes the formulation of a reorganization plan. In the first place they are probably willing to put up new money in an effort to retrieve what they have lost. Second, they elected the management to which the senior security holders must probably look for success in recovering at least part of their principal and original fixed return. If the seniors press the juniors too hard in the negotiations, the latter may say: "All right, take the property. We don't care to participate in the reorganization on such onerous terms." Since the senior security holders do not want the property on which they have a claim, such a threat usually brings them to terms. The stockholders are thus ordinarily permitted to participate in a reorganization on a fairly generous basis.

End of Receivership

When the receiver has sufficiently restored the physical condition of the property in his charge and its earning power, when the security holders have fought out their divergent views as to a reasonable reorganization plan and have finally reached an agreement, the end of the receivership is at hand. The plan is now submitted to the security holders. Probably most of them have already deposited their securities with the various protective committees which represented their interests in formulating the plan. Under the normal procedure these will now have an opportunity to withdraw their securities in order to signify dissent. Failure to withdraw within a limited time will automatically signify assent. Few will withdraw in the normal course of things, but, on the contrary, non-depositing security holders will now deposit until perhaps 90% to 95% of the various securities have agreed to the plan. The plan has also been submitted to the court having jurisdiction and has received its approval.

Legal Steps

Substantial agreement of all parties in interest having been obtained the new company which is to take over the property is organized. In order to retain the good-will of the old company it is usually of the same name with some minor variation or has exactly the same name, but is incorporated in a different state. The reorganization committee now proceeds to foreclose one of the mortgages securing a bond issue of the old company, the court fixes an upset price below which the property cannot be sold, a public auction is held at which usually no other bidders appear and the committee bids the property in at the upset price. Securities of the new company are now issued in accordance with the terms of the plan and it is started on its career. All concerned hope that it will have a more prosperous one than its predecessor. It is at least equipped with properties in sound condition and adequately supplied with working capital. Its management is doubtless inspired with new zeal and perhaps has the benefit of an engineering survey of the property which should assist materially in the effort to achieve efficiency of operation.

When Time Works Against Speculator

An element in speculative calculations whose importance is often underestimated is the time element. When a large corporation goes into receivership the speculator may be inclined to buy its securities on the theory that the bad news is all out, that the next change in the corporation's affairs will surely be for the better. In general this is a fairly sound theory, but the speculator should remember that the receivership may be a prolonged affair during which news regarding the company may be extremely meager and general public interest in its securities at a low ebb. During this period, moreover, he will be foregoing any return on his commitment. Presumably the speculator will not regard his operations as successful unless he makes a better return than 6% on his capital. He should always bear in mind in buying a non-income-producing security that he could increase his capital fairly rapidly by buying a sound investment issue yielding 6% and reinvesting the income. If he buys a bond at 50, say, on the eve of a three-year receivership, he should remember that the bond must be worth at least 59¾ at the end of the period to show him a return equal to 6%, compounded semi-annually. Ordinary mathematics thus favors a delay in making a commitment in the securities of a corporation in receivership at least until the terms of reorganization are known.

Discouraging Delays

Legally receivership and reorganization involve many complications. Even after substantially all the security holders have assented to the plan, it has been declared operative, the new corporation organized and the foreclosure sale held—there may be delay in actually issuing the stock of the new corporation and in calling on stockholders of the old corporation for payment of

221

their subscriptions to new securities. In common conservatism, the new company will hardly inaugurate dividends on its stock until some months later still. The first enthusiasm which greets the plan of reorganization, whose announcement is an implied expression of faith in the future of the enterprise by the bankers and others closest to it, is thus likely to be followed by discouragement. The fact that between the announcement of the plan and its final consummation the shares are traded in on a "when issued" basis also acts to facilitate a decline in the market for the new securities shortly after they are issued. Many speculators whose credit is stronger than their bank accounts make it a practice to buy "when issued" securities when trading begins. They are likely to sell when these contracts are finally settled and their brokers call on them for real money.

NORMAL SEQUENCE OF MARKET MOVEMENTS

There is thus a strong tendency for the stock of a reorganized company to enjoy a preliminary rise when it is in the "when issued" state, to decline after the first enthusiasm has worn off and before the new company is showing real results. If the company has been soundly reorganized, however, stripped of some of its unprofitable properties, its capitalization substantially reduced, its treasury greatly strengthened, there is nevertheless an excellent prospect that the new securities will increase substantially in value in a few months or years. The investor who must have income and the impatient speculator have alike been eliminated by the tedious process of receivership and reorganization. The new securities are probably pretty well concentrated in "strong hands," large holders who have not bought them for a few points profit and who have the ability to make the company worth substantially more than at the low point of its fortunes.

The Bankers' Prestige

There is an added factor tending to make the securities of a reorganized company increase in value. This factor is the desire of the banking house identified with the company to maintain its prestige and good-will. Having sold an issue of bonds and thus become identified with a given company, the average large banking house feels a high sense of responsibility to its clients for the continued prosperity of the company and the ultimate fate of the bonds. If a default occurs, a thoroughly responsible house will devote time, money and effort out of all proportion to the profit originally made on the financing in an effort to make good the losses suffered by its clients. Banking houses differ widely in this respect, but a speculator should ascertain the reputation of bankers for a given company in this connection.

In looking for profits in reorganization securities, the speculator will be sure first that the reorganization plan is a sound one, second that the outlook for the industry in which the company is engaged is reasonably bright. If the reorganization is of a sick company in a chronically sick industry, the stockholders of the old company who are putting more money into the new company may be actuated by hope rather than by good judgment. There is nothing in such a situation to interest the intelligent speculator. On the other hand, a reorganization plan may be only moderately drastic, but if fundamental conditions favor the new company large profits will be made in its securities. The analysis of conditions in a given industry has been touched upon in another place and requires no further comment here. The analysis of reorganization terms is a subject deserving some attention.

Standardized Reorganization Terms

The experience of the financial world in reorganizations in recent decades has been so extensive that practices have become fairly well standardized. Given a company in receivership with a certain capital structure, certain normal earning power, certain requirements for additional capital and the intelligent speculator does not need to have a dictaphone installed in the office where the various protective committees meet in order to be able to tell pretty well what the final reorganization terms are likely to be. Railroad reorganizations are perhaps most standardized. The bulk of the railroad mileage of the United States has been through receivership at least once, a considerable part of it twice. Details of the reorganizations of various roads are readily available for study, the results of reorganizations are known and certain general principles may be applied in any case.

RAILROAD REORGANIZATION

In the case of a railroad of any size it may safely be assumed that operation of the property will be continued, no considerable mileage abandoned. Certain property is so essential to the road that bonds secured by first mortgage on it will go through receivership and reorganization undisturbed. This is almost invariably true of equipment trust obligations, usually true of first mortgage bonds on the most important mileage. A glance at the map and a reasonable knowledge of the geography of the territory served will tell what mileage probably carries the heaviest traffic. Since receivership was caused by insufficiency of net earnings to meet fixed charges, however, some bonds must suffer in the reorganization. The issues whose holders must make sacrifices will naturally be the junior mortgage bonds, the debentures, the bonds secured by unimportant mileage. These may have to be exchanged for income bonds, on which interest will be paid only when earned, or for preferred stock or for both. If an income or adjustment bond issue is created, provision will also probably be made for the authorization of a new mortgage which may be used for financing future improvements.

To provide immediate cash requirements the stock will probably be assessed, stockholders being given new bonds at par for their assessment. The stock whose holders pay this assessment will then be exchanged for stock of the new company, though perhaps a fewer number of shares. Stock whose holders do not pay the assessment will be scaled down in a greater measure. By these means the fixed charges of the new company will be brought well within the normal earning power of the property. With increased earning power resulting either from the growth of gross revenues or more efficient operation following improvement of the property the adjustment or income bonds may then receive their interest and in time the various stocks be placed on a dividend basis.

Early Troubles of Atchison

Atchison, today perhaps the strongest railroad in America, was reorganized twice in the closing years of the nineteenth century, once without foreclosure in 1889 and once through receivership in 1894. The latter reorganization was a drastic affair, replacing $232,000,000 bonds and $102,000,000 stock with $97,000,000 general mortgage 4s, 1995, $52,000,000 adjustment 4s, 1995, on which interest was payable only when earned, $111,500,000 5% preferred and $102,000,000 common stock. Besides the drastic cut in fixed charges, the way to financing of improvements was opened by the reservation of a large block of general 4s for this purpose and by creation of a prior-lien mortgage. With the position of the bonds assured by the great reduction in funded debt which had occurred it remained for the normal growth of the road's business under sound management to make the junior securities valuable. The new preferred stock sold at the outset as low at 14⅛, within two years it doubled, by 1900 it had reached approximately the levels which it has held ever since as an investment issue. Just after Atchison was reorganized the new common stock sold as low as

8¼ within two years it almost trebled, in 1901 it reached 91 and likewise entered investment ranks.

Industrial corporations are a much less homogeneous group than railroads and reorganization procedure is far less standardized. In general any plan adopted to terminate a receivership is likely to be much more drastic than in the case of a railroad. Funded debt may be eliminated entirely, as in the Virginia-Carolina Chemical reorganization in 1925. If any bonds are permitted to remain outstanding, the reorganizers will probably be very particular to see that fixed charges of the new company will be well within the limits of probable earning power. Skilled reorganizers will likewise insist that the new company start business with a more than adequate supply of working capital. The speculator will study the plan with these two points especially in mind.

COMPARING MARKET VALUES

One interesting comparison may be made between the old company and the new company to the advantage of the speculator. What was the old company worth at a fair market valuation as measured by average prices for its securities in a normal year? Deduct from this figure a fair estimate of the value of the properties eliminated in process of reorganization. The change in working-capital position will be of particular interest. Now compare this figure with the market value of the securities of the new company. The latter total will probably be much smaller than the former, the difference measuring the possible appreciation in securities of the reorganized company with a recovery to its former position in the industry and in the estimation of the investment and speculative public. The speculator must weigh the chance for such a recovery in the light of his estimate of the prospects for the industry and his appraisal of the ability of the management.

Chapter XVI

Trading in Unlisted Securities

"Inever buy unlisted securities," says many an investor or speculator, thereby eliminating from his field of operations many thousands of securities which afford substantial opportunities for sound investment or for speculative profits. If he sticks to his position, he thereby ignores almost entirely such important classes of securities as bank and insurance stocks, many sound public utilities, a host of industrial issues of greater or less value. To include so great a number and variety of stocks in one sweeping condemnation would seem altogether too drastic a policy. The intelligent speculator, on the contrary, will seek to understand something of the unlisted securities market, to understand wherein trading in it differs from trading in listed securities.

Accuracy of Quotations

The first and most obvious difference between trading in listed and unlisted securities is the difficulty in getting accurate quotations on the latter. A complete report of sales on the floor of the New York Stock Exchange is published daily by *The Wall Street Journal* and by the leading daily papers of New York and other important cities. These quotations are compiled with the greatest care and are more than 99% accurate. They represent actual public transactions in a market where buyers and sellers are restricted and hedged about by all sorts of regulations for the protection of the trading and investing public. Similar quotations of actual sales on the New York Curb and out-of-town Stock Exchanges are almost as easily available and are nearly as accurate.

WASH SALES

Obviously the fact that a given stock actually sold at a given price at a certain time means something to the speculator. He has some idea at what price he can buy or sell shortly thereafter. In the case of unlisted securities the speculator has no such authentic information regarding prices. A good many unlisted securities are, to be sure, bought and sold in the weekly auctions held in Boston, New York and Philadelphia and records of these transactions are available. Transactions in individual stocks occur at irregular intervals and even then are not always an indication of the true market. While wash sales are almost impossible in trading on the floor of the Stock Exchange under the strict rules to which members are subject they are by no means uncommon in the auctions. A wash sale is a sale by a trader to himself, used to establish a market. A trader who had accumulated a large block of a given stock might bid well above its true value at a public sale in order to establish a public record which would be useful in distributing his holdings. For a very different reason many worthless or nearly worthless securities are sold annually in the auctions to establish losses for income tax purposes. A published record that an unlisted stock sold at a certain price in the auctions by no means establishes a real market for the stock at or near that price. The interested speculator should ascertain whether the quotation was the result of a single bid or whether a number of bidders sought to purchase the block.

ERRORS IN BID AND ASKED QUOTATIONS

Ordinarily the only available quotation of an unlisted security is a bid and asked quotation. Leading daily papers in financial centers are now publishing once a week or oftener such quotations for a long list of the more important unlisted stocks and bonds. These quotations are furnished by leading firms specializing in "over-the-counter" business. They are not brokers receiving a definite commission on each transaction, but are largely traders on their own account, seeking to buy as cheaply as possible and to sell as dearly as possible, both from the public and from each other. Sometimes they take a commission for executing an order for a customer, but more often they seek to make a quarter of a point or five points or whatever the traffic will bear. For this reason they naturally tend to give the bid and asked figures with a spread wide enough to allow a reasonable profit plus a margin for errors. Another source of errors in published bid and asked quotations is the probability that at any given moment a particular house may not know of the absolutely best bids and offers in the market. The net result of all these sources of error is the fact that the speculator must regard published bid and asked prices as only approximations indicating the level at about which purchases or sales may be made.

Choosing an Unlisted Broker

The speculator who is interested in an unlisted stock must naturally first get a quotation showing its approximate price and then choose the firm with which he proposes to deal. This is a matter of some difficulty. The old legal maxim *"Caveat emptor"* is applicable to the unlisted securities market with full force. Going without introduction to a firm by whom he was not known a speculator would probably pay the top price in buying and get the lowest price in selling. If he went to half a dozen firms, his inquiries might have a disastrous effect on the market. Inquiry for even a ten-share lot from several different firms might give the impression that there was active bidding for the stock and have worse results than simply throwing oneself upon the mercy of one firm. In dealing with a firm to which he was a stranger the speculator might, of course, use the simple expedient of concealing his position on the market in making his first inquiry. If he wished, for example, to buy 100 shares of a given unlisted stock, he might inquire at what price he could dispose of such a block of stock. The broker having committed himself to a bid quotation in answer would hardly be likely to name an asked figure at too great a spread from the first quotation given.

Rather than trust to any such ingenuity or to luck in seeking a trading house with which to deal the speculator would probably desire to find the most reliable firm available. To this end he would perhaps ask his bank and several brokerage firms for the names of the two or three most reliable trading houses, in their judgment. The firm getting the most votes in such an informal poll would presumably be worthy of a considerable degree of confidence. One thing the inquiring speculator would not do in the course of his investigations, that is, ask anyone whether such-and-such a firm were "all right." Unless the person asked were on the most intimate terms with him, or the firm about which he asked of notoriously bad reputation, the answer would probably be so cautious as to be of little value.

The difficulty of choosing a trading house might be obviated, if the broker through whom the speculator deals in listed securities maintained a trading department. Many of the leading Stock Exchange houses do maintain such departments for the convenience of their customers. While it is likely that on any given stock such a trading department may not have as close a market as some one trading house it is at least in a better position to trade than the individual customer and is at his service as a rule on a commission basis.

ALWAYS A SPREAD

Perhaps the principal objection to unlisted securities voiced by the speculator who is accustomed to dealing in listed stocks is the excessive spread between the bid and asked price. In point of fact this spread is not usually excessive and the critic often fails to realize that there is a comparable spread in listed stocks. The average trader, however, is accustomed to seeing quotations of listed stocks in terms of sales, seldom seeing the bid and asked figures, while in the case of unlisted issues he usually sees the bid and asked figures, almost never sales prices. At any given moment, however, there must always be some spread between bid and asked figures. The size of the spread is in inverse ratio to the activity of the stock. In the case of a very active stock like United States Steel, the spread may be only one-eighth or one-quarter of a point. A fairly active stock may be quoted from one-half to two points lower on the bid than on the asked side. If a stock only sells one or two hundred shares a day, the spread may reach four or five points. In the case of that large number of listed stocks which sell only infrequently there may be a spread of ten or even twenty points. For example, as this is written Fidelity-Phoenix Fire Insurance is quoted at 180 bid, 190 asked on the floor of the Stock Exchange. A trader in the stock could do better than this in the outside market, where it is simultaneously quoted 183 bid, 188 asked.

The Banker's Attitude

Another objection of the speculator to unlisted securities is their relatively limited acceptability as collateral for bank loans. The banker who is lending the money of his depositors on collateral security is interested primarily in the marketability of the collateral rather than in its quality. He prefers a highly speculative active listed stock which he could sell at a few minutes' notice to a high-grade investment issue with a narrow market which he could sell only with difficulty. It is much easier for the banker, furthermore, to determine how much he can safely loan on a listed stock whose quotation is immediately available than on an unlisted stock of which he may never have heard. It is a great deal easier to pick up *The Wall Street Journal* on his desk and see where a given stock actually sold on the Stock Exchange than it is to find the market for an unlisted stock and having found it to determine roughly how broad or narrow it may be. In the case of an unlisted stock with a narrow market the conscientious banker might feel impelled to give some weight to the factor of intrinsic value. He would thus be involved in the necessity of a still more tedious investigation. All in all, it is not surprising that the listed stock is preferred by the banker who is approached for a time or call loan.

"Hard-Boiled" Brokers Preferred

If the banker prefers listed securities as collateral, it follows that the broker shows the same preference. The broker who carries accounts on margin for his customers gets a substantial part of the necessary funds by repledging their securities at the banks. If he accepts from his customer securities upon which he cannot get a loan from his bank, he will quickly get into a dangerously "frozen" condition. Under these circumstances all the good collateral in his office might be in the banks and the bulk of his own capital tied up in unacceptable securities. A sudden break in the market which wiped out some of his large customers and put their accounts "under water" might in that case be disastrous. In general the speculator who trades on margin will find that the broker who is most "hard-boiled" in requiring him to maintain an adequate margin, most strict in his requirements of marketability in the securities offered to him as collateral, will be the safest broker with whom he can deal. In time of stress it is not such a broker who closes his doors. The broker who accepts business on dangerously thin margins, or on poor collateral in an effort to get greater volume, is not the safest broker to tie to.

Bargains in Obscurity

Despite the obvious disadvantages of the unlisted securities market, the fact that the number of securities available far exceeds the number of listed securities should alone cause the speculator to pay some attention to this field. Failure to do so will result in his missing many bargains. Moreover, all but an insignificant fraction of the stocks of financial institutions, on the whole the best investment stocks available and frequently the best speculations available, find their sole market off the floor of the Stock Exchange. The very obscurity of the outside market is an advantage to the alert speculator. Stocks often sell at ridiculously low levels for considerable periods merely because few people know anything about them. The speculator who discovers a stock in this situation does not need to know the general trend of the market, he does not need to foresee future growth in the company's earnings. If the stock is selling well below the level which current earnings and position justify, and there is nothing in sight to impair its position in the near future, he may be sure that others will discover it and that in time it will rise to a reasonable price level. Activity in the unlisted market is often the forerunner of introduction to Stock Exchange trading. A large part of the money made by bulls on stocks which have this history is frequently made before listing takes place.

Financial Institution Stocks

Perhaps the safest speculation obtainable is the stock of a financial institution, purchasable as a rule only in the outside market. With the growth of a community or of the country in wealth and population, banks and insurance companies grow even faster. The financial organization of society becomes more intricate as material civilization advances and the services of such institutions become constantly more indispensable. A large

233

bank or insurance company is thus almost bound to grow in size and in the value of its stock over a period of years. The far-sighted investor who buys the stock of such an institution and holds it will almost surely reap handsome profits in a few years. This is hardly speculation in the ordinary sense of the term, but the trader who is looking for more immediate profits at least has the satisfaction of knowing, if expected profits fail to materialize quickly, that he has a sound investment and that his profits are merely postponed.

BANKING: NOT A ROUTINE MATTER

Naturally the speculator interested in bank and insurance stocks will want to select his stocks intelligently, as he would in any other field. Superficially, banking, for example, looks like a very simple business. The banker accumulates deposits on which he pays 2% or less and then lends the bulk of them to his customers at 4% or 6%. Given the capitalization of the bank and its volume of deposits, it would seem that simple arithmetic should show the rate of earnings. As it happens, banking is no more conducted on a dead level of uniformity than any other business. Given two banks with substantially the same capital, same surplus and same volume of deposits, one will probably earn far more than the other—its stock sell considerably higher.

THE BANK'S FINANCIAL STATEMENT

A bank's financial statement differs from that of another sort of business enterprise in that its principal items are in terms of money or the equivalent of money. The following is a typical statement of a strong national bank:

Assets

Loans and discounts.....................	$42,086,204
United States bonds......................	9,412,296
Other bonds and securities...........	3,177,938
Banking house.............................	2,736,202
Cash and due from banks.............	17,534,164
Customers' liability a/c acceptances	1,870,380
	$76,817,184

Liabilities

Capital	$3,000,000
Surplus..	2,000,000
Undivided profits	4,690,687
Deposits	61,972,206
Bills payable	1,000,000
Bankers' acceptances endorsed......	2,252,587
Acceptances outstanding	1,901,704
	$76,817,184

CASH AND CASH EQUIVALENTS

With two exceptions all the items on the assets side of the balance sheet represent cash or loans of cash. The exceptions are the banking house, a permanent investment which may fluctuate in value considerably, and "other securities." Bonds, of course, are merely long-time loans of cash. Stocks, however, do not carry the assurance that their holders will receive a given sum in cash on a fixed date. On the liabilities side all the items represent cash owed by the bank, on demand or on fixed dates, except the three net-worth items, capital, surplus and undivided profits. These represent the stockholders' equity in the bank. In a bank statement surplus is normally a round amount, representing a definite fund established by the sale of the stock at a premium and increased by definite appropriations from undivided profits. It is usually considered as sacred as capital itself. Undivided profits, on the other hand, represent accumulated earnings not appropriated for dividends or additions to surplus.

THE DEPOSITOR'S ANALYSIS

It has already been noted that from a depositor's viewpoint the statement reproduced exhibits a condition of strength. The analysis is simple. Leaving out the acceptances, which are contingent liabilities, the bank owes just under $63,000,000, of which probably a substantial part is not payable on demand but on specified dates. To meet this debt, it has over $17,500,000 cash in its own vaults or deposited in other banks. It has just under $9,500,000 government bonds which could be sold at a *few* hours' notice or used as collateral at the Federal Reserve Bank. Here is a total of $27,000,000 surely available to meet unexpected withdrawals. This is equal to 43% of the amount owed by the bank. In addition, an unknown portion of the loans and discounts items consists of call loans secured by Stock Exchange collateral and payable on demand. A further large portion consists of loans eligible for rediscount at the Federal Reserve Bank. When it is considered that a large part of the deposits were owed to customers who were also borrowers for an even larger total, it will be seen that the position of the bank on the date of the statement was impregnable.

From the stockholder's standpoint the statement was also one of great strength. Surplus and undivided profits were more than double the amount of stock outstanding, giving the stock a book value of more than $320 a share. Deposits were equal to 6.4 times the total net worth. If we assume that the bank can lend its funds on the average at 4% and pays on the average

2% on its deposits, gross earnings will be 4% on net worth plus the difference between the two rates or 2% on deposits. Since deposits are 6.4 times net worth, total earnings on net worth will be 16.8%. Multiply that by 3.2 to get gross earnings, theoretically, of 53.8% out of which the bank must absorb its losses, pay its taxes and expenses. Having started on a career of assumptions let us further assume that these require 1½% on resources. Deductions from gross income will then be 35.6% on capital, leaving a net of 18.2% on the par value of the stock. Some such calculation could be made for any bank.

A WIDE RANGE OF ACTIVITIES

Any such theoretical calculations are largely vitiated by the factor of management. The ratios of losses and expenses vary widely as between different banks and so does the ratio of gross earnings to resources. In a large modern bank there are many possibilities for activities outside the field of taking deposits and making loans. The bank may have a foreign department, buying and selling foreign currencies for its customers, a trust department, acting as executor and trustee of estates, a corporate trust department, holding property in trust for bondholders under corporate mortgages, a transfer department, handling corporate transfer books and paying dividends for corporate customers, a bond department and many others. It may have a securities subsidiary which takes part in bond underwritings and similar activities. Having approximately the same financial set-up a strictly commercial bank will probably not enjoy the earning power of a bank which goes the whole distance in branching out into other fields.

A bank statement offers few points for analysis. The principal asset, loans and discounts, may in any given case be 99.9% equivalent to cash or it may consist to a considerable extent of frozen loans to borrowers who are in financial difficulties. In the statement itself the analyst will find no hint as to the quality of the loans and discounts. In general he may assume that the loans of a large bank are good. This statement may not be 100% accurate in a year like 1907 or 1921, but it is nearly enough so for practical purposes.

DETERMINING BOOK VALUE

In analyzing a bank's statement the speculator will first determine book value of the stock. Normally the stock will sell well above its book value. He will next find by a comparison of successive statements how the deposits are growing, whether the bank is growing faster or more slowly than its principal competitors. Next he will compare the undivided profits items of successive statements. The increase in undivided profits and surplus plus the amount of dividends paid equal the net earnings for the period. The speculator will naturally wish to buy the stock of a strong bank which shows rapid growth and large and growing earning power.

It sometimes happens that a comparison of balance sheets does not reveal the full earnings of a bank. The National City Bank of New York, for example, largest of America's banks, owns all the capital stock of the National City Co., leading distributor of bonds to the investing public. It is possible to determine the earnings of the National City Bank itself by a comparison of its statements, but the earnings of the subsidiary bond-selling organization are not disclosed. Similarly the Fletcher Savings Bank & Trust Co. of Indianapolis owns all the capital stock of the Fletcher Joint Stock Land Bank. Earnings of the latter cannot be ascertained from the statements of the former, though in this instance separate statements of the subsidiary institution are available. Where such hidden assets and hidden earnings exist the speculator must guess as best he can their importance. Such mysteries are the breath of life to many speculators.

The Fire Insurance Company

The bank owes its depositors fixed sums of money at any given moment; the fire insurance company carries a possible liability equal to many times its entire resources. It never knows when it may be called upon to make good a substantial portion of that liability. By scattering its risks, however, by not insuring too much property in the same community, too many houses, even, on the same street, too much property of the same kind, by risking only a small fraction of its resources on any one property, the fire insurance company eliminates risk in large part. Its business looks like an enormous gamble, but actually the large fire insurance company is one of the safest vehicles of investment. It makes profits in two ways. First, the premiums received should exceed the losses sustained and expenses of running the business, thereby yielding an underwriting profit. Second, it has at any time a large volume of premiums in hand which together with its capital and surplus are largely invested in stocks and bonds. These investments, if well made, yield it interest and dividend income and capital gains. Security holdings are revalued annually and surplus adjusted accordingly. In the case of the best-managed companies profits accrue from this source with considerable regularity.

The following statement exhibits the condition of a large fire insurance company as of July 1 for two successive years:

Assets

	Later year	Earlier year
Bonds and stocks	$60,641,147	$50,315,929
Real estate	1,709,574	1,663,630
Loans on bond and mortgage	5,200	338,488
Premiums and cost of collections	4,238,261	4,011,455

Accrued interest and dividends	553,605	490,944
Cash	1,773,059	2,223,881
	$68,930,846	$59,044,327

Liabilities

Unearned premiums	$27,140,738	$23,217,408
Losses in process of adjustment	2,940,498	2,644,180
All other claims	757,415	876,893
Reserve for div. and contingencies	1,735,000	1,600,000
Reserve for market fluctuation in		
securities	3,000,000	....
Capital stock	10,000,000	10,000,000
Surplus	23,357,195	20,705,846
	$68,930,846	$59,044,327

SOME TECHNICALITIES

The meaning of the various terms in these balance sheets is clear enough for the most part. "Premiums and cost of collection" represents premiums in the hands of agents, not yet remitted to the company. On the other side of the balance sheet "losses in process of adjustment" represents damages by fire to insured property reported to the company for which it has not settled on the date of the balance sheet. The most mysterious item to the layman is that of "unearned premiums." Clearly the company does not actually owe its policy-holders the hundreds of millions of dollars which would be required to pay for the simultaneous destruction of all the property insured. This is only a contingent liability, only a small fraction of which will conceivably become actual liability. It does, nevertheless, owe its policy-holders a definite amount, the sum which they could demand by asking cancelation of their policies. If a given building is insured for one year for a premium of $3600 and a balance sheet is drawn up thirty days later, the company will have earned only $300 of the premium, the balance will be an unearned premium liability.

The volume of business which a company does is indicated by the size of its unearned premium reserve. In the merger of two companies the purchaser is usually willing to pay a substantial sum for this business. The book value of an insurance company stock is capital plus surplus divided by number of shares outstanding. The liquidating value of the company is the book value plus 40%—as a fairly accurate rule of thumb—of the unearned premiums. In calculating earnings, similarly, it is customary to add dividends paid during the period, the increase in surplus and 40% of the increase in unearned premiums. The company whose statement is shown paid 24% on its capital in dividends and increased its surplus by an amount equal to 26.50%. Forty per cent of the increase in unearned premiums was equal to another 15.60%, giving total earnings for the period of 66.10%, after deducting $3,000,000 as a reserve against depreciation of securities.

OFFICIAL REPORTS

Fire insurance companies must report their affairs in great detail to the insurance commissioners of the various states. Hence the speculator can ascertain whether the company in which he is interested makes on the average an underwriting profit or an underwriting loss over a period of years. More companies sustain losses than make profits on underwriting, but the best-managed companies make small profits in the long run. He can also find whether the company is regularly increasing its volume of business, standing still or losing ground. He can then compare value of securities held with their cost and obtain some light on the ability of the management in this important aspect of its operations. The stock of the company which makes the best showing in these three important respects will make the greatest appeal *to* him.

Life Insurance Liabilities Certain

Life insurance differs from fire insurance in that the liability to policy-holders can be accurately calculated on the basis of mortality tables. The companies fix their rates in accordance with old mortality tables and also select their risks by medical examination so that there is a hidden surplus in the policy-holders' reserve in this case also. It amounts to perhaps 10% of the reserve. Liquidating value of a life insurance company stock and earnings of the company are calculated in the same way as for a fire insurance company except that this ratio instead of 40% is applied to the reserve. Life insurance is a much safer business than fire insurance, its continued growth is a remarkably stable phenomenon. From the standpoint of the speculator or investor it is a pity that there are only a few life insurance stocks available.

The stocks of financial institutions form the blue-ribbon group among unlisted securities. In the over-the-counter market there are also hundreds of industrial and utility stocks worthy the attention of the intelligent speculator.

CHAPTER XVII

Options and Arbitrage

P uts, calls, spreads and straddles are a mysterious subject to the ordinary speculator in spite of the fact that they afford one of the best possible media of gambling on a shoe-string with any chance of success, offer the only form of insurance against loss available to the margin trader, give absolute protection to the short seller against the threat of a corner. While every British stock trader is familiar with the theory and the practical usefulness of options, many Americans have speculated for years without having learned more of options than their names.

What Options Are

Briefly an option is a right to buy from or sell to the maker a given amount of a given stock at a stipulated price within a limited period or to do either. The maker or writer of a call, for example, permits the holder to call upon him for a specified number of shares at the specified price during the life of the option. The maker of a put agrees to purchase from its holder at any time within the option period. The maker of a spread agrees either to purchase from the holder at one price or to sell to him at a higher price. The maker of a straddle agrees either to buy from or to sell to the holder at the same price.

In the New York market 100 shares is the unit of trading in options. Options for 25 or 50 shares may be purchased, but at a less advantageous price. Occasionally options are written on a large scale, 1,000-share options being not uncommon and 10,000-share options not unknown. The great bulk of the business is done at a fixed price, the purchaser of the option paying $137.50 for a put or a call on 100 shares (plus a $2 tax in the case of a call) or double that sum for a spread. Of this amount the maker of the option gets $112.50 and the balance is divided equally between the purchaser's broker and the specialist.

THE WRITER'S POSITION

At first sight it might appear illogical that one should be able to buy an option on 100 shares of any stock for a fixed amount. The option, however, is not written at the market at the moment it is made, but at a price some distance away from the market. Options are thus commonly quoted so many points up or down for thirty days, the standard term of the great bulk of options. For example, options on United States Steel common may be quoted four down and six up at a given moment. Suppose that at that moment Steel is selling at 140. The quotation means that for $139.50 a trader may buy a thirty-day call on 100 shares at 146, for $137.50 a thirty-day put at 136 or for $277 an option permitting him either to sell 100 shares to the maker at 136 or to purchase 100 shares from him at 146—in other words, a spread. In the case of a stock selling around 20 the quotation of a put or call might be as close to the market as half a point. In a highly excited market options might not be available closer to the market than ten or twelve points even on a stock selling under par. Naturally the writer of such privileges would not make them if he thought there were much chance of their being exercised. Some business is done in options at the market, but in this case the cash cost to the purchaser will be much greater than $137.50 for 100 shares for thirty days. It will probably be several hundred dollars, varying with the state of the market in general and of the optioned stock in particular. Some business is also done in options running longer than thirty days, but this also is exceptional.

Speculating on a Shoe-String

From the standpoint of the man who buys options as a means of speculating on a shoe-string, their advantages are clear. To the average broker and the average trader, anyone who trades in lots smaller than a hundred shares is a piker. On a stock selling at any respectable figure, a sound brokerage house will require a minimum margin of $1000. The man with only two or three hundred dollars and the itch to speculate usually does not have patience to accumulate such a sum before embarking on his venture nor does he wish to be a piker. Options offer him his opportunity. For $137.50 he can "control" 100 shares of almost any active listed stock for thirty days. Suppose that he selects Steel as the vehicle for his operations, believes that it is cheap and buys a call, six points above the market. He may be perfectly correct in his belief that the stock is intrinsically cheap, but he is gambling on the prospect that it will have a fairly extended movement within a comparatively short period. On his initial venture he will probably come to a realization for the first time of how short a period thirty days really is. Before he even begins to get back the price of the option the stock must rise six points. Another 1⅝ -point rise will be necessary before he will have retrieved his initial capital and the commission on selling in the open market the stock which he is to buy from the maker of the option. When the stock has risen 7⅝ points, however, even a moderate further rise will mean doubling and trebling the amount risked in the operation.

Limited Risk

While the chances are that in the case of any given option the stock optioned will not move far enough within the life of the privilege to yield its holder a profit, such a method of trading has at least the virtue of involving the trader in a very limited risk of loss. If he pays $139.50 for a call on 100 shares of Steel at 146 and the stock moves absolutely contrary to his expectations and goes to 130 within the life of the privilege, he has merely lost its cost. If he had bought 100 shares of Steel on margin, his loss would have been far heavier, though in the later case he would be able to cling to his position for an indefinite period, perhaps only on condition of putting up more margin. This advantage of the margin trader as against the option trader is not so great as it looks. The option trader who found himself out the cost of his option at the end of thirty days in such a case as that cited could buy another call, at a better price, and still be out of pocket much less than the loss suffered by the margin trader in the case we have assumed. In fact, a ten-point loss to the margin trader would equal the cost to the option trader of extending his option over a total period of seven months.

TRADING AGAINST AN OPTION

In the case cited it has been assumed that the holder of the option merely waited until the day the option expired and then exercised his option, if the market permitted him to do so profitably, and otherwise did nothing. It by no means follows that this is the course the option trader will pursue. Suppose that within a week or ten days after the trader bought his call on Steel that stock had risen to but not beyond the option price. In the meantime he had changed his views as to the market and believed that a reaction was impending. He would then sell 100 shares of Steel at the option price, being protected against loss on his short commitment by his option. A price fifteen points under the option figure on the expiration date of the privilege would then mean for this trader not a loss but a handsome profit. It will be noted further that on the short sale the broker would not require more than a point or so of margin, since his customer would be protected by the option.

Converting a Call into a Straddle

Vary our suppositious case again and assume that when Steel had risen to the option price the trader was beset by doubts as to its probable movement during the remaining life of the privilege. In this condition of uncertainty he would logically sell short only 50 shares of Steel at the option price. The direction of the stock's movement would now be a matter of indifference to him. He would profit whichever way it moved, granted only that it moved far enough. If the stock fell, he would cover his short sale of 50 shares and permit the call to expire unexercised. If, on the contrary, it advanced, he would exercise his option on the 100 shares, delivering 50 shares against his short contract and selling 50 shares at a profit. Such an operation in reality constitutes the conversion of a call into a straddle. The same result would be achieved by buying half the shares covered by a put at the option price. Conceivably the holder of an option might trade against it a number of times during the course of its life.

Options as Insurance

Thus far options have been considered as a means of speculating on limited capital with risk of loss definitely limited and potential profits unlimited. As a matter of fact, only about one-quarter of the business in options is done with such speculation in view. The bulk of the purchases of options are made as a means of cheap insurance against excessive losses. Suppose that a trader is short of Steel at 140 and not too sure of his position. He can protect himself in one of two ways. He may enter a stop-loss order a few points above the market or he may purchase a call. Suppose that two traders are in this position. One of them buys a call six points above the market, the other enters a stop-loss order at 146. Carry our assumption a step further and assume that within thirty days Steel advances to 147 and then abruptly reacts ten points. Under these circumstances the trader who tried to protect himself with a stop-loss order automatically covered at 146 and on a 100-share trade took a loss of $600 plus commissions. The other trader was protected by his call so that he could not lose more than $600 plus the cost of his call no matter how high the stock went. He was thus able to watch the advance to 147 with equanimity and to take advantage of the subsequent decline, covering his short sale at three points gross profit or a net profit of $300 less the cost of the call and commissions.

Steel is a comparatively slow-moving issue, yet even in that stock wide movements may take place which offer the holder of an option substantial opportunities for profit or at least valuable protection against loss on margin trades. In June, 1926, for example, Steel fluctuated by weeks as follows :

Week of	June 1-5	June 7-12	June 14-19	June 21-26	June 28-30
High	126½	137	139¾	139¼	144
Low	122½	125⅜	134½	136¼	137¼

More volatile stocks frequently offer far greater opportunity for profit to the trader in options.

MOTIVES FOR WRITING OPTIONS

One thing which often puzzles the student of options at the outset is the apparent imbecility of the writer of the option. Why should anyone, it may be asked, write a call on 100 shares of a certain stock a few points above the market for a compensation of $112.50 when his potential loss in case the market goes against him is unlimited and may easily reach $1000 or more? On a little analysis his position is not so absurd as it looks. Suppose that a trader holds 100 shares of Steel now selling at 140. He believes that it is fully worth that price, but is willing to sell it six points higher. He might express his willingness by giving his broker a selling order limited at 146 or by writing a call at that price. In the latter event he receives $112.50—additional profit if the call is exercised, velvet if it is not. A trader who had taken a short position on Steel might write a put from similar motives.

BUYING ON A SCALE DOWN

A trader may make an option from a different motive. Suppose that he is bullish on Steel and is seeking to accumulate 1000 shares as cheaply as possible. He may put in limited buying orders at prices below the market or he may write puts. He is as likely to get his stock by one method as by the other, but in the latter case he gets the premium paid for the options as partial offset to the purchase price of the stock or as consolation prize in case the puts are not exercised. The trader who wishes to take a short position might similarly prefer to write calls than to place limited selling orders above the market.

It sometimes happens that the maker of options has an opportunity to reinsure by the purchase of similar options at more advantageous prices. Suppose that he has sold a call on 100 shares of Steel at 146, a reaction has occurred and he can now buy a call on 100 shares of Steel at 142. By so doing he will be out of pocket only $25, the commissions to his own broker and the option specialists on the call he wrote. If Steel advances beyond 146, both calls will be exercised and he will have $400 gross profit. If it advances beyond 142 but not to 146, he will have a small profit on the call he purchased. If it does not advance, he will have had insurance against loss on the call he wrote at negligible cost.

In the limits of a short chapter it is not possible to treat adequately the possible ramifications of trading in options. The speculator who experiments in this field will find fascinating opportunities for the exercise of his ingenuity. There are one or two technical points, nevertheless, that require mention. The matter of dividends is one important detail. When a stock sells ex-dividend during the life of a privilege the option price is reduced on that date by the amount of the dividend.

The Maker's Responsibility

Of obviously vital importance to the trader in options is the responsibility of the maker of the option. In the New York market an option is not considered good unless it is guaranteed by a member of the New York Stock Exchange. When such a guaranty is attached to it the responsibility of the maker is no longer in question. This point is particularly important because options afford an excellent field of operations for the bucket-shop operator. Such a member of the financial underworld may advertise in mediums which are not too particular in some such fashion as this: "Do you know that for $25 you can control 25 shares of any listed stock?" On replying to such an advertisement the small trader will be offered a seven-day option on his favorite stock. If he makes any money on the trade, he will not receive cash at once, but instead will be urged to purchase other options. If his customers become too successful and too insistent, a "broker" of this kind will simply close his doors.

Long-Term Options

Within the past two or three years a new type of option has appeared on the market in increasing quantities. This is the long-term stock purchase warrant, usually attached to a bond as a "sweetener" to assist its flotation. While no individual in his senses would write an option good for years instead of a month or two, a corporation may properly give long-term options on its own stock as an extra inducement to secure additional capital. One of the earliest important instances of such financing occurred with the offering of 100-year 6% debentures of the American Power & Light Co. to its stockholders in 1916. As an added incentive for their subscriptions—at a price of 93—the company attached to each $1000 debenture a warrant entitling its holder to subscribe for 10 shares of the company's common stock at $100 a share at any time up to March 1, 1931. It was six years before this privilege had any more than a nominal value. Many of the warrants were detached by the bondholders and found a separate market at a few dollars apiece. In 1922 the stock crossed par and the option warrants began to have real value. In the following year the stock reached 177 and in 1924 a high of 500 on the eve of a ten-for-one split-up. At $500 a share for the stock the option warrant originally attached to a $1000 debenture and valued by the market as low as $30 in 1921 became worth $4000.

In every month of the six years during which American Power & Light warrants had no substantial value, that company reported a gain in gross revenues over the corresponding period of the previous year and in all but one or two months a gain in net. Under these circumstances, it is rather remarkable that anyone was ever willing to part with a fifteen-year call on the stock.

Detached Warrants Scarce

Option warrants are usually detachable in form. In such a case there will ordinarily be a separate market for the bonds with warrants, bonds without warrants and the warrants separately. Since warrants attached to a bond issue cost the original purchaser, nominally at least, nothing, he will ordinarily be reluctant to detach them and sell them separately. Not only will the intelligent bondholder be unwilling to swap a handsome potential future profit for a small present certainty but the careless bondholder will be prevented by mere inertia from selling his warrants. Accordingly the marketability in such case will be much better for bonds with warrants than for bonds without warrants or for the warrants themselves. It is sometimes possible to buy bonds with warrants, detach the warrants and sell the bonds without warrants to the sinking fund, but in general it is frequently not an easy matter to buy warrants. In some cases, furthermore, option warrants are non-detachable in form and will be honored, either for a limited period or for the life of the warrants, only if presented with the bonds to which they were originally attached. It may sometimes be worth while to detach non-detachable warrants where the prohibition is limited in time. In December, 1925, for example, an issue of five-year notes of the Rand Kardex Bureau, Inc., was sold carrying stock purchase warrants detachable after one year. A few months later a block of these notes minus the stock purchase warrants was reoffered by one of the firms in the original syndicate. Under the circumstances the warrants detached did not become good for several months, but then they had a four-year life without penalty.

Variety of Terms

The terms of option warrants possess an infinite variety. Some option warrants are issued with a life of only a few months, others are good in perpetuity. In the latter category are the option warrants originally attached to Southeastern Power & Light debenture 6s, 2025. Each debenture was accompanied by ten warrants permitting the holder to subscribe to one share of common stock at any time for $50. That portion of the public interested in warrants took the lesson of the American Power & Light warrants so to heart that as this is written the Southeastern warrants are quoted 9 bid, though the stock itself may be purchased as low as 28. Ordinarily warrants run several years, but a period of more than ten years is an unusual life for these privileges.

Option warrants are frequently issued on a sliding-scale basis, good at a certain price for a year or two and then at a higher price. Universal Pictures warrants issued with preferred stock, for example, entitled their holders to buy the company's common stock at $35 a share for three years, then at $40 a share for two years. Another sort of sliding-scale arrangement is typified by the warrants attached to an issue of German General Electric 6½ s sold late in 1925. The bond issue was for $10,000,000 and each $1000 bond carried one warrant. The first 2360 warrants presented entitled their holders to purchase 18 shares of common stock at $24 a share, the next 2150 called for 18 shares at $26.50 a share and so on, the last 1750 warrants being good for 17 shares at $34 a share. In such an arrangement there is an obvious incentive to a speedy exercise of the privilege.

THE PATIENT SPECULATOR

The option warrant as a speculative medium obviously makes a strong appeal to the man with plenty of patience and limited funds available for speculative ventures. The young man with a moderate income, for example, may find that his surplus after living expenses and the essential appropriations for life insurance premiums and cash reserves in savings banks and other sound investments is decidedly small. If he wishes to speculate with this small margin, the option running several years on a promising common stock at a fairly reasonable price offers a very attractive vehicle. If he has, for example, $500 a year with which to speculate, he might buy 50 shares of stock on a ten-point margin and probably lose his money or he might buy options on perhaps 100 shares. If he has the will power to let them "ride" and has selected them with reasonable discrimination, there is at least a fair prospect that in some bull market before they expire his warrants may have a value several times $500.

DISADVANTAGES OF OPTIONS

The disadvantages of options are obvious. They have limited marketability and ordinarily no value as collateral for a loan. They practically never yield their holders any income, though interest-bearing warrants are not absolutely unknown. For these reasons option warrants should never be purchased separately unless there is a fairly reasonable likelihood that they will be worth several times their cost. This factor of the carrying charges of speculation is one to which the average trader gives too little attention. Presumably no one enters on speculation without anticipating an average return over a period of years of at least 10% on his money. At 10% compounded semi-annually money doubles itself in a trifle more than seven years. In buying so highly speculative a security as an option warrant the speculator will naturally convince himself that he has an opportunity to double and treble his money in a considerably shorter period.

MENTAL INERTIA

The very useful knowledge of the possibilities in options is sometimes withheld from a trader by mental inertia on his part. Holding the unfounded belief that the subject is too technical and complicated to be comprehended without an undue amount of mental effort, he may remain in wilful ignorance. The same barrier sometimes prevents a speculator from making a proper and profitable study of arbitrage. Briefly defining it, arbitrage is the simultaneous purchase and sale of identical or equivalent securities in different markets at a profit. Where the same security is the vehicle of trading in two widely separated markets, an opportunity for arbitrage trading obviously arises. Before the war arbitrage operations between New York and London were conducted on an extensive scale. At a given moment an active stock like Steel might be selling higher in one market than in the other by enough of a margin so that sale of a block in the higher market and purchase in the lower market would cover commissions, cost of transportation of the certificates and loss of interest on the money involved during transit, cable costs and other expenses and leave a profit. Such operations are sure to be undertaken whenever there is trading in a security in two markets. One of any two markets will be the more active in any given stock. Designating this as the primary market and the other as the secondary, it is obvious that the arbitrage traders perform a valuable service for traders operating in the secondary market in keeping prices there closely in line with prices in the primary market. This sort of arbitrage trading is a field for the specialist and not for the average trader.

Arbitrage in Equivalents

Arbitrage in equivalent securities is a rather different matter and affords an opportunity for the non-professional. The simplest example of "equivalent securities" is afforded by the issuance of subscription rights for the purchase of new stock. American Telephone, for instance, has financed a large part of its new capital requirements for many years by the offer of additional stock to its shareholders at intervals. Usually such offerings carry the option of payment in full on a given date or of payment in installments. Instead of taking an actual offering it will be simpler to illustrate by a suppositious case. Assume that American Telephone announces late in April an offering of new stock at par to stockholders of record May 15, stock to be paid for in full June 15, in the ratio of one new share for each five shares held. A stockholder of record May 15 will then receive for each share held one "right" or subscription warrant. He will need five rights in order to be entitled to subscribe to one new share at par. Suppose that on the day the offering is announced Telephone is selling at

135. Trading at once begins in the rights and every broker at once proceeds to calculate the value of the rights. In doing so he must remember that the value of each share of stock includes until May 15 the value of one right. The calculation is then very simple. The difference between the market for the stock and the subscription price divided by the number of rights required to buy one share plus the one right included in the market price equals the value of the right. The equation in this case would be:

$$\text{Value of right } \frac{\text{Market (135)—Subscription price (100)}}{\text{Number of rights required (5)+ 1}}$$

Each right is then worth under these circumstances $5.83. To the nearest sixteenth this is 5 13/16. In a less active stock than American Telephone the minimum fluctuation in the rights would probably be an eighth of a point. After the stock sells rights, the premium over the subscription price would be divided by the number of rights required to subscribe for one share.

From the standpoint of arbitrage transactions it makes no difference whether one is buying or selling the stock itself or the rights. Each right with enough others to permit a subscription to one share is equivalent to a share for future delivery minus the subscription price. When rights make their appearance, interested brokers immediately compile a table of equivalent values for all prices at which the stock and rights are likely to sell. Whenever there is a discrepancy thereafter until the rights expire floor traders conduct arbitrage trades which bring the two back into line. This is another type of arbitrage trading suited only to the professional.

Another case of equivalent securities occurs when a stock is split by payment of a large stock dividend or reduction of par value or both. Between the declaration of such a dividend or the announcement of a split-up and the actual consummation, there may be several weeks during which the old and new stocks will sell side by side on the Stock Exchange—perhaps the old on the Stock Exchange and the new for a time on the Curb. If the two get out of line on the basis of their equivalent values, there will be another opportunity for arbitrage trading.

ARBITRAGE IN REORGANIZATIONS

Reorganizations and mergers offer the non-professional trader his best opportunities for profitable arbitraging. In a complex reorganization involving a number of different securities, it sometimes happens that the various old securities and new securities involved sell out of line with each other for weeks. Where an arbitrage trade involves buying old securities and selling against them new securities which are traded in on a "when, as and if issued" basis there is, of course, a certain risk that the reorganization plan may not finally be adopted, that the "when issued" trades may be canceled as a result and that the speculator may thus be stuck with the outstanding securities, which he would not have purchased except as part of an arbitrage transaction. Ordinarily a reorganization plan which has been announced in all its details by a committee including the bankers most interested in the company will go through without trouble so that this risk is very slight, but it does exist. Occasionally it is possible to arbitrage in securities which are all on a "when issued" basis. Then, if the plan fails of adoption, the arbitrageur has lost nothing but paper profits. Early in 1925 such an opportunity presented itself in connection with the reorganization of the Wickwire-Spencer Steel Corp. Under the plan, preferred stockholders were given the right to subscribe to new 7% five-year notes at par in the ratio of $1000 notes for each 50 shares and also to receive 175 shares of new common stock. For a considerable period the preferred rights and new common had a good market on a "when issued" basis. At one time the preferred rights were selling around 8 and the new common around 5. Disregarding commissions, this was equivalent to a price of 52½ for the new notes. The arithmetic is as follows:

Cost of 50 rights @ 8	$400.00
Subscription $1000 notes....................	1,000.00
Cost $1000 notes and 175 shares com.	$1,400.00
Proceeds sales 175 shares @ 5..............	875.00

While the new notes had practically no market at this time, it was clear that such obligations of a newly reorganized company would be worth substantially more than 52½, especially if the new stocks were worth $5 a share. So it turned out and for a considerable period after the reorganization plan went into effect, the 7% notes sold around 75.

ARBITRAGE ON A MERGER

Announcement of a merger plan sometimes creates opportunities to arbitrage, particularly if the plan involves several different securities. The proposal of the Van Sweringens to create a new railroad system by leasing the Chesapeake & Ohio, Erie, Hocking Valley, Nickel Plate and Pere Marquette to a new company, stockholders of the five roads to exchange their stocks for stock of the new road in various ratios, made an excellent opening for arbitrageurs. For a year and a half before the Interstate Commerce Commission turned down the plan, the old stocks continued to sell on the Stock Exchange while the new stocks sold on the Curb. Prices were frequently far out of line with each other. For many months it was possible to buy Erie common and sell the equivalent amount in new Nickel Plate stock against it at a profit of several points. By a smaller margin Pere Marquette usually sold under its equivalent value while Chesapeake & Ohio usually ruled above it. As it happened the market's appraisal in this instance was correct. The plan was disapproved by the Interstate Commerce Commission and the arbitrageurs' paper profits were wiped out. The stocks concerned quickly recovered, however, to levels equal to or higher than those at which they had sold while the plan was in prospect. The incident nevertheless suggests a lesson for the speculator. In buying a stock for an arbitrage profit through selling its equivalent in a "when issued" stock he should be sure that if the "when issued" stock should never be issued, he would be content to take his chance on the old stock.

HEDGING

Akin to arbitrage is hedging. This consists in buying one stock and selling another. A speculator may be led to this procedure by uncertainty as to the trend of the market. Perhaps he is interested in the motors, but is not sure whether the group has reached a market peak or whether still higher levels are in sight. Under this circumstance it would be logical to buy the strongest stock in the group and go short an equivalent amount of an intrinsically weaker issue. If the market turned downward, the profit on the short commitment should outstrip the loss on the purchase, and vice versa. Hedging may also be adopted where one of two kindred issues seems intrinsically very much cheaper than the other. In a previous chapter the diverse trends of Bethlehem Steel and United States Steel for the years 1921-26 have been analyzed. Hedging operations in those two stocks would have been profitable at almost any time during that period. If the speculator uses bad judgment in a commitment of this sort, he may suffer the misfortune of being whipsawed, of losing money on both sides of the transaction. This fact constitutes no argument against the practice, however. To lose money is the conventional penalty for bad judgment in speculation.

CHAPTER XVIII

When Speculation Becomes Investment

"Your articles deal with speculative investment rather than with speculation," said an astute observer of both fields of activity when he had read the greater part of this series of articles. To this charge the writer was forced to plead guilty. After all it is by no means easy to draw the line between investment and speculation, between speculation and gambling. If one is to discuss the topic of speculation and perhaps thereby induce some readers to attempt it who might otherwise have left speculation alone, it is much more helpful to the average reader, much less dangerous to the reader who might misinterpret what he reads, to discuss that sort of speculation which is on the borderland of investment than the more dangerous and less useful type of speculation which borders on gambling.

FANTASTIC POSSIBILITIES

Probably the average man who opens a margin account with $1000 has at least subconsciously the idea that if he doesn't double his money in a year he will be disappointed. If he could really do this consistently and kept his profits in his operations, he would be richer than any man now alive in less than twenty-five years. Stated in this way the thing is an absurdity. In real life the man who starts speculating with a thousand dollars will either be unsuccessful or he will make something more than pure interest on his money and gradually accumulate a moderate fortune. As he grows older his natural tendency probably will be to take fewer and smaller risks, to become more an investor than a speculator.

BUSINESS MANAGEMENT

Perhaps the best sort of speculation, and the kind that is most likely to be successful, is that which regards it as the business management of a fund. With the modern tendency of business to become concentrated in larger units there is less likelihood that an ambitious individual will become sole owner and autocratic manager of a great business enterprise. There are still and always will be opportunities for a business genius to exploit a new idea of business management or a new product with phenomenal success, to duplicate in another field the success of Henry Ford with motors or F. W. Woolworth with merchandising. Comparatively few businesses can expand entirely out of earnings so that even the business genius is likely to find himself sooner or later the employee of a large group of stockholders. Anyone possessed of talent of a lesser order is almost sure to find himself in a salaried executive position, subject to a greater or less degree of control by others. In the management of his personal funds, however, any individual can give his business judgment and initiative free rein.

MEN, MATERIALS, MONEY

What does the manager of a business do? He controls men, materials and money, seeking to handle them in such a way that the business will produce a profit. If the business is to be more than a fleeting success, he must in so doing render some real public service either in transforming the materials into a form more useful to the ultimate consumer or in rendering them more readily available. Conceiving the speculator as manager of a business it will be seen that he also controls men, materials and money. The money is the starting point of his business, the materials are the securities which he buys and sells, the men are the directors and managers of the companies in whose securities he invests. His materials are not, to be sure, transformed in his

261

hands, but his very activities in buying and selling tend to make them more or less readily available to the conservative investor. In the same way he exerts an indirect influence over the men who serve him. The compensation and the tenure of office of the directors and executives of even the largest corporations depend in the long run upon the satisfaction that their services give to the intelligent speculators and investors interested in their securities. If the speculator detects evidences of incompetent management in a given corporation, he cannot "fire" the offending management, but he can give silent evidence of his disapproval by selling the corporation's securities or by leaving them alone.

Ten Commandments for Speculators

As in any business there are standards of management which cannot be disregarded by the business man, so in speculative investment it is possible to formulate certain rules which must be followed intelligently if success is to be attained. The speculator will never be a success if he attempts to follow any set of rules blindly. There will always be exceptions, he must apply his intelligence keenly in any given situation. Nevertheless, so far as the technical details contained in the seventeen previous chapters may be summarized in a few paragraphs, it may be useful to do so.

Ten precepts for the speculative investor may be stated as follows:

1. Never hold fewer than ten different securities covering five different fields of business.

2. At least once in six months reappraise every security held.

3. Keep at least half the total fund in income-producing securities.

4. Consider yield the least important factor in analyzing any stock.

5. Be quick to take losses, reluctant to take profits.

6. Never put more than 25% of a given fund into securities about which detailed information is not readily and regularly available.

7. Seek facts diligently, advice never.

8. When stocks are high, money rates low but rising, business prosperous, at least half a given fund should be placed in short-term bonds.

9. Borrow money sparingly and only when stocks are low, money rates high but falling, and business depressed.

10. Set aside a moderate proportion of available funds for the purchase of long-term options on stocks of promising companies whenever available.

MINIMIZING CHANCE

The first rule given suggests a minimum standard of diversification. It is just as important in speculation as in investment that a given fund be divided among several baskets. Diversification accomplishes three important results for the speculator. It minimizes the factor of chance, allows for an occasional error of judgment and minimizes the importance of the unknown factor. As in every other field of human activity, chance plays its part in speculation. An earthquake or some other unforeseeable "act of God" may make a mockery of the best-laid plans. No such accident will affect all securities equally, however, and diversification affords the best possible protection against the effects of accidental factors. Errors of judgment are likewise inescapable. Even the most astute speculator is likely to arrive at wrong conclusions from the data in hand 20% to 25% of the time. If he stakes his entire fund on *one* security about which his conclusion is wrong, he will be wiped out.

On the other hand, a 25% margin of error in judgment will not seriously affect the speculator who has scattered his commitments among ten different securities.

The most important factor affecting the value of any single security at any given moment is the unknown factor. Not even the president of a company knows all the facts affecting the intrinsic value of its securities. The speculator must allow a considerable margin for the *unknown,* even in the case of companies which make frequent reports of their condition and make an honest attempt to keep their stockholders and the public fully informed regarding their affairs. By sufficient diversification these unknown factors affecting individual securities cancel each other. The loss which is due to the unknown factor in one case will be counterbalanced by an unexpectedly large profit in another.

A Psychological Difficulty

It is conventional advice to the investor that he should go over his holdings in search of weak spots at least annually. The speculator will naturally watch his holdings much more closely. The second rule means something more than a mere scanning of his list of commitments and calculation of the paper profit or loss that they show. It means that the speculator should seek so far as possible to re-analyze each commitment from a detached standpoint. Psychologically this is a very difficult thing to do, to consider dispassionately a venture in which he has already risked his funds. Nevertheless, the speculator should make a determined effort to do just this. If he has 100 shares of a given stock, for example, which is selling at 90, he should disregard entirely the price that he paid for it and ask himself this question: "If I had $9000 cash today with which to purchase some security, would I choose that stock in preference to every one of the thousands of other securities available to me?" If the answer is strongly in the negative, he should sell the stock. It should make not the slightest difference in this connection whether the stock cost 50 or 130. That is a fact which is entirely beside the point, though the average individual will give it considerable weight.

Patience Essential

It is not suggested that the speculator undertake this process of re-analysis much more frequently than once in six months. If he tries to do it oftener, he is likely to fall into the evil and usually fatal habit of frequently switching his commitments. One of the essential qualifications of the successful speculator is patience. It may take years for the market in a given stock to reflect in any large degree the values which are being accumulated behind it. Twenty years of plowing earnings back into property were followed in the case of the Southern Railway by an advance in its common stock from 25 to 120 within two years. Careful analysis may detect values far in excess of market price behind a given stock. The market may not reflect these values until the combination of a bull market and a change in dividend policy supplies the necessary impetus. Even in a bull market a sound stock may lag behind the procession in a discouraging manner for weeks or months. The trader who is always looking for "action" in the market will usually jump from one stock to another during the course of a bull movement only to find at the end that he has made far less money than he would have made by putting his money in ten or a dozen carefully chosen issues at the beginning and holding them.

Necessity for Caution

The adjuration contained in the third rule, to keep at least half the fund in income-producing securities, is based on the fact that income-producing securities are as a class of higher grade than non-income-producing securities. In them the risk of severe

265

loss is far smaller than in the latter group, though the potentialities of profit are also, as a rule, smaller. It is the part of wisdom, however, for the speculator not to venture too far from shore in his operations. In case of a sudden storm it will contribute much to his peace of mind to know that at least a substantial part of his holdings consists of securities of investment grade. Not primarily for the income to be derived from them but because of the investment quality inherent in a large proportion of them is it suggested that the speculator stick to income-producing issues in large degree.

Four Classes of Stocks

Thus explained there is no conflict between the third and fourth rules. In fact, they are entirely consistent, since the best stocks normally show the lowest yields. In buying stocks for speculation it is to be assumed that the purchaser does not need income from the funds involved. Otherwise he cannot afford to speculate at all. Granted this assumption the dividends he may expect to receive are a minor consideration. He is seeking an increase in the market value of his stocks. Theoretically one might divide common stocks—the principal vehicles of speculation—into four classes. These are: (1) dividend-paying stocks of high grade, representing ownership in strong companies with good future prospects, ordinarily selling on a low-yield basis; (2) low-grade dividend-paying stocks, affording high yields because their dividends are in doubt and future outlook uncertain; (3) non-dividend-paying stocks of companies which are making definite progress in strength and earning power and are headed toward dividend ranks; (4) non-dividend-paying stocks of companies showing no evidence of growth in strength and earning power, headed perhaps for receivership. On theoretical grounds stocks of classes (1) and (3) are the stocks to buy. From one type the immediate return will be low, from the other nil.

TESTING A THEORY

Is it possible to test this theory as to the type of stock to buy in relation to income? The problem might be investigated by selecting a substantial number of stocks at random, dividing them into high-yield and low-yield groups and following their fate over a period of years. For this purpose all the industrial common stocks alphabetically from A to G, inclusive, quoted in the ten-year price range in Moody's Manual were investigated. It was assumed that a speculative investor purchased as many shares of each as $1000 would buy at the average of their 1913 high and low quotations. On the basis of total cash dividends paid in 1913 the yield at the average price was calculated and two groups of stocks selected on this basis, those yielding more than 8% and those yielding less than 6%. There were thirteen issues in the former group, fourteen in the latter. It is further assumed that the commitment was closed out in each case at the average between the high and low of 1922. Despite the fact that the year of purchase was immediately followed by a severe stock market and business depression, that the year of sale was immediately preceded by a similar period, the total commitment in each class of stocks showed a profit upon liquidation. The interesting fact disclosed by the following table is, however, that the low-yield stocks not only showed a far larger profit when sold but that in the aggregate they even showed a larger return on the commitment for the entire period. The table shows the gain in value as follows:

	Sold 1922	Cost 1913	Profit	% Profit
Low-yield stocks	$19,356.13	$11,307.39	$8,048.74	71.2
High-yield stocks	$14,635.13	$13,026 56	$1,608.67	12.3

The second table gives the yield in cash dividends in percentage on cost each year:

	1922	1921	1920	1919	1918	1917	1916	1915	1914	1913
Low-yld. stks.	8.23	9.43	12.82	9.44	9.27	8.82	6.71	4.30	4.28	4.00
High-yld. stks.	5.17	6.38	9.04	7.55	7.24	8.32	6.83	6.38	7.57	10.83

There can be no question which commitment would have been the more satisfactory.

AN ASTONISHING RESULT

Among the non-dividend-paying stocks, it is impossible to distinguish dispassionately between those which a trained observer would have considered promising and those which he would have considered hopeless. Accordingly it is only possible to take the whole group of non-dividend stocks and trace the fate of a commitment in them. There are twenty-seven issues in this group, involving an assumed original commitment at the average between the 1913 highs and lows of $26,645.34. There was, of course, no dividend return from these stocks in 1913, but in the following year three of them paid dividends, affording a return of .8%. In 1915 the dividend income increased to 1.19%, in 1916 to 5.96%. Thereafter the increase was rapid to a maximum of 30.9% in 1922. Even eliminating a large extra paid by Cramp Shipbuilding, in the latter year the return was 18.9% and the aggregate return for the entire period well in excess of the yield afforded by the stocks which were on a dividend basis when purchased. Assuming sale of these twenty-seven stocks in 1922 at the average between the highs and lows for the year, the capital gain was $56,400 or 211% on the commitment.

This figure was so strikingly high that revised study was undertaken of results under the most unfavorable conceivable circumstances. For this purpose it was assumed that each of the twenty-seven stocks was sold at its lowest 1921 quotation, at the bottom figure of a year of extreme depression. The chances are something like a million to one that a trader would be unable to get the lowest figure of the year for twenty-seven stocks if he tried. It is further assumed that the two stocks for which no 1921 quotation is available were written off as total losses. Even under this excessively unfavorable assumption the commitment would have been liquidated for $47,542.75 or at a profit of 79.6%. This is larger than the profit yielded by the dividend-paying groups under much more favorable assumptions.

The study cited amply justifies the injunction to consider immediate return a minor factor in deciding whether or not to embark on a given speculative venture. It is not sufficiently thorough to warrant the conclusion that non-dividend-paying stocks should be purchased in preference to dividend-payers. Indeed, for the reasons already given it would seem most inadvisable for a speculator to venture his entire resources on such issues.

Realized Profits Not the End Sought

The fifth rule suggested for the guidance of the speculative investor would seem to contradict a proverb which every trader hears almost as soon as he first enters a brokerage firm's board room. "You'll never get poor taking profits," runs this saying. As a matter of fact, the trader can insure his ultimate failure no more certainly than by taking profits. He should understand clearly what he is attempting to do. He is not seeking realized profits on which he will have to pay an income tax, but the maximum capital appreciation for his funds. If in the course of his operations he does sell certain securities at a profit and switch to other securities, the realization of profits involved is entirely incidental to his main purpose of achieving the greatest possible growth in the value of his speculative fund.

What should be the attitude of the speculative investor toward changes in the market value of stocks which he holds? Presumably he has bought a given stock because on mature consideration he believed it to be undervalued. He may profit through (1) more general recognition of the values behind the stock or (2) increase in the earning power and assets behind the stock. Such an increase in the earning power behind a stock is the normal result of sound management. So long as this increase is in process there is no reason why the stockholder should terminate his commitment. The only logical reason that the speculative investor can have for selling a stock he holds is a change for the worse in the position of the stock. Far from indicating such a change, an increase in the market value tends to confirm the soundness of the judgment which led to its purchase. On the contrary, a decline in the market for the stock tends to indicate that the judgment of the speculator was wrong. This is not necessarily the case and he may be well advised in a given case to hold a stock through a declining market with confident expectation of eventual profit. If he were to base his decision solely on the action of the market, nevertheless, a moderate decline in a stock would afford a much sounder reason for selling it than a moderate advance.

IMPORTANCE OF INFORMATION

Rule No. 6 lays further stress on the importance of the "unknown" factor in analyzing a security. So far as he is dealing with the unknown the speculator is gambling. He must seek by every means to reduce the element of gambling to a minimum. To do this he must confine his transactions for the most part to securities about which he may obtain at fairly frequent intervals and, with a minimum of trouble, adequate information. There are many good stocks about which adequate information is not available and money is often to be made in them. Where the information which is forthcoming is favorable or where sufficient information may be obtained by taking some trouble it may be advisable to purchase such a stock, but it is sound policy not to place too great a proportion of a given fund in an issue of this type.

It is sometimes worthwhile to go to some trouble to obtain sound information. For example, a certain moderate-sized manufacturing company publishes only a condensed annual balance sheet by way of informing its shareholders regarding its operations. For some years this balance sheet has shown an item of accounts receivable entirely too large for the size of the business. This fact suggested that the stock might not be a bargain after all at a price equal to half the net quick assets behind it despite a good record of earnings and dividends. A reporter who was also a stockholder attended the 1926 annual meeting. He and one other stockholder outside the management who took the trouble to attend were permitted to see a detailed balance sheet showing that over two-thirds of the accounts receivable item, as of December 31, 1925, consisted of United States Treasury notes. Here was a stock genuinely undervalued, though the company's statements, so far as they were readily available, themselves suggested serious doubt as to the values behind it.

Each to His Own Decision

No one ever attained a fortune by seeking the advice of others. This is the basis for the seventh rule. An efficiency expert may point the way to technical improvements in the conduct of a business, but he can do no more. The responsibility for the success or failure of the business must rest in the final analysis on the energy, character, ability and force of decision of one man. The Fords, Rockefellers, Morgans have not dominated their chosen fields by seeking the advice of "experts," but by following their own judgment, though it may have meant on occasion flying in the face of precedent.

The venerable Chauncy M. Depew once gave an interview to an inquiring reporter who wanted to know what had been the greatest mistakes of his life. In reply Mr. Depew detailed three. Financially his greatest error was his failure to purchase a sixth interest in the infant which later became the American Telephone & Telegraph Co. for $10,000. Strongly attracted to the venture Mr. Depew yet deferred action until he had consulted expert advice. To this end he approached a personal friend, the president of the Western Union Telegraph Co., doubtless the best qualified expert available to anyone. In all sincerity he was told that the telephone was impracticable and that in any event Western Union owned patents giving it a better claim to the invention. Mr. Depew lived to see Western Union a subsidiary of American Telephone.

LACK OF CONVICTION FATAL

In Wall Street—and in the financial district of every large city—one hears on every hand bond salesmen asking brokers' clerks, and vice versa, "What do you think of the market?" or "What do you know that's cheap?" or "What do you hear that's new?" Thus half-baked opinions, rumors, tips, gossip are circulated, usually to the cost of everyone who pays any attention to them. Such questions betray a lack of conviction which is almost fatal to success in speculation. The trader either does not have sufficient knowledge to form the basis of intelligent opinions or lacks the backbone to pursue a reasoned program when he has formed it. Such a trader is doomed to failure. Let him who would succeed in speculation seek all the facts diligently, for with inadequate or erroneous information even the most intelligent speculator may reach a wrong conclusion, but let him remember that in the end he must decide for himself what and when to buy and to sell.

A COMPROMISE

The eighth rule is a recognition of the cyclical nature of stock market movements and also a compromise between two schools of thought regarding long-pull speculation. Some students hold that the long-pull speculator should trade on the long swings of the stock market, endeavoring to buy stocks near the bottom of a bear market, then to sell his entire holdings near the peak of the ensuing bull market and to hold the proceeds in short-term securities until another bear market has run its course. Others believe that he should buy sound common stocks and hold them, selling only when the bright prospects of a given issue appear dimmed and then switching to some other promising issue. In this and previous chapters theoretical instances of both types of trading have been given, with satisfactory results over a period of years despite entirely random selections. The ideal program would seem to be a compromise between the two extremes. While the speculative investor is primarily interested in buying stocks likely to appreciate in value rather than in the trend of the market, he cannot reasonably ignore the long swings of bull and bear markets. When a bull market has attained considerable stature and the foundation of easy money has begun to crumble, he might well go over his holdings with a view to disposing of a considerable part of them. In so doing, it cannot be too strongly emphasized—the cost of any given security is a factor of no importance.

OVERTRADING TO BE AVOIDED

A chief fault of the average trader is his propensity to overtrade and it is against this tendency that the ninth suggested rule is directed. The analyst of securities soon learns that the best managed companies frequently have much more cash on hand than there seems to be any necessity of their having, that they seldom borrow money and never up to the limit of their credit. The speculative investor can apply this principal of good management to his own venture. While a bank may be perfectly willing to lend him 75% to 80% of the value of sound, marketable stocks he would be very foolish to use such borrowing power up to the hilt. If he did so, a moderate decline in the market would so endanger his capital as to disturb seriously his judgment of values. Instead of falling into this common error, the shrewd speculator will borrow on a far more limited scale and only occasionally. Obviously the best time at which to borrow is when stocks in general are low. An advance in the market then increases the borrower's equity and strengthens his position. During the course of a bull market he will find it wise to use one of his peri-odical house-cleanings to liquidate his loans, a later one to shift in part into short-term bonds.

So huge are the possibilities for profit in long-term options to buy stocks of promising companies that the tenth rule should be a part of the operating policy of every speculative investor. The two words "promising companies" are an important part of the rule. Option warrants are an increasingly popular attachment to bond and preferred stock issues. They will be offered in many cases merely to give a talking point for bond salesmen, their prospects of attaining value being microscopically small. In the case of promising companies, however, the shrewd speculator will strive to acquire as complete an assortment as possible with an eye to long-range profits.

A PROFITABLE AVOCATION

Investment pure and simple involves no serious problems for the possessor of funds. Savings banks and kindred institutions, endowment life insurance policies, government bonds, the trust departments of strong banks offer solutions for the man seeking safety above everything or the busy executive who lacks the time to give his funds proper supervision. The business man who can devote the necessary time to the control of his personal finances will find speculative investment a fascinating undertaking keeping him constantly in touch with the material progress of the world. He will take an intelligent interest in economic history in the making. By the application of the principles discussed in these chapters, he should make this undertaking a profitable as well as an interesting avocation.

The End

Other Investing Classics available at Traders' Library...

Tape Reading & Market Tactics
by Humphrey B. Neill

1970 edition of the 1931 classic. Neill tells not only how to read the tape, but also how to figure out what's going on behind the numbers. Full of graphs and charts, this book contains excellent sections on human nature and speculation. This is a not-to-be-missed bestseller about the mechanics that drive price action.

ISBN: 978-1-59280-262-3
$13.50

Think and Grow Rich by Napoleon Hill

Since its release in 1937, this book has been an influence on more successful people than almost any other title. Written from research in interviews with the industry giants like Thomas Edison, John D. Rockefeller, Alexander Graham Bell, and many others, this guide breaks the path to success into 13 steps. Find out what these steps are and how they can transform you life.

ISBN: 978-1-59280-260-9
$13.50

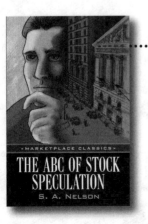

The ABC of Stock Speculation
by S.A. Nelson

Originally a primer for traders in the early 1900s, this book outlines the history of trading and provides the essentials that still stand true today. Great insight into Dow Theory, market swings, stop orders, from a close friend of Charles Dow. This classic includes original editorials written by Dow himself. A must-have for any investor or trader.

ISBN: 978-1-59280-263-0
$13.50

WWW.TRADERSLIBRARY.COM